GW00685908

THE BOOK
of the
Liffey
from
source
to the sea

Elizabeth Healy

Christopher Moriarty

Gerard O'Flaherty

Design: Jan de Fouw

WOLFHOUND PRESS

O

tell me all about
Anna Livia! I want to hear all

about Anna Livia. Well, you know Anna Livia? Yes, of course, we all know Anna Livia. Tell me all. Tell me now.

Anna Livia Plurabelle
Joyce's Universal River

Gerard O'Flaherty

Soft morning, city! Lsp!

James Joyce

I am leafy speafing.

This is the Liffey in *Finnegans Wake* giving a final greeting to the city of Dublin. Those who are familiar with the river can readily recognise the damp overcast feeling that permeates the quays early on an autumnal morning.

It took James Joyce nearly a third of his life to write *Finnegans Wake*, which was meant to be his masterpiece. Unfortunately, when it was published in May 1939 it was regarded by the great majority of the reading public as being incomprehensible because of the dream language in which it was written. However, over the years it has come to be regarded as a great comic novel, having for its principal characters the city of Dublin, standing for all cities, and the Liffey, representing the rivers of the world.

Joyce does not describe the Liffey, his words *are* the river as, while in exile, he listened to it 'as she bibs us, by the waters of babalong.' He was so obsessed by the river that he had the map of its course woven into a carpet for his living room.

Finnegans Wake is the dream of a publican, H. C. Earwicker, in Chapelizod as he lies in bed beside his wife Anna Livia. In the dream Earwicker becomes the personification of the city of Dublin beside the Liffey, with his head at Howth and his feet in Castleknock. Earwicker is unreliable, hot tempered, despotic and

. . . mid piddle med puddle, she ninnygoes nannygoes nancing by . . .

given to debauchery. He came as a wild Viking rover to establish a city on the banks of the Liffey . . . 'I laid down before the trotters to my eblanite my stony battered waggonways, my nordsoud circulums, my eastmoreland and westlandmore, running boullowards and syddenly parading,'. [Stoneybatter, North and South Circular Roads, Eastmoreland Street, Westland Row and Sydney Parade.] There is some doubt as to whether or not the Viking married the lady of the river; if he did it would be appropriate that the ceremony should be in a church dedicated to our first parents 'was her banns never loosened in Adam and Eve's or were him and her but captain spliced?' We will never know.

Anna Livia is not just the Liffey, she is the universal river 'The Log of Anny to the Base All'. She remembers how she was a little cloud in 'My great blue bedroom, the air so quiet, scarce a cloud. In peace and silence . . . First we feel. Then we fall.' Within the Anna Livia Plurabelle episode there are the names of hundreds of rivers buried or hidden in the text. The narrative opens with two young washerwomen, one on either side of the stream, at the source of the Liffey near Kippure. In the course of their chatter Anna Livia is discussed at great length and she herself thinks back over her life and remembers how she has been a cloud, a shower, a rivulet, a brook before becoming a river.

First she fell as a shower 'little . . . Anna Rayiny, when unda her brella, mid piddle med puddle, she ninnygoes nannygoes nancing by . . . . Upon Benn Heather, in Seeple Isout too.' [Howth and Chapelizod]. Later she falls 'on the spur of the hill in old Kippure, in birdsong and shearingtime, but first of all, worst of all, the wiggly livvly, she sideslipped out by a gap . . . while Sally [the Sally Gap] her nurse was sound asleep . . . fell over a spillway before she found her stride and lay and wriggled in all the stagnant black pools of rainy . . . and she laughed innocefree with her limbs aloft and a whole drove of maiden hawthorns blushing and looking askance upon her.'

But 'she was just a young thin pale soft shy slim slip of a thing then, sauntering, by silvamoonlake . . . before she ever dreamt she'd lave Kilbride and go

. . . sauntering, by silvamoonlake . . . before she ever dreamt she'd lave Kilbride . . .

foaming under Horsepass bridge'. [Horsepass Bridge is now under the Blessington Lakes].

As the river grows, so too does Anna Livia become a woman, 'ducking under bridges, bellhopping the weirs, dodging by a bit of a bog, rapidshooting round the bends, by . . . the pools of the phooka and a place they call it Blessington . . . as happy as the day is wet, babbling, bubbling, chattering to herself, deloothering the fields on their elbows leaning with the sloothering slide of her, giddygaddy, grannyma, gossipaceous Anna Livia.' And 'her muddied name was Missisliffi'.

The river flows out of Wicklow and on through Clane, Kildare to the 'strawbirry reds'. The city is reached in the late evening, 'Look, look, the dusk is growing! . . . It's churning chill. Der went is rising.' The washerwomen have grown old and in the gathering darkness they appear to be a tree on one bank and a stone on the other, while the Liffey goes 'home slowly now by own way' until it is lost 'Beside the rivering waters of, hitherandthithering waters of. Night!'

Later, the old river is flowing to her father, the sea, and she is yielding place to her daughter who is 'just a whisk brisk sly spry spink spank sprint of a thing' so it is time to 'let her rain now if she likes.' Anna Livia has 'a hundred cares, a tithe of troubles' and she asks, as Joyce did, 'is there one who understands me? . . . I am passing out. O bitter ending! I'll slip away before they're up. They'll never see. Nor know. Nor miss me . . . A way a lone a last a loved a long the'. And here the book ends, but we know that the narrative loops around to the beginning again to 'riverrun, past Eve and Adam's, from swerve of shore to bend of bay, brings us by a commodius vicus of recirculation back to Howth Castle and Environs.' Yet there is a moment in time between the beginning and the end, be it a second or a million years, which allows the river to become a cloud, a shower, a stream and a river again.

'Anna was, Livia is, Plurabelle's to be.'

'Anna was. Livia is. Plurabelle's to be.'

The support of the
Electricity Supply Board
(the ESB), is gratefully acknowledged.

First published 1988 by
WOLFHOUND PRESS
68 Mountjoy Square,
Dublin 1.

© 1988 Wolfhound Press

Text and illustrations
© individual contributors

British Library Cataloguing in
Publication Data

The book of the Liffey:
from source to the sea.
    1. (Republic) Ireland. Liffey River.
    Visitors' guide
    I. Healy, Elizabeth
914.18'304824

ISBN 0-86327-167-7

Design by Jan de Fouw.
Typesetting by Redsetter Ltd.
Colour separation and film by
Graphic Reproductions Ltd., Dublin.
Printed by TechMan Ltd., Dublin.
Bound by Library Bindings Ltd.

Introduction

The Liffey is Dublin's river, as the Thames is London's and the Seine that of Paris. But a Capital City may be inclined to forget that its river has a life apart from its city streets. The Liffey belongs at least as much to County Wicklow, where it rises, and even more to County Kildare where it runs most of its course.

The Liffey rises in a dark peaty pool high in the Wicklow mountains, a short distance from Sally Gap on the flanks of Kippure, not more than ten miles from the sea. One can almost see Dublin Bay from its starting point. But, as if reluctant to make so precipitate a descent, it turns inland instead, to set out on a wandering journey of 80 miles through three Counties before finally submitting to the sea.

Its course forms a great circle. Leaving the high wilderness of its birth, it meanders south and westward down the heathery flanks of the mountains to spread wide in the Blessington Lakes. The lakes were created by man as part of the process of harnessing the Liffey to make power to light the streets and homes of Dublin, and to supply it with sweet water to drink. Only incidentally has the reservoir given Dublin's hinterland the additional bounty of a wonderful playground for sports and pleasures of all kinds, as well as enhancing an already beautiful landscape.

At the lakes the Liffey has reached the plains. Now it turns northwards to flow through the limestone grasslands of Kildare, rich country for raising fat cattle and fast racehorses. Here there are many large private estates and the riverside is not always accessible to pedestrians, but bridges and roads cross and re-cross it so there are plenty of points of contact and exploration.

Finally the Liffey swings eastwards towards the Capital. At Islandbridge there is a great change. The fresh waters of the river meet up with the tidal waters of the estuary and the water that flows through Dublin has a different personality: Anna Liffey goes mature and stately through the city streets.

It is appropriate that Anna Liffey ends, as she began, in a Dark Pool, the *Dubh Linn* which named the city a thousand years ago.

It is that length of time since bands of Viking sea-rovers settled, first at Islandbridge, then farther down the shallow and muddy shores of the Liffey mouth. Down through the centuries Anna Liffey has been tidied and constrained, deepened and corseted by quays, as Viking, Norman, English and Irish came and went, fought, intermingled and built, while the city expanded to eventually hold a third of the population of Ireland. By contrast, the silent moorland where the infant stream emerges has hardly changed at all, nor have the level grasslands of the plains of Kildare, apart from the growth of a few modest towns and a succession of fine manor houses. The river manages to largely avoid heavily-trafficked roads. So, in a way, a journey with the river, from source to the sea, is like a journey in time as well as space.

The Book of the Liffey is offered as a companion/guide to a journey of discovery. If readers get even half the pleasure that we have had exploring Anna Liffey, they have happy days ahead. •

CONTENTS

The phrases in the opening and closing sequences are from *Finnegans Wake* by James Joyce.

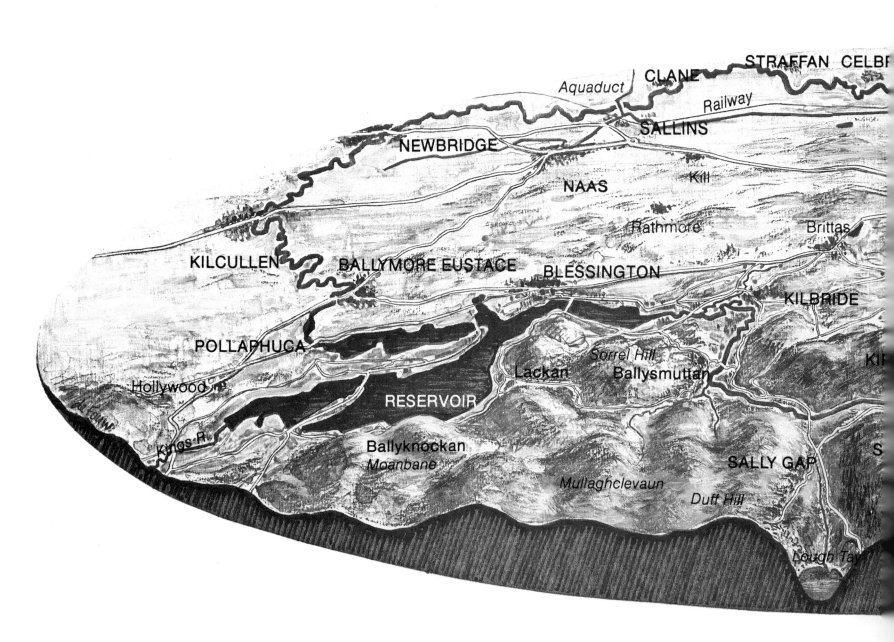

riverrun, past Eve and Adam's, from swerve of shore to bend o

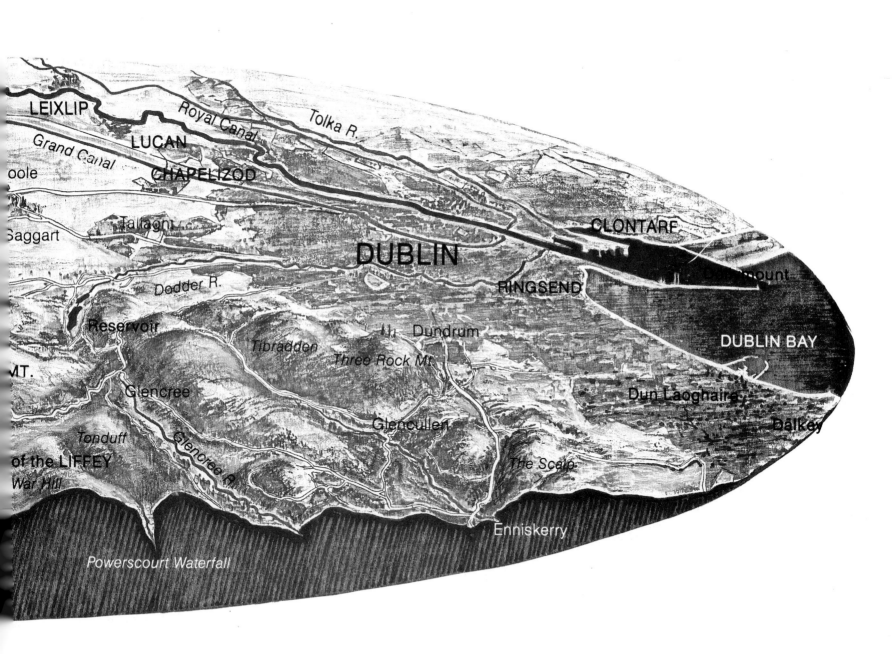

uy, brings us by a commodius vicus of recirculation back to . . .

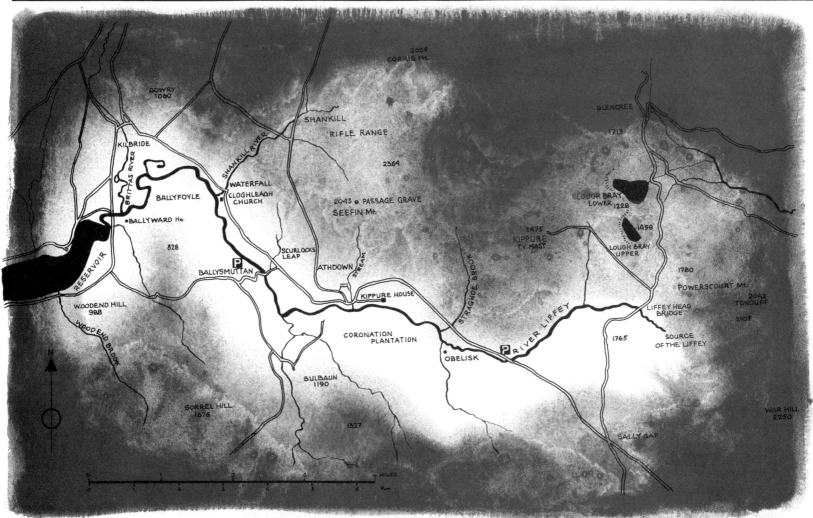

The Land above the Liffey

The Source of the Liffey is only ten minutes walk from the road at Liffey Head Bridge. Above it lie heavenly miles of lonely moorland which no discerning wayfarer can resist.

Two green tracks lead up the slope. They mark the paths of streams which run underground, except where potholes open and you can hear the water gurgling two metres down below the base of the peat blanket. Immediately upstream of the Source there lies a broad, shallow pond. The streamlets actually tunnel beneath this and enter the Source pool below the surface so that it is strangely calm. In wet weather the streamlets divide vertically: some of the water goes through the pond, while the rest flows beneath the peat.

Beyond the stream lies an almost level tract of moorland where the Dargle and the Vartry flow towards the eastern slopes of the Wicklow Mountains. It is a wonderful place, a land of miniature lakes where there is peace and solitude.

On all sides are round or oblong pools, the biggest about 20 metres long and plunging to dark depths of a metre and more, but with the shallows carpeted in pale green moss. On a sunny day they present a succession of sparkling blue mirrors in the midst of brown sedge and heather.

Peat covers all the higher slopes, except at the very tops of some of the mountains. Deer grass is the dominant plant on the wet parts, with frequent bog cotton. In places there are great patches of asphodel, the most brilliant of all the bog plants, with spikes of bright yellow, star-like flowers in July and August. Ling heather grows all over the drier slopes and survives in little tussocks on the wet ones. Beyond the reach of the casual turf-cutter and too poor to interest the sheep, this is the real wilderness where wild nature rules supreme.

Christopher Moriarty

The Liffey of the Wilderness

The Source of the Liffey is a deep, dark pool between the mountains of Kippure and Tonduff. An enchanting place, the pool lies at the base of a black amphitheatre of peat and from it the stream gushes, between banks of green grass.

If you climb by the edge of the amphitheatre, all of two metres high, you can see the mast at the summit of Kippure and from that, should you climb it, can be seen the path of the river through the city of Dublin: Dubh Linn, the Dark Pool where the Liffey ends as it began.

The way to the source

Dubliners attain the birthplace of their river by following the Military Road past Glencree and Lough Bray and over the shoulder which divides the catchments of Liffey and Glencree Rivers. There is an almost imperceptible dip in the road, 500 metres past the gateway to the transmitter. Two inconspicuous rows of granite blocks, one on each side of the road, form the parapets of Liffey Head Bridge, a resounding name for a curious piece of civil engineering.

There is room to park one car about 50 metres up the hill past the bridge. The walk from the bridge to the Source is an easy 600 metres, made easier by the wearing of wellies. The bridge is supported on each bank by great, rough blocks of granite. It probably boasted a round arch in its heyday, but the present structure comprises three concrete drainpipes, piled one atop the other. In dry weather, the lowest of the three copes with all the water and the wayfarer can cross the infant river in a single stride.

The water is brown, but clear, coloured by humic acids leached out of the peat. It flows over a stony bed with, now and then, patches of sparkling gravel, formed from shiny crystals of mica and quartz, liberated from the granite by rain water. Two underground streamlets enter the infant river between the Source and Liffey Head Bridge. Both of them flow out from round holes in the peat banks. A bracken plant grows at the mouth of the more downstream of the two, its fronds, fresh and green, standing out against the black peat.

Upstream of the bridge, the banks of the stream are green, with grass, mostly fescue and a variety of mosses. Common rush and the great woodrush, with its broad green pointed leaves, grow in clumps amongst the grass and by the water's edge. They contrast with the brown bog flora of the moorland just above. There the dominant plants are ling heather on the drier parts and bog cotton on the wetter. Green, with white tufts in summer, the bog cotton leaves turn red in autumn. The heather blooms fresh and green in spring, with pale mauve flowers in late summer. But its underlying woody growth provides an impression of brownness at all times.

Anna Liffey

Anna Liffey – *Abhainn Lifé* – may be translated simply as the River Liffey. Once upon a time it was known as *Ruirtheach*, the flashy torrent. According to legend, Lifé was the daughter of Cannan the Pict, and the wife of Deltbanna mac Drucht, 'the Spencer of Conary Mór, King of Tara'. As this couple were travelling from Tipperary towards Tara, they crossed the plain in Kildare through which the Ruirtheach flowed. Lifé was so delighted with the beauty of the plain that she asked if it might be named after her, at which request 'Deltbanna dealt out no more liquor for the men of Erin until the plain was called by his wife's name', hence *Magh Lifé*, Lifé's Plain. The plain gave its name to the river.

Granite and peat

The mountains to the northeast are Tonduff and Maulin, forming the near side of the Glencree valley. To the southeast are War Hill, Djouce and the delightfully named 'Luggala or Fancy'. They stand just at the edge of the granite 'batholith' which forms the main part of the Wicklow Mountains.

Their geology is very interesting. After the Ordovician period, more than 600 million years ago, folding of the rock strata took place along a northeast to southwest axis. At a great depth, granite intruded in the shape of an elongated dome, extending from Dalkey to the Blackstairs.

Between this dome and the older slates and shales which surround it, lies a 'metamorphic aureole' of mica schist, a flakey rock sparkling with small crystals of mica. It was formed by chemical action between the hot granite and the surrounding slate.

In the course of time, many rock strata have been deposited on top of the granite dome and its covering slate. And they have all been worn away again, so that the granite root of the mountain system now lies exposed. Where this matters in the context of the scenery is that granite, unprotected by the schist, weathers to form gentle, rolling hills.

The schist on the eastern edge of the granite presents an altogether tougher exterior. Tonduff, lying within the granite, accordingly has gentle slopes, but Maulin and Djouce are of schist and are steep and rugged. The summit of Luggala is granite, but the beetling cliffs on its edge are schist. The upper Liffey flows over the granite and that is why it lacks the grand waterfalls of the smaller, eastern rivers.

But to return to more recent happenings, the superficial appearance of the upper Liffey valley results from events which took place less than ten thousand years ago. That date marks the end of a period when glaciers moved over the higher hills, breaking off and scattering boulders large and small. High rainfall and the acidity of the granite then combined to allow the growth of sedge and moss which ultimately formed the peat.

Trees, rocks and cascades

Downstream of the bridge the first tree in the Liffey valley grows. It is a willow, making the most of the shelter afforded in the angle between the embankment of the bridge and the steep-sided valley. Two ferns, male fern and polypody, grow there as well, besides the bracken.

The stream turns a corner and loses itself completely in the moorland. The valley is very narrow, less than 10 metres wide, and heather grows close to the banks: deep, springy heather, a pleasure to walk on. In the course of the first mile or so, the slope falls gently and the valley is completely hidden, with no land visible but the slopes of Kippure. Then the more distant summits of Sorrel and Mullaghcleevaun appear.

The bed of the stream is mainly coarse gravel, with a large boulder now and again. Then the first major outcrop of solid granite appears and the river, now swollen by tributaries and no longer an infant stream, plunges merrily over cascades and cuts itself steeper valleys where rowan trees grow.

Turf-cutting

A little way up from the valley, transformations of the landscape have begun. The traditional turf-cutting, which depended on a man's ability to walk over the bog and cut

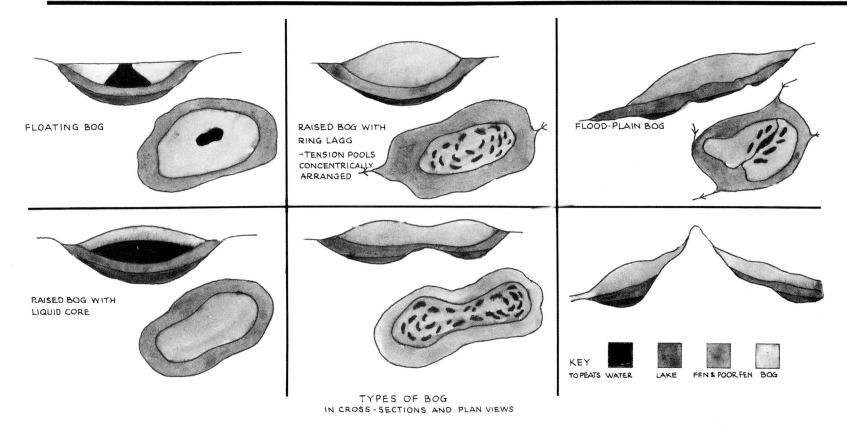

FLOATING BOG

RAISED BOG WITH
RING LAGG
–TENSION POOLS
CONCENTRICALLY
ARRANGED

FLOOD-PLAIN BOG

RAISED BOG WITH
LIQUID CORE

KEY
TO PEATS   WATER   LAKE   FEN & POOR FEN   BOG

TYPES OF BOG
IN CROSS-SECTIONS AND PLAN VIEWS

with a slean, has been replaced by mechanised exploitation. The 'sausage machines' crawl over the bog, exuding sausages of peat, in place of the hand-cut sods. The old system moved so slowly over the moorland that heather, sedges and grasses can regenerate on the cutaway surfaces: there are many traces of the old diggings elsewhere in the valley and that system is still in use to the west of the Military Road.

If all goes well, the slopes will survive the faster operation, but nobody yet knows whether the enterprise will succeed. At least some of the sheep farmers who share the valley are delighted to see the development. They welcome anything other than State forestry. Visitors, who don't have to make a living from the land, look on aghast and hope that the entire heather-clad slopes will not be washed into oblivion.

Coronation Plantation

The Liffey passes through the peat cuttings and emerges from its hidden valley where the road heads downstream towards Coronation Plantation. A flat bridge, supported by three pillars of granite, carries the road across the stream. There is room to park cars and picnic beside it. Downstream the valley opens out a little and gravel has been deposited by floods in the past. This gravel drains easily enough to prevent the ground from getting waterlogged. Grasses rather than sedge or moss grow there and gorse makes its appearance.

The City Bog-Men

When you drive over the moorland by the Sally Gap, you're likely to see brightly-coloured bundles of plastic bags laid out on the bog. The bags are full of turf 'saved' by Dublin clerks and lawyers and plumbers and businessmen, who come up here from the city to bend their backs and heave the sacks, not through need but for pleasure. **Noel Masterson** *recalls the days when necessity was the motivating factor.*

I can still see that line of walking cyclists stretching along the Featherbed road to the skyline – some towing turf barrows, some with spades and sleans tied to the crossbar. A string of Dublin turf-cutters pushing their way on worn-out war grade cycle tyres to the Featherbed bog. The year 1942.

It was a 12-mile 'ride' from Clanbrassil Street, mostly up hill, with a glass of buttermilk at the last cottage before Featherbed corner, price 1 old penny. The road surface was badly damaged with

The coronation was that of King William IV in 1831. Irish forestry at the time was enjoying a period of expansion which had begun in the latter half of the 18th century and was to continue until wholesale felling without replanting began in the 1880s. Coronation Plantation has achieved the immortality of being named on the Ordnance Survey maps but nowadays it is more of a region than a managed forest. The land is held as commonage by five sheep farmers and the trees are left to fend for themselves.

If, therefore, you look for a plantation you will be disappointed. But if you would prefer a beautiful landscape with a character all of its own, you will be richly rewarded. Instead of the dense green of mature forest, the hillside is dotted with tall, isolated Scots pines: green all the year round but with leaves sparse enough to reveal the rich orange-red colouring of the bark on the branches. There are many great oaks in the forest, too, adding splashes of green or gold. To some extent the surviving trees follow the valleys of the tributaries on the left bank of the Liffey so that the forest extends away into the hills, thinning out and disappearing in the distance.

Energetic people, prepared to jump the damp patches, can enjoy a walk by the riverside, where it borders the Plantation, in shoes. Boots are essential for the leisured classes.

Downstream of the flat bridge, an anonymous tributary enters the Liffey on the left and just below it the Plantation begins. The Ordnance Survey of 1838 marks the forest boundary, stretching from this point away up the hill towards the southwest. It extends in a straight line for more than 1 km, forming a great rectangle with its base along the river. In fact it never happened that way and the eventual planting was on a more modest scale.

The Liffey descends gently, making its course over white granite boulders. Scots pine predominates, splendid tall trees, each standing far enough from the next to exist as an individual with its very own shape. There are occasional wild rowans and a good few oaks, some poor and stunted, some magnificent. Bracken grows on the lower slopes amongst the trees.

The bracken-clad hillsides are a haunt of the whinchat, a robin-sized bird with brown and chestnut colouring and a pale but conspicuous stripe above the eye. It is something of a rarity in Ireland but comes to breed every summer in and around the Plantation.

There is a slightly sad side to the forest. As in communities of ageing people in other remote parts of the country, there is no sign of the younger generation. The herds of sheep and occasional deer destroy all the seedlings. Meanwhile, the old trees one by one fall before storms or, occasionally, die where they stand and stay for years as lonesome skeletons.

A little more than 1 km downstream of the bridge comes a clearing in the forest and a change from bracken to pasture. Gravel, deposited by the main river and by Lugnalee stream on the left, overlies the peat and makes a well-drained patch. Here stands a long, low cottage, marked 'Game Keeper's Lodge' on the old map. A few beech trees make their appearance - they insist on good drainage.

Up the hill, behind the cottage and a little way to the west is the quaint granite obelisk commemorating the beginning of the plantation. The inscription, in very neatly executed Roman letters, is difficult to read now. It remains undamaged by the hand of man, but overgrown with a mottling of lichens which in places fill the hollows of the letters. Fortunately, Weston Joyce in *The Neighbourhood of Dublin* quotes it in full, having made a drawing of the monument in 1890:

large depressions where turf-laden lorries had sunk through the thin surface the previous autumn. You were on unmetalled sand road when you crossed the Dublin-Wicklow boundary.

Ho Chi Minh and his cyclists would have liked the passage to the bog and the spirit of the turf cutting Dubs who, to begin, hardly knew a slean from a slash hook. It was all a part of the 'emergency' spirit which even I, a 12 year old boy, could sense. I felt I was part of a family survival, maybe even a national survival movement which embraced growing your own food in allotments, joining the part-time defence forces and, for my 60 year old father and me, the bizarre concept of 'saving' our own fuel.

On a calm June day as you neared the Wicklow boundary and the sand road, you could smell the turf smoke and see dozens of blue drifts from the tea fires all the way up to Kippure and the road to Liffeyhead – no bottled gas then. I was chief cook, barrower and footer of our two-man team, tasks for lesser mortals, such as sons, daughters and wives. The superior task of sleansman was reserved. No way could you let an inexperienced amadán muck up a nice straight cutting. The boss might be a printer or a bookie's clerk, but this was year two and he knew a thing or two about turf cutting and you couldn't let that culchie from Donegal or Connemara have a free laugh at your Dublin man's crooked bank.

The hard work, the clean dirt, the gritty eyes were all part of it. The talk around the tea fire was men's talk, turf talk. How somebody struck a gusher of water at 6 spits and was denied the heavy coal-like stuff that burned with a blue flame, or the story of the man who tried to bring down

Coronation Plantation
Lordship of Blessington
County of Wicklow
This Plantation in the Brocky
Mountains of 500 Irish
Laid out by the
Most Honourable the Marquis of Downshire
The fencing commenced in August, 1831.

*   *   *

It was called the
Coronation Planting, in honour of his Most Gracious
Majesty
King William IV
The Most Noble the Marquis of Anglesey being
Lord Lieutenant of Ireland.

*   *   *

And for the future supply of useful
timber for the
Estate
And improvement of the
County and the
Benefit of the
Labouring Classes

*   *   *

This planting
finished on the
day of   18

two bags of turf on his bike and the brakes broke on the Hell Fire Club hill. Great stuff for a boy, mixed with mouthfuls of sausage and turf mould and weak ration tea, strengthened by the colour of the bog water. And the journey home, freewheeling nearly all the way with maybe a glimpse of the Mournes, and a slap-up meal of eggs and more sausages which remained plentiful when bananas were an exotic memory.

But the great day was when the hired lorry with its special petrol allowance for turf carrying was unloaded at your front door, the neighbours gazing with envy at this mountain of dry turf which would burn with heat and cook meals when the gas gave out. (The 'bought' turf only steamed.) All the family, cousins and all, rallied round to bag it through the house and into the back, and afterwards the *meitheal* sat down to a meal of joy, the harvest festival must have been a wonderful event in times past.

The 1980s now, and some of the boys of the 40s and others are at it again. The turf is the same. The road is a good road now. The turf cutters' cars are parked all along the side and calor gas doesn't smoke. The need to cut your turf is gone and I wonder what the purpose is now. Maybe it's to hear the larks singing all day as before, though even this is threatened, for the

The unfinished inscription makes a silent comment on the failure of the great enterprise. Joyce remarked in a footnote that the plantation was being cut down in 1920 and J B Malone in *Ramblers in Wicklow* made a similar comment with reference to World War II. Even so, many trees have survived to commemorate a century and a half of forestry.

A footpath from the keeper's cottage leads down to a bridge over the Liffey and up the right bank to the road, meeting it just beside another of the tiny 19th century farmsteads. Like the Keeper's cottage, it stands surrounded by a patch of gravel deposited by a tributary, the Straghoe Brook. The brook is spanned by a well-built bridge of granite with a round arch, buttressed by concrete and steel in more recent times. The house was inhabited for many years, until he died in 1986, by old Joseph MacLoughlin and his dog. The highest house in the valley, it was being repaired by new owners in 1987.

Continuing downstream, the main river cuts deeply into the bank in places, revealing peat to a depth of about 2 metres, lying on gravel as deep again. In dry weather the Liffey keeps to its bed, with plenty of stones exposed and, now and again, a long island of gravel. The scene is transformed after heavy rain, when the river rises by more than 2 metres, festooning the bushes with grass and beating down the rushes and bracken on either side.

near KILBRIDE

Kippure House

The edges of the valley grow steep in places and alder and willow thicket appears on the left bank. On the right, a pine forest begins, enclosed by a wire fence. This stands in the old demesne of Kippure House, the highest big house on the Liffey. The 1838 map shows a large demesne extending for 1.5 km between road and river, the seat of George Moore, Esquire, Member of Parliament. A police station, now a sturdy granite ruin of one storey, stood at its eastern end, by the road. Less than half the demesne was forested in the old days and the pinewood belongs to a more recent planting.

The ruins of Kippure House and its farm buildings stand on the right bank, with a great, walled orchard now containing an elderly apple tree. Beech, ash and cypress were planted near the house. The farm buildings are still in use in part. To the west of the yard, a slightly ruined lime kiln stands in the field.

Limestone, available in the river valley 5 km downstream, was burned in the kiln to transform it to the corrosive 'quicklime'. This in turn was spread in heaps to be 'slaked' by the rain. In this form it was safe to handle and add to the soil. The introduction of ground limestone put an end to the tradition of lime burning. The kilns, however, were of rugged construction and many survive lower down the valley.

The western boundary of the Coronation Plantation lies across the river from Kippure House. At this point, too, the geology makes a brief departure from the ubiquitous granite. Rapids in the stream flow over a very small outcrop of mica schist and some of the boulders are of porphyry, a form of granite with extra large crystals of felspar.

On the right bank, the Athdown Stream joins the Liffey, flowing down through old demesne woodlands with many beeches and some Spanish chestnut. Where the road crosses the stream, at Kippure Bridge, the trees are particularly fine and a picnic place has been provided by the Forest Service. This is part of Kippure Forest, a plantation of sitka spruce which climbs high on the slopes of Seefin Mountain.

The moss cushions

As you go downstream on the main Liffey, the slope is decreasing and the stream is quieter. The pines on the left bank give way to ash and birch. A little farther down, there is a small floodplain of gravel which is gradually being overgrown by soft little cushions of a bright green moss. This is *Polytrichum* and each frond looks like a pine tree in miniature. The fresh, green colouring on an autumn day when nearly everything else is brown is lovely to see. It is also a very interesting illustration of how the peat bog developed on the granite gravel in times long gone when the climate was moister.

In those times, some 5,000 years ago, the moss grew faster than its dead remains could decay. An organic soil therefore grew up, covering first the gravel left by the glaciers, then the large stones and ultimately forming the blanket bog which covers so much of the uplands. Nowadays the mosses grow only in the wettest places, in this particular case by the riverside where flooding is frequent. Further downstream, in places, the bank has been cut away by the river and shows a pattern of alternating layers of peat and gravel. If they don't get swept away by a high flood, the *Polytrichum* cushions will ultimately form a peat layer. This may in time be covered by gravel from a new flood. Then moss will grow again, forming more peat until the next flood. And so on.

After the *Polytrichum* patch, the Liffey descends into something approaching a

sausages are back on Kippure in plenty but this time it's by way of a corduroy pattern of turf laid down by a growling tractor. The tracks eat into the heather and scar the face of Kippure.

A Dublin man would have to work very hard now to escape progress. I wonder is there any way you can progress backwards.

Footnote

If you'd like to join the bog-men, contact the Powerscourt Estate (Tel. 01-867676) around March or April, and arrange to meet a ranger who will allocate you an area on the mountain. If you are going to do your own cutting, your bank will cost you about £25 for the season, and you should expect to take 4 to 6 tons of turf out. Nowadays a lot of the turf is sold 'on the spread', that is, already cut (or, rather, extruded) by machine. Buying it this way, an area which will yield 7 tons will cost you about £110, including vat.

Noel Masterson

gorge and the character of the banks changes dramatically. The ground is too steep or too wet for grazing and a thicket of birch, willow and alder appears. Honeysuckle and bramble trail amongst the branches. Across the river, the slope is drier and there is a grove of hazel, with blackthorn and hawthorn. It is rich in bird life, a haunt of long-tailed tits and goldcrests and, in summer, willow warblers.

Childhood to youth

The lower end of the gorge is marked by a large outcrop of granite. On both sides lie deep deposits of gravel where quarrying is in progress. This spot is a milestone in the geography of the Liffey. The upland reach has come to an end, leaving behind the barely viable farmland, its dwellings either abandoned or rebuilt by weekenders. Industry and prosperous agriculture have begun in the lowlands and the slopes are dotted with well-kept farms. The Liffey itself changes: from a sparkling brook to a more sedate river in a flood plain, with many long pools, silent and deep. It has passed from childhood to youth.

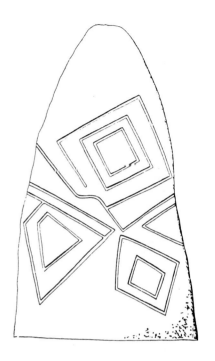

It is easy to ford at the quarry and the right bank is very much easier walking than the left. An old, abandoned road runs close to the river, passing by an enclosure surrounded by Scots pines with ash and hawthorn. The old map marks it as a graveyard. One small granite pillar stands within the enclosure. This was not a country for rich people with money to pay for memorials.

The mountain to the east is Sorrell, corrupted from the Irish 'samhraig', the hill of summer. The Liffey flows north to skirt it and then goes south again, so that the view from the top is of both upland and lowland river. The lower slopes of Sorrell are green and fertile in parts, with a lovely network of old stone walls. The well-drained green fields with their sycamore and ash trees along the boundaries alternate with bog and birch. Spruce forest grows high up the slopes. Sheep, cattle and horses graze the land. Horses are immune to the liver fluke which does so much harm to sheep in the damp, riverside pastures.

Seefin and the stone age

There was a ford at Ballysmuttan in the old days, but no trace of a road on the 1838 map to join the hamlets of Ballysmuttan and Scurlocks Leap. The bridge which stands there now was built, according to a stone at the base of one of its piers, in 1848. Compared with the older bridges, times had changed. Granite is still used, but as a very accurately cut stone to form two vertical piers. These support a flat roadway of concrete and steel, with sides of cast iron lattice, almost eaten away by rust in places. The railway engineer had taken over from the stone mason.

The mountain standing over Ballysmuttan bridge to the northeast is Seefin, its upper slopes barren, with many boulders showing above the bracken. A little way to the

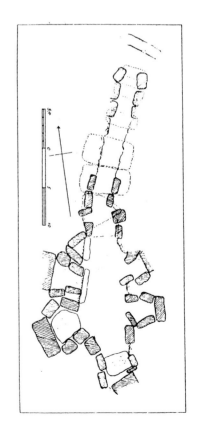

The mound near the summit of Seefin mountain contains a passage grave of a style related to the great prehistoric tombs of the Boyne Valley. The corbelled roof has fallen in and much stone debris has accumulated inside, but you can still make out some of the five burial recesses. A number of decorated stones and marks such as illustrated above have been recorded, but are difficult for the amateur to locate.

left of its summit is a small and important hump. It is a passage grave, related to the great tombs of Knowth, Dowth and Newgrange, even if rather smaller. The cairn, according to Michael Herity in *Irish Passage Graves*, is circular and 26 metres in diameter. It contains a good deal of quartz in addition to the main building stone which, not surprisingly, is granite. The passage and chamber measure 9 metres. The chamber has a complex plan, with no fewer than four side branches. Some of the stones are decorated and the style compares with sculpture at Fourknocks and Newgrange and also with a passage tomb across the sea in Anglesey.

The builders were Neolithic farmers living down in the fertile valley, between four and five thousand years ago. Although large blocks of granite are abundant round about, it must have been a considerable undertaking to carry them up the steep slope. Where the sculptors worked, no-one knows. They may have decorated the stones in the comfort of the lowlands before they were carried up to that very exposed hilltop. The white quartz rocks used are fairly plentiful in granite regions.

The Seefin tomb is the best known, but not the only passage grave above the upper Liffey valley. Others listed by Michael Herity are on Seefingan and, above the Blessington Lakes, on the slopes of Sorrell and Lugnagun. Evidently the builders sought to give their monuments a commanding view of the farms down below. There is little doubt that they were shrines in fertility cults. It seems reasonable to suppose that the communites took comfort from being able to look up at the resting places of their ancestors, clearly marked by the hilltop cairns.

Ballysmuttan

The right bank downstream of Ballysmuttan has small, green fields, bounded by stone walls. Small mounds of football-sized lumps of granite stand in some of the fields. Apparently, these mounds were simply dumping places for the stones which at one time were scattered all over the surface of the land.

The river rushes around the larger boulders in its bed: brown, peat-coloured water set off against the shining, eternally-splashed rock. The stones of the walls and the mounds are darker, encrusted with lichens of various shades of grey-green, grey or black. Lichens literally subsist on air, with the help of a little sun and rain. Running water or frequent floods are too much for them and therefore the stones in the river are white on top. The lower parts of these boulders, however are green or blackish. Where they are permanently washed, algae coat the stationary stones below the surface. The gravel and smaller stones, the rolling stones indeed, are clean because the stream moves them too often to allow the algae or mosses to grow.

The ground on the left bank is generally moister than on the right. The contrast between the well-drained green pasture and the boggy fields is very striking. It is hard to believe that no serious attempts to drain the damp areas were ever made and the explanation probably lies in differences in the size and abundance of stone in the soil. Too many large boulders would make it impracticable to dig drains by hand.

The right bank is dotted with long-established farmsteads, many of them partly hidden amongst fine, old beech trees. The farms on the left bank, however, are far removed from the valley. Thickets, just about penetrable, of blackthorn and hawthorn, hazel and willow abound, and the riverside walk has little enough to recommend it. The wet pasture eventually yields to spruce forest, mature and undergoing clear-felling in 1987.

Ballysmuttan Bridge

The road stays close to the river for 3 km from Scurlocks Leap to Knockatillane and gives a good view of it all the way, over low banks rather than through hedges. The river meanders down below, restricted on both sides by the steeper slopes and forming little gravel flats within the bends.

Cloghlea and the Shankill River

Cloghlea is the site of the first church in the valley: a ruined one is marked on the old map and a new one was built close by in the 19th century, with a sexton's house beside it and a rectory across the road. A holly tree grows near the church. That would not be at all remarkable, since holly is a common tree in the old woodlands. What is surprising is that it is the first which I have been able to find in my journey down the river. There are probably others, but the species is unusually scarce in the upper valley.

Cloghlea Bridge crosses the lovely little tributary called the Shankill River. The bridge is an old one, with a round arch and a balustrade made of square pillars of granite. Its setting in a steep valley, shaded by beech, oak and Spanish chestnut, is incomparable. Jays add colour to the bird life.

The Shankill River plunges down over a series of cascades to join the more placid Liffey below. The granite in the Shankill bed is much more finely grained and harder than that of the surrounding country. Quartz is present to a greater degree than usual. This vein of unusual rock attracted some unfortunate mining prospector in the 19th century in a vain and slightly misguided search for iron ore.

The Shankill was under hideous threat for some time of being called upon to supply water for the region. It could probably have done so in wet weather, but the abstraction would have reduced the flow almost to nothing in a dry period. So the bright waterfall would have disappeared in fine weather when it looks its best and the neighbourhood would probably have had water shortages anyway.

The Ice Age

Where the Shankill River joins the Liffey lies evidence of geology of far greater significance than any abandoned iron prospecting. Pebbles of limestone, grey and smooth, appear in the stream bed. They have been found farther upstream, but become plentiful at this point. The nearest solid limestone outcrops at Saggart, 9 km to the north. The explanation of the presence of these 'erratics' is as simple as its influence on the whole story of the Liffey is profound.

During the Midlandian stage of the Ice Age, between 40,000 and 15,000 years ago, an ice sheet extended over the northern half of Ireland, on the east coast stretching as far south as Wicklow Head. As the ice flowed southwards, it scraped the underlying rock surfaces, gathering a conglomeration of clay, gravel and stones which it carried along. The ice, with its burden of 'till' filled the lower parts of the valleys of the Wicklow Mountains, besides covering the plains. In this way, stones were transported far from their parent rock and thus limestone gravel coats the lower slopes.

Limestone till usually forms an easily drained and fertile soil so the lower slopes are incomparably richer than the uplands. The water of the river also changes its character; the brown tinge is typical of acid, peaty conditions, with no lime in solution. Where the lime begins to be dissolved, the water loses its brown colour. Lime-rich water supports a much greater variety of plant and animal life and allows fish to grow bigger and faster.

Leaving the granite

The Liffey takes a sharp turn to the west around the bottom of the hill of Ballyfoyle where the forest grows. The landscape changes dramatically. It is nearing the western edge of the granite massif and the hills are lower. To the west, the river runs slowly through a broad plain with great meanders. The nearly level ground with its fertile soil provided a good living and the farm houses change from small hillside dwellings to spacious mansions. There are two of them on the plain: Ballyward on the left bank and Kilbride on the right.

Modern maps mark a curious feature of the river just south of Kilbride. A blind

CLOGHLEA CHURCH

The Liffey of the Wilderness

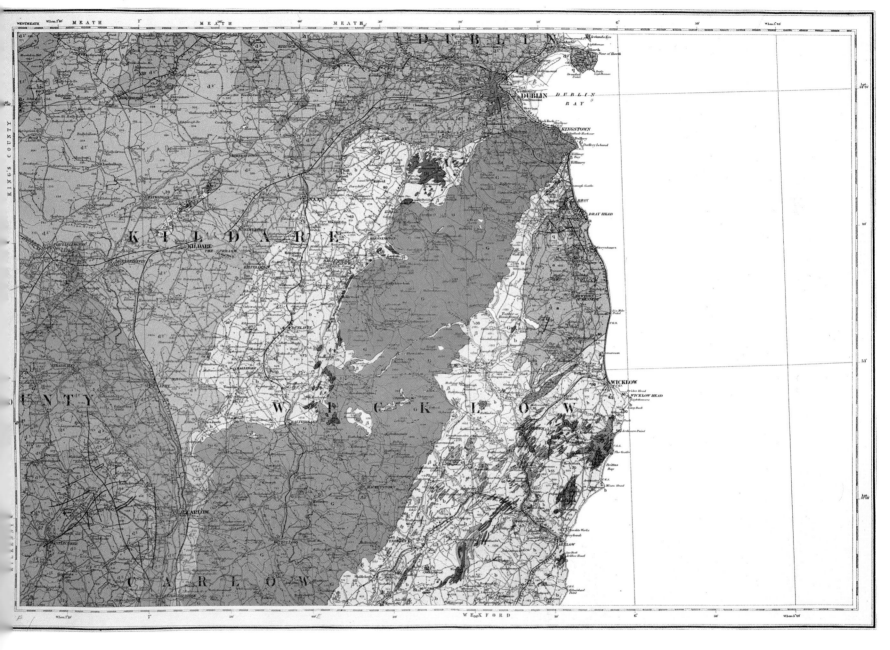

Geological Map compiled by the Geological Survey in 1911 and published by H.M. Ordnance Survey in 1913.

Grey/Green and **Yellow** represent Cambrian rock – slates, quartzites etc.

Reds are Igneous rocks: Geranium red is granite, dark red is diorite.

Mauves/pinks: these are Ordovician and Silurian rocks – schists, slates, sandstones.

Blues and **Greens** represent Limestone. The green is shaly limestone, best developed in the Dublin area.

Brown: Old Red Sandstone. Outcrops occur on the Hill of Allen and NE of Naas.

The soft moss cushions, *Polytrichum*, forms the basis of peat bog.

The very young river, near Liffey Head Bridge

Evening light transforms extruded turf-cuttings into layers of gold.

The Coronation Plantation.

Ruined house near Kilbride.

branch runs north and then east, ending in a hook. It is not a tributary in the normal sense of the term, but is all that remains of a meander marked as the main river on the 1838 map. The river burst its banks and adopted a shorter course. The path of the old valley can still be made out by the line of bushes which ran beside it.

The Brittas River

After Cloghlea Bridge, the road stays high on the hillside, above the valley and passes a sturdily built old National School on the right. A pinewood, on the left a little farther on, gives a good view of the Liffey and its meanders. One kilometre northwest of the pinewood there is a crossroads, with a 'Cul de Sac' notice at the left turn. This road runs to its end where an important tributary, the Brittas River, joins the Liffey. It passes the grey Tudor-style Manor Kilbride and ends in a conglomeration of earth-moving machinery.

The Liffey hides behind a line of bungalows, but the Brittas River runs past the gateway at the end of the road. Its importance lies in the fact that it has run through the limestone gravel over its entire 5 km and carries lime in solution which enriches the lake. It is also a haunt of the freshwater crayfish, a small, lobster-like creature, almost exterminated elsewhere in Europe by disease.

Immediately after the crossroads, the main road passes an inn on the left with a courtyard and a lovely old residence. It was recently restored by its owner to reveal the original granite stone work, hidden by a covering of plaster for long years. The next turn left enters the village of Kilbride with its neat stone church. Then the road goes more or less straight to cross the Liffey at Ballyward Bridge.

Ballyward

It was a very beautiful bridge, with a large, round-headed arch in the centre and one smaller arch on each side. It stood for perhaps a couple of centuries until the floods, which accompanied Hurricane Charlie in September 1986, carried the central span away. Travellers of today clatter across the river on a Bailey bridge, offering fervent prayers that the Wicklow County Council will be able to find the money for the restoration which the bridge so richly deserves.

The banks upstream of the bridge carry notices to discourage visitors who can admire, from the roadside, the line of beeches and poplars which follow the right bank. Ballyward House, a rather severe classical building of three storeys, stands tucked in under the hill of Ballyfoyle, looking out over the flood plain.

The downstream side of the bridge is more inviting, and there are stone steps jutting out from the wall of the bridge on the left bank. The steps lead down to an almost semicircular field, bordered by a loop in the Liffey and by the road. A small tributary, the Ballyward Brook, joins the river 200 metres to the south, flowing beneath a much smaller, but equally attractive stone bridge. The pebbles in the river and in the brown, glacial till of its banks are mostly limestone, with a sprinkling of granite and quartz and an occasional piece of red sandstone. The pebbles are coarsely angular, not smooth or rounded. This is a feature of ice-carried stones: those carried by water become smooth.

Above the right bank at Ballyward Bridge, a narrow, winding road goes off towards Blessington, leaving the river bank for a little only to return to it again at one of the loveliest, but most easily overlooked, viewing points. The spot is marked by a small

BALLYWARD HOUSE

concrete enclosure on the left. It may have housed a village pump.

The river runs at the base of a steep bank cut in the glacial till. Ancient Scots pines and beeches grow on the right bank on its less steep parts, small willows struggle desperately for a foothold elsewhere. The Liffey is broad and shallow, sparkling over a bed of gravel. On the left bank is a beautiful stand of Scots pines, planted in 1970 and 1971. They are young trees yet, and should be truly magnificent when they approach maturity in thirty or forty years.

Our descendants will have to resist the urge to fell them for timber when that time comes and leave them to make a wonderful park. The beauty of a riverside forest is that the trees are able to develop their lower branches to the full. This little stretch of the Liffey somehow seems to belong more to Canadian forests than to Ireland.

Golden Hill is the name of the slope to the right, so named in honour of the sheets of gorse which cover it. It stands on the western boundary of the granite mass and also watches over the transformation of the untamed Liffey of the uplands. The water slackens its pace and grows deeper, ready to open into the placid waters of the Blessington Lakes. ●

Cascade among the trees, at Cloghlea, where the small Shankill River joins the Liffey.

The Blessington Lakes

The Blessington Lakes look as if they belong there. And the forests that surround them blend perfectly with the mountain scenery. It is hard to believe that, up to a point, they are a recent artificial creation, owing as much to engineers, foresters and landscape planners as to nature.

The recent history is that the lakes were created in 1940 when the dam was built at Pollaphuca. The forests, mostly sitka spruce and Japanese larch, began to be planted in 1959. Curiously, the ancestral trees hail from both sides of the Pacific Ocean, from the State of Washington and from Japan respectively.

The valley in the Ice Age

Perhaps the most surprising fact is that the lakes are not as artificial as they seem. The Midlandian ice sheet, that which deposited the limestone till over the lower slopes, retreated slowly towards the north. For a long period it formed a dam along the line of hills to the north and west of the present lake. This dam impounded an enormous area of water, extending from Brittas to Hollywood Glen, some 20 km overall.

Evidence for the former existence of the lake lies in the nature of the gravel and silt deposits in the valley. Details of its history and eventual fate are given in a paper by Anthony Farrington in 'Irish Geography' (1957). The lake varied in extent in the course of many thousands of years, eventually coming to occupy an area very much the same as the present day reservoir. With the withdrawal of the ice sheet, the great glacial lake also disappeared. Then, in 1940, the Electricity Supply Board (ESB) built the dam at Pollaphuca, which re-created it.

Two more aspects of happenings in the Ice Age need to be mentioned to explain the scenery around the lakes: the outwash gravels and the deltas. Even during the Ice Age there were summers as well as winters. In summer some of the snow would melt, producing torrential rivers. The meltwaters carried silt, gravel and stones, depositing them in mountainous heaps whenever the speed of the current slackened. Whereas the ice-born till is a conglomeration of particles of all sizes, from fine silt to large stones and even boulders, the outwash gravels are sorted according to particle size. The larger stones were carried the shortest distances by the water, the silt was held for longer.

Where a torrent entered the lake, the material was deposited in a delta, a fan-shaped area of clean gravel or sand. Beyond the delta the clay particles slowly settled on the lake bed. They form a grey or brown mud, slithery and glutinous when damp. As

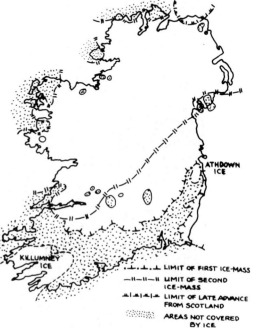

LIMIT OF FIRST ICE-MASS

LIMIT OF SECOND ICE-MASS

LIMIT OF LATE ADVANCE FROM SCOTLAND

AREAS NOT COVERED BY ICE

The Blessington Lakes.

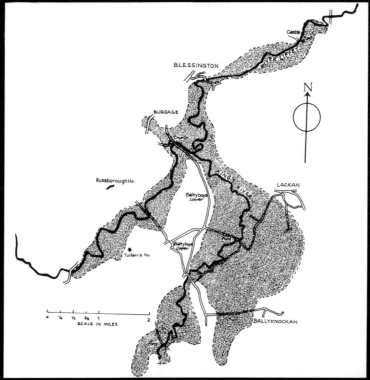

The course of the Liffey and the King's Rivers before the flooding of the valley by the ESB in the 1940s.

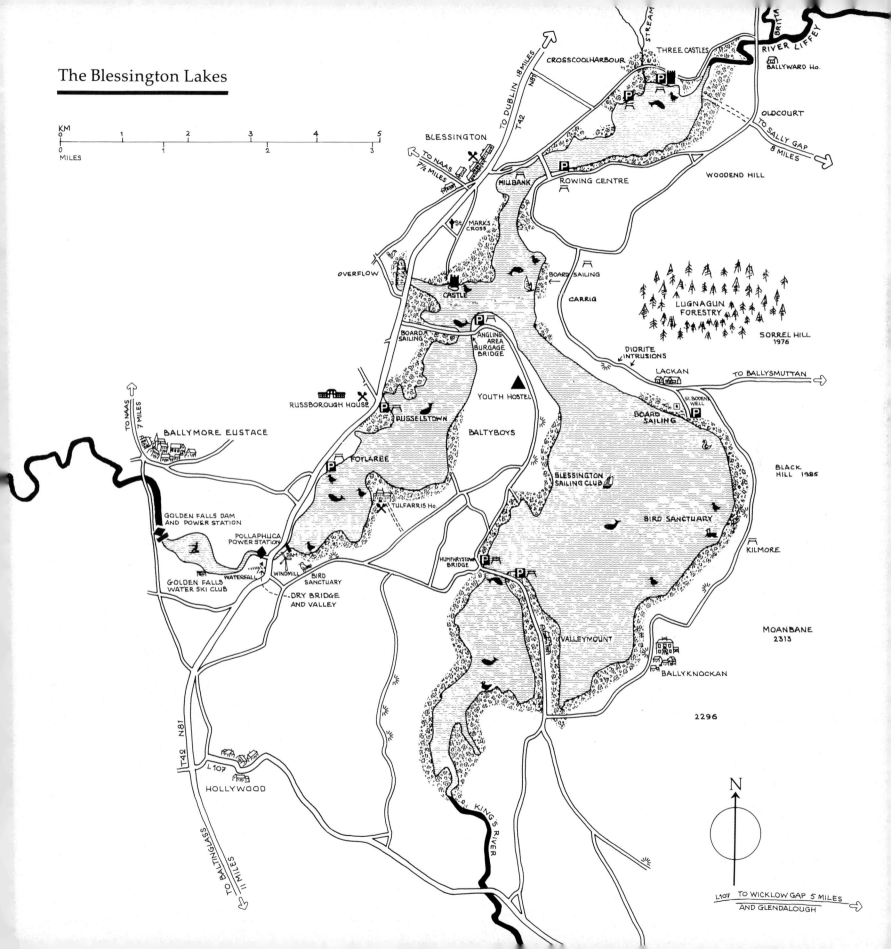

The Blessington Lakes

KM
0 1 2 3 4 5
0 1 2 3
MILES

TO DUBLIN 18 MILES
N81
T42

CROSSCOOLHARBOUR

STREAM

THREE CASTLES

BRITH

RIVER LIFFEY

BALLYWARD Ho.

P
P

OLDCOURT

TO SALLY GAP
8 MILES

BLESSINGTON

TO NAAS
7½ MILES

MILLBANK

P
ROWING CENTRE

WOODEND HILL

St MARKS CROSS

OVERFLOW

BOARD SAILING

CASTLE

CARRIG

LUGNAGUN FORESTRY

SORREL HILL
1976

BOARD SAILING

P
ANGLING AREA
BURGAGE BRIDGE

DIORITE INTRUSIONS

LACKAN

TO BALLYSMUTTAN

YOUTH HOSTEL

St BODENS WELL

P

BOARD SAILING

RUSSBOROUGH HOUSE

P
RUSSELSTOWN

BALTYBOYS

TO NAAS
7 MILES

BALLYMORE EUSTACE

P
FOYLAREE

BLESSINGTON SAILING CLUB

BLACK HILL 1985

GOLDEN FALLS DAM
AND POWER STATION

TULFARRIS Ho.

BIRD SANCTUARY

KILMORE

POLLAPHUCA POWER STATION

DAM

WINDMILL

BIRD SANCTUARY

HUMPHRYSTOWN BRIDGE

P

P

MOANBANE
2313

GOLDEN FALLS WATER SKI CLUB

WATERFALL

DRY BRIDGE AND VALLEY

VALLEYMOUNT

BALLYKNOCKAN

2296

N81
T42
L 107

HOLLYWOOD

KINGS RIVER

TO BALTINGLASS
11 MILES

N

L 107 TO WICKLOW GAP 5 MILES
AND GLENDALOUGH

children we used it as pottery clay, baking our wares in the turf fire. Sadly, we never discovered how to make them waterproof. In places, the seasonal effect of the flood can be traced as 'varves' in the clay, giving it a layered appearance, one layer for each annual flood.

The lake circuit

It is possible to walk very nearly all the way around the lakeshore. But it would be rather longer than the 50 odd kilometres of gravelly beach. Several tributary streams inhibit an easy passage and therefore it is more satisfactory to make the circuit by road.

The shore can be approached easily at the nine 'Amenity Sites' provided by the ESB and at the bridges and other convenient spots. Each of the amenity sites has parking space, picnic tables and easy access to the shore.

The roadway has the added advantage that it leads through the villages, most of which grew up high above the floor of the valley, making use of the drier and less hilly ground. This was an important social and economic benefit when the valley was flooded, since only 76 homesteads stood below the planned level.

A perfectionist who wishes to follow the road all the way around the lake in one trip must make a long diversion at the southern end. Ordinary mortals may enjoy a somewhat shorter tour which keeps as close as possible to the lake and measures 34 km. It misses out the extreme southern portion by crossing the bridge at Valleymount. The main part of this chapter describes that tour, beginning at the head of the lake at Three Castles, a place of treasured memory of days spent birdwatching, fishing and boating many years ago.

This circuit, however, does leave aside some of the finest scenery and a number of pleasant points of access. These are covered in an addendum in the form of a 29 km trip beginning and ending at Blessington.

Three Castles

One castle stands beside the road in the townland of this name. The words appear in Irish in the *Annals of the Four Masters* but otherwise there is no trace of the whereabouts, or even the existence, of its companions. It is a solid structure, the walls mainly of sandstone and limestone blocks, but with neatly carved granite surrounds for the doors and windows. Restored and repaired now, it stands with doors and windows barred to the exclusion of cattle and people alike. It was once accessible to both and, by climbing a wall to the first floor, you could reach a spiral staircase and the roof. The view from the top is magnificent, commanding the valley of the Liffey for miles in both directions.

Its importance lay in its position, very close to the edge of the fertile land of west Wicklow and Kildare. Across the Liffey lies poorer, acid land, not worth the colonist's trouble and expense to annex. There dwelt the O'Tooles and O'Byrnes and other dispossessed Irish clans. They lived, as have mountain men all over Europe, to some extent by pillaging the rich settlers of the lowlands. Hence the castle, from which it was possible to spot musterings on the far side of the river.

Weston Joyce in *The Neighbourhood of Dublin* quotes at some length from the State Papers of King Henry VIII for 1538. The passage describes a bloody skirmish between John Kelway, Constable of Rathmore, a strategic town on the hills to the west, and Tirlagh O'Toole. Kelway took refuge in 'a small pile called the Three Castles' but the

THREE CASTLES

The Blessington Lakes

O'Tooles 'a thatched house joining to the same pile put afire, so that the head of the same pile, being covered with thatch lacking battlement took fire, and so all burned. . . .' The interesting point in the quotation is that it may explain the present day appearance of the castle. The wall facing south is not the original exterior, but has broken walls on each side. Could these have belonged to the 'thatched house' destroyed in that action four hundred and fifty years ago?

Whatever the explanation, the castle was still in use 18 years later when the Annals record a defeat of the Fitzgeralds by a surprising alliance of the English and the O'Tooles. Life is more peaceful by the Castle nowadays. The silence of an autumn morning when I visited it recently was broken only by the call of wild geese on the lake and the footsteps of a cock pheasant at the edge of the woodland.

Common Teals

The water's edge

A path leads down from the main road, south of the castle, to the 'old road' which ran eastwards to a bridge over the Liffey and so up the hill to Oldcourt on the opposite bank. This road runs first between banks and old hedges, exceptionally interesting in being allowed to grow in peace, safe from the savage attentions of mechanical hedge-trimmers. Ash and elder are the dominant trees, with wild rose and hawthorn.

Below the castle, the old road leads on through a larch wood, planted in 1962, passing by snowberry and a horse chestnut tree, remnants of landscape planting long years ago. The track ends abruptly at the water's edge, where the river is broad and silent at its entry to the lake. When the lake level is low, there is a firm, stony beach by its margin. At high water, the beach is covered and the route by the shore goes through the tall reeds which cover a great expanse of flat land between the lake shore and the old road.

In winter the lake shore plays host to a great gathering of wildfowl. Black-headed gulls, curlew, lapwing, mallard, teal and wigeon are all plentiful. But grey lag geese are the pride of the Blessington wildfowl. They arrived in the region in the 1940's, soon after the lakes had been created.

Winter wildfowl

Grey lag geese were common in Ireland at the time and it was not surprising that a party of them should make their winter home by the new lake. However, in the course of the next thirty years, the Irish grey lag population declined seriously, so that they became relatively rare. All this time, the Blessington flock maintained its strength and even increased in numbers, thanks to the very carefully controlled hunting around the lakes. When they were counted in March 1986 they numbered 260. Three Castles is their favourite haunt and the best place to look for them, but they move off to forage in the surrounding fields, returning to the lake for rest and refuge.

The reed swamp

The reed swamp, like the grey lag geese, is another of the contributions made by the reservoir to the natural flora and fauna. Willow trees have grown in places in the swamp, but its general appearance is of an uninterrupted plain. Pheasants live amongst the reeds, redpolls and reed buntings perch in the willows. A wellie-clad walk along the bank down the river and then westwards by the lake shore and back to the old road and

GREYLAG GOOSE

the castle, allows a close approach to the wildfowl which congregate at the water's edge.

Following the old road to the west from the car park is not quite as straightforward as the eastward track just described. The road forks beside a heap of moss-covered masonry, the remains of a farm house. The right hand fork was a driveway, the left the main road. Nowadays the latter heads into a stagnant pool through a bed of nettles. The more amenable route to the lakeshore therefore is to take the driveway, cross a tiny stream and follow the edge of the larch wood towards the shore which the old road, accessible again, now follows.

Deer live in the larch wood and the scent of fox hangs in the air in places by the roadside. The reed swamp continues to the north, interrupted by a large, shallow pool when the lake is high, by an expanse of mud at other times. The lake itself over most of the region is shallow and from time to time recedes completely. Either way, the area is a haven for wintering birds.

Most of them depart in spring for breeding places far to the north. All need large breeding territories and therefore few can remain by the lake. Some, such as the wigeon, geese, whooper swans and Bewick's swans, do not normally breed in Ireland anyway. Mallard, teal, curlew and lapwing all nest near the lake as do many of the smaller birds. In summer, they are joined by swifts, swallows, sand martins and house martins gathering to feed on the insects which emerge from the lake or breed in the swamps.

Great-crested Grebe.

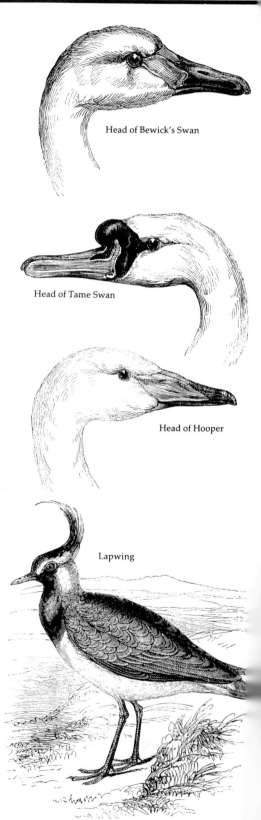

Head of Bewick's Swan

Head of Tame Swan

Head of Hooper

Lapwing

Crosscoolharbour

Progress along the lakeshore is halted, tantalisingly, by a deep tributary stream flowing down from Golden Hill. The stream leads northwards to the new road, built by the ESB in the 1940s. This goes southwest for a little less than 1 km through the townland with the wonderful name of Crosscoolharbour. There it joins the old road at a point of considerable antiquarian interest. Just behind one of the bungalows is a ring fort, with elderly trees growing on its banks. Next to it is an old, disused and rather neglected cemetery. About 100 metres to the west of it was Scurlock's Holy Well, venerated in the month of June but with little sign of latter-day pilgrims.

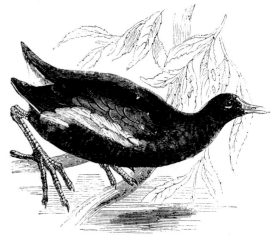

Moorhen

Picnic tables stand amongst the larches farther down the road, giving a lovely view across the lake to the low hill of Woodend on the left and Sorrell on the right. Steps lead down to the beach, and a very interesting beach it is, too. Amongst the usual limestone pebbles are patches of grey, slithery clay and, just 125 metres southwards from the steps, the clay appears in a bank at the back of the beach. It has a layered structure, almost like the pages of a book, and is an excellent example of the varves formed in the lake beyond the ancient delta. More of the clays are exposed at the point to the northwest of the steps. Here they can be seen lying in position on top of the glacial till.

From Crosscoolharbour the road runs southwestwards towards Blessington, bounded by hedges on both sides, interrupted by unusual gateways. Some of them conform to the local standards with gate posts either of hewn granite or of living ash trees. The odd ones have railroad sleepers. These represent the last mortal remains of the Dublin and Blessington Steam Tramway which plied its way nearby from 1888 to 1932. The steam engine, resplendent with a tall smokestack, hauled two double-decker passenger carriages.

The road to Blessington

Where the road approaches the Blessington bridge, there are mountainous gravel quarries to the north. These are part of the delta system, deposited by torrents coming through a gap in the ridge of hills at Blessington. The ESB bridge replaces the older Blessington Bridge which crossed the river lower down in the valley. A water mill stood beside it and, for many years after the flooding, the two gables and chimneys of the tall mill building rose defiantly above the water.

The new bridge provided a quite unexpected home for birds. Soon after it was built, house martins came to nest beneath it. They have very specialised needs: a smooth ceiling with a vertical wall to attach their cup-shaped nests to. The eaves of some old, but very few new, houses suit them. The bridge, with its flat and angular surfaces was ideal. The lake provided all the insects the birds could possibly need. Totally secure from cats and out of reach of people, the house martins fly in and out betwen the pillars, catching flies and feeding their nestlings.

House Martin.

The gravel pits also provide nesting places, but for sand martins, not house martins. The sand martins need a bank of a certain consistency of sand. It must be firm enough to allow them to dig horizontal burrows of up to one metre long. Thanks to the way in which the water sorted and graded the sand, there are several suitable banks. The sand martins are sociable birds and in places the cliff face is honeycombed with their nesting holes.

The way from the bridge to Blessington is a tree-lined one, shaded by stately beeches. At the Health Centre just before you come to village, a discreet laneway leads down towards the lake at Millbank. This is another of the old, abandoned roads. It is bounded first by a wall of limestone blocks, next by a damp mud cliff, with a covering of green liverworts and finally by a granite wall. The river ran close to the bank here, cutting away to form the steep slopes where it took a sharp turn to the left. The estuarine muds of the former lake were plentiful in places and have made the bank unstable. Down by the lake shore, broken pieces of concrete tell of a failed effort to prevent the cliff from slipping farther.

The village of Blessington

A short distance up the road from Millbank lies the wide street of the village of Blessington. It is a delightful place, with an old-world hotel and numerous pubs. The village was developed in the 17th century by Michael Boyle, Archbishop of Dublin.

The church was founded in 1682 and, not long afterwards, provided with a peal of six bells. They are rung at half past six every Saturday evening. Ringing these old bells has become so popular that the parish even boasts a junior bell-ringing team to supplement the main one. The bells are all the original ones, never recast. The church clock makes a claim to be the oldest public timepiece in Ireland.

The Archbishop owned estates centred on Blessington, but stretching far away to near the source of the Liffey. These passed by marriage to the Hill family. Wills Hill crowned a highly successful career in politics by being created the first Marquis of Downshire in 1789. His inheritance included a mansion to the northwest of the village, where the old gateway still stands.

The mansion was destroyed by an accidental fire towards the end of the 18th century. The village itself was devastated in 1798 when most of the houses were burned. The stately appearance of Blessington was decreed by the 3rd Marquis, an outstanding landlord who worked ceaselessly to keep his colossal estates in order. The bizarre fountain opposite the church bears a suitably loyal inscription. In this case it may indeed reflect the sentiments of the tenantry. The Marquis died in 1845 at Blessington in the course of a tour of his estates. Downshire correspondence, mostly dealing with the running of the estates and amounting to 30,000 letters, is preserved in the Northern Ireland Public Records Office.

Monument to the 3rd Marquess of Blessington in the centre of the village. The inscription, on three sides, is as given below.

A TRIBUTE OF RESPECT FROM THE TENANTRY ON THE WICKLOW KILDARE AND KILKENNY ESTATES OF THE MARQUIS OF DOWNSHIRE

ERECTED ON THE COMING OF AGE OF THE EARL OF HILLSBOROUGH 27 Nov. 1853

THE WATER SUPPLIED AT THE COST OF A KIND AND GENEROUS LANDLORD FOR THE BENEFIT OF HIS ATTACHED AND LOYAL TENANTS

Burgage

From Blessington the main road heads straight towards the south for exactly 1 km where a turn to the left goes down to the 19th century cemetery of Burgage. At its southern end stands a great cross of granite, in some ways like the typical high crosses, but with no trace of sculptured figures. It does have the usual circle between the arms, but in the form of a solid disc, not a ring. It is called St Mark's Cross nowadays, having been known as St Baoithin's up to the 19th century. The cross formerly stood some way to the south, close to a holy well and a cemetery beside the ruined church of Burgage. The bodies from the old burial ground were reinterred and the cross re-erected in the newer and higher cemetery.

A narrow lane leads from the cemetery to the lake shore and a ruined tower. The preferable way of continuing around the lake is to go back to the main road which crosses a culvert at a place curiously known as the Overflow, a large pool to the west of the road. In a way it does look as if the lake had overflowed to fill it, but in fact it is simply the flooded bed of a tributary stream. Swans usually nest there and moorhens abound. Herons, which nest nearby in the grounds of Russborough, visit it frequently.

A long, narrow bay of the lake comes up to the road opposite to the Overflow and gives one of the most picturesque views of the whole region. On the left stand the remnants of the ancient tower of Burgage which looks like a castle – and a very romantic one, too – but was in fact a church. To the right is the wooded hill of Baltyboys and, across the lake, the long, green shoulder of Lugnagun, with Sorrell Hill behind it.

Russelstown and Russborough

To make the longer circuit of the lakes, we must head southwards, resisting the temptation to cross the Burgage Bridge. The next stopping place is on the left in the townland of Russelstown. The turning enters woodland and goes quickly to the shore of the most delightful bay in the entire lake system. It is a narrow, winding inlet, sheltered on all sides by spruce and larch woods, screened by alder and poplar. The floating jetty is used for boats servicing the trout cages out on the lake.

The view across the water is of Baltyboys Hill. Almost completely covered by the limestone drift, it has fertile pasture on its slopes, divided into generously sized fields with neat hedges. It is named on the map as 'Boystown or Baltyboys', a confused corruption of the Irish name. The 'boys' part of the name comes from the Irish 'bui' meaning yellow, but often rendered 'boy' in the anglicised form. The Bal part of the name can indeed be translated as town and 'Boystown' seems to be a cross between a translation and a phonetic spelling.

Russborough, greatest of the great houses of the upper Liffey, stands in its spacious demesne on the right of the road, a little farther on. It demands a special visit (see p.103), but even passers-by can admire the house in the middle distance. Building began in 1741 and the house survived 1798 intact. The high wall which surrounds most of the demesne has been lowered in front of the house, allowing the plain people to admire it. On the left of this gap, elderly trees, including a lovely weeping willow, surround a hidden pond. Herons nest in the higher trees above it.

Russborough
2 miles south of Blessington

Russborough is the home of Sir Alfred and Lady Beit. Through their generosity it is now owned by the Alfred Beit Foundation, to provide a centre for exhibitions and functions, and to make it accessible to the public.

The rooms are not enormous, but are beautifully proportioned. The Salon has some of the Francini brothers' finest plasterwork; there is a Music Room with a vaulted ceiling to enhance the sound; the Dining Room and Tapestry Room are full of charm and interest. The house is a perfect setting for the Art Collection which is one of the most important in these islands. Even though some of the most priceless paintings were presented to the National Gallery in 1987 for security reasons, the collection remaining is worth travelling any distance to see, especially to see paintings of this calibre in a domestic setting, rather than in the somewhat unnatural setting of a gallery. Works by Vernet, Guardi, Bellotto, Gainsborough, Raeburn and Ruisdael still grace the walls, and there is also a display of carpets, tapestries and Italian bronzes.

The house is open every afternoon during July and August, and on Sundays and Bank Holidays during the rest of the year, or by special arrangement. There is a tea room, a shop with souvenirs and craft items, a children's playground and a fine wooded parkland to wander in. Bus No. 65 stops at Ballymore, less than a mile away (and it's a nice walk after that). Telephone 045-65239.

The end of the lake

Less than a mile south of Russborough is the picnic place of Foylaree, standing high above the lake at the top of a gravel cliff. In the distance, to the left across the lake, are the floating trout cages. To the right the lake ends abruptly at the dam, which can be seen more clearly by driving on and parking just in front of a little pinewood on the left.

Across the road from it stands a tall, pale yellow building with high windows, surrounded by mature pine trees. It is the Valve House owned by Dublin Corporation. The valves control the water drawn off from the lake to be piped to the treatment plant down the hill at Ballymore Eustace (see page 61).

Above the lake shore the steep banks of glacial till are different from those at the northern end. They contain slatey sandstone rather than limestone as the more plentiful rock. The rock itself outcrops at this point. Just around the corner stands the dam, blocking the narrow gorge through which the Liffey plunged in its days of freedom.

From the road, Pollaphuca looks pleasant, with its fine old trees, but scarcely gives a hint of its grandeur. You must walk along the road, peer in through the ESB gateway and then crane your neck over the high walls of the bridge. The gateway discourages access to the power station, almost completely hidden down in the valley, except for the great cylindrical tower whose top stands above the level of the lake. It is a hollow cylinder, designed to withstand the surge of water which comes when the generators are turned off.

The house on the left bears a sign saying 'Tram Shop' and retains something of a railway station look. This was the end of the line for the steam tramway, which was extended from Blessington in 1895, seven years after the Dublin to Blessington route began.

The Pooka's Pool

From the recess on the bridge just past the Tram Shop, overlooking its little garden with a dejected apple tree, there is a splendid view of the upper part of the gorge. The left bank is very steep, going down to a vertical cliff of slate, encrusted with pale green lichens. Male fern and bluebells grow on the lower banks and beeches and pines on the upper, with laurels a little way upstream.

Downstream of the bridge, the gorge widens out. Down at the bottom on the left bank are the remains of a turbine and across the river in the distance stand pale green fibre-glass fish tanks used for rearing young salmon. A gateway leads to a footpath running along the edge of the gorge to take you by the back entrance to the pub.

The footpath gives a view through the trees of the bridge, built by Alexander Nimmo in the 1820s, of blocks of sandstone with granite finishing. The arch is gothic and the bridge is decorated with crosses and blind arches. It stands 40 metres high and spans 20 metres. It is possible to climb down the slopes to the pools beneath but, as the notices say, extremely dangerous, especially in wet weather when leaves and clay conspire to accelerate the descent.

Where dark pools now lie and the water trickles, the Liffey used to rush (according to Joyce) saying, or perhaps roaring: 'Poulaphouca, Poulaphouca'. The ESB and the Dublin Corporation have swallowed it up and reduced it almost to silence.

There were three cascades and three pools, of which the middle one was the property of the Pooka himself. He was a sprite with a warped sense of humour, usually

Poul a Phuca C Wicklow.

Pollaphuca: an engraving of the gorge shortly after the building of Alexander Nimmo's bridge in the 1820s. The photograph (far left), taken in the 1930s, shows how recently it has become almost totally overgrown.

appearing in the form of a horse. If he chanced on a somnolent drunk, he would hoist the luckless sleeper on his back and take him for an unmerciful gallop. This, of course, would explain the victim's dishevelled appearance and severe headaches the morning after.

While the gorge is a place of outstanding beauty, it is geographically quite normal. The water of the Liffey is held at a high level, 200 metres or more, between the granite to the east and the ridge of sandstones to the west. Where the ridge gives way to a plain, some 50 metres lower down, the water plunged over the rock barrier, cutting the deep cleft in the course of time.

The dry valley

The next bridge, 150 metres down the road, spans a quite extraordinary valley. As at Pollaphuca, the walls of the bridge prevent a casual motorist from seeing what lies below. Indeed, I had passed it many times before noticing it. The valley is deep and green but completely devoid of a river. In wet weather pools form, but even these are temporary and grass grows all over the valley floor. Once upon a time the Liffey did flow there, but it abandoned its course to cut the great gorge.

For the road engineers it was nearly as challenging as the gorge and they solved the problem in a spectacular way, inspired perhaps by the builders of the tower houses like the one at Three Castles. In effect they filled the valley with a castle, using a barrel vault to support the road. A second vault at a lower level stands beside the main one, but it is hidden by side walls so that the bridge appears from the outside to consist of a single, pointed arch. Provided you don't mind sharing the floor of the bridge with the cattle, which appreciate its shelter, you can enter the chamber beneath the arch. Otherwise, take a short walk along the driveway to the secluded pub of Pollaphuca House, admiring pine and oak trees by the way, and enjoy a dry view of the dry bridge.

The Piper's Stones of Athgreany

At this point a diversion of 5 km to the south, along the main road for Baltinglass, might just be permitted, even though it makes a perilously close approach to the valley of the Slaney. The road goes through the townland of Athgreany where, in a landscape of ancient hawthorns, stand the Piper's Stones; a very fine circle of 13 boulders where it is well known that the phantom piper will oblige from time to time.

The circle probably dates to the Bronze Age. The archaeologist Peter Harbison made the interesting discovery that , although there are a great many stone circles in Ireland, it is only in this region that they are associated with a piper. The tradition dates to the 17th century when puritanical settlers brought with them the improving tale of a group of wayward people who went dancing on the Sabbath and were turned to stone.

'The Piper's Stones' at Athgreany.

Baltyboys

After the Dry Bridge, two unobtrusive left turns continue the journey around the lake. The road rises after the second turn and gives a good view where it levels out at a gate, back to the upper end of the dry valley, to the wind generator on the left and the cliffs of glacial till above the lake to the right. The generator was built as an experiment in 1982 and produces 55 kilowatts. The next turn to the left leads to Tulfarris House,once an affluent farmstead, in 1988 an up-market hotel.

The road past Tulfarris runs beside a lovely row of very old beech trees. On the right are the ruins of two large houses: as time goes by, it takes more and more land to keep a rich family in their accustomed style. So the farms grow bigger and nobody wants to buy the old homesteads.

The geological boundary between sandstone to the west and granite to the east runs close to the road. The boundary itself is invisible, but it probably accounts for the very existence of Baltyboys Hill. The resistance to weathering of the schist layer between sandstone and granite prevented the Liffey from wearing the rock away and capturing the King's River to the east.

The lake in 1943, just after the flooding. Note the shoreline, with grass to the water's edge and no sandy shore.

Just over the hill, surrounded by granite walls and with neatly carved gateposts, is a cemetery, commanding a lovely view across the lake to Ballyknockan. Many of the headstones use the local stone, indeed it is the burial place of the quarrymen. It is a rather curious graveyard, with a cluster of graves at each end and a green sward in the middle. The reason is that the rock in the middle is so near the surface that nobody can be buried there.

From the cemetery, the road goes down the hill towards the shore of the greatest of the three lakes and takes a right turn towards Humphrystown Bridge and Valleymount. There are pleasant parking places at both ends of the bridge. The lake shores are sandy with the glacial till exposed above the high water mark. Sandstone, limestone and granite are all present in the till.

Towards the north and west the lake is held within a magnificent curve of mountain slopes. The long ridge of Lugnagun has a cap of spruce forest extending downwards to the 300 metre contour. This marks the limit of the fertile land which depends on the limestone till. Above it the hillside was poor, acid pasture which the owners were prepared to sell for State forestry, while the fields below were worth keeping for grazing.

The taller hills nearby are Sorrel, Black Hill and the two-headed Moanbane. Mullaghcleevaun in the distance peeps through the gap between Black Hill and the northern summit of Moanbane. Away to the south, beyond the top of the lake, the higher hills are Church Mountain and Corriebracks, which separate the catchment of the Liffey from the Slaney.

Valleymount

The village of Valleymount nowadays stands on a long, narrow peninsula, having been built at the top of a ridge with extensive bog on either side, now submerged. It marks the boundary of the granite lands which centre on the next hamlet of Ballyknockan. The achievements of local stone masons show in every old house where fan lights and lintels and window sills are all of cut stone. Abandoned and unroofed cottages of granite stand firmly amongst the new houses, resolutely refusing to be destroyed by the elements.

The west front of the little church is delightfully ornamented, with granite pilasters and a slender cross, the latter carved with a succession of dates in the life of the church: 1846, 1875 and 1938. Inside there are four beautiful windows by Harry Clarke. Three are memorials to named families, but the fourth has a special dedication:

> 'Erected by the Quarrymen of Ballyknockan in memory of their deceased parents and relatives'

From this point onwards the work of the quarrymen dominates the scenery, with more and more stone appearing as you approach the quarries themselves, perched on the slopes of Moanbane.

At the left turn out of Valleymount, the walls are neatly built and the barbed wire above them is attached to tall stone pillars, built into the wall every 6 or 7 metres. Foxgloves and pennywort, with its tuppenny-sized pale green leaves, grow along the walls. Ballyknockan and the quarries spread over the hill above the lake.

Heron.

The quarries of Ballyknockan

The road crosses a small tributary which the lake has flooded to produce a swamp with alder and hazel. Then it rises gradually, with the stone walls growing ever more stony and spectacular. The quarries centre on a mass of granite described in the Geological Survey map as 'Rather fine-grained granite, nearly equal parts of felspar and quartz. Mica black. Quarried in joints and runs in an ENE direction'. It has for centuries been a highly prized architectural stone, gracing many of Dublin's most important buildings and even exported to England.

Close to a tall, new crane in the quarries stand the Virgin and Child of Ballyknockan, a charming sculpture in stone. The Virgin looks across to the distant Church Mountain, with the Child standing beside her. There is a memorial tablet in the wall beside the group. It may once have said something about them, but the words now are quite illegible.

At least two stories are told of why she stands there. The first is that the Child is on the wrong side — in which case Raphael and others had it wrong, too. The second is that whoever commissioned the work refused to accept it and the quarrymen subscribed to pay the sculptor and keep it. Looking at her you can easily see why some aficionado of plaster Madonnas might have rejected this much more original work. I feel sure that she is happier where she stands, under the sky, venerated by villagers and by people who love the mountains.

A track leads past the Virgin, up the hill and forks a little way farther on. The right hand path leads for a long way through the moorland and up Moanbane which has a rather soggy summit, but gives a splendid view. The left hand track ends at two gateways. The wooden gate on the right marks the way up the hill, following a high stone wall into the next field where stands another and very much older sculpture by the Ballyknockan people. It is a small cross, standing in a hollowed stone. Its tale is that the sheep were smitten by a plague which was stemmed by prayers said at the cross.

Just beside the cross, the stone wall is broached by a very curious small gateway. Made of two uprights and a lintel of stone, it is high enough for a sheep to pass through, but far from comfortable for the shepherd.

From this height on the hillside, there is a distant view across the lake and away to the plains of Kildare where the Liffey flows. The symmetrical, pointed hill is the Hill of Allen (page 88), a prominent part of the ridge which separates the Liffey from the Slate River, a tributary of the Barrow. Before leaving Ballyknockan, feast your eyes on the stone walls of the old cottages.

The granite lion sits on the roadside near the Ballyknockan stone quarry. Two of his brothers guard Stormont Castle. This one, apparently rejected, still manages to retain his dignity.

Stone and sheep

Sadly, the village no longer supports as many families as in times gone by. So there are many roofless dwellings and deserted gardens. But quite a few of the best houses survive, some with neatly carved decorations. The old houses are too small and too crowded for present day tastes. Ballyknockan is a rare thing in the Irish countryside, the centre of a region which enjoys the basis of a small rural industry. The people have a source of income other than what can be made from sheep farming.

The grazing in the hinterland by and large is not quite good enough for cattle which can thrive only on the lower slopes. In the days of subsistence farming, many families could survive on their own potato crops and a few animals. For anything approaching

The one remaining castle at 'Three Castles' on the lake shore NE of Blessington.

View of the lake, looking SE towards Moanbane Mountain with Ballyknockan to the right.

Humphreystown Bridge.

The Virgin of Ballyknockan. Though she looks rather neglected and abandoned on a wayside track, there is usually an offering of fresh flowers at her feet.

contemporary living standards, the grazing area per family needs to be very large and therefore few people can live off the land.

For different reasons, the farms on the rich land across the lake are also few and scattered. The land there is good enough to make the farmers wealthy. It has been the preserve of the well-to-do for many generations, considered worth granting in the 17th century to the people who were on the right side of the current ruler.

A memorial to the harsh realities of 19th century life stands near the lake shore at the end of the old road which linked Ballyknockan and Valleymount. You find it by following the main road below the village, passing both pubs and stopping where the road swings to the right, with a marvellous view across the water to Lugnagun.

The old road is now a bumpy track, leading downhill between the granite walls with their ferns and foxgloves. A solitary gable stands in a small field and a neatly carved stone bears this inscription:

> THE EMERGENCY LAND-
> -GRABBER
> DEFEATED HERE 1882
> GOD SAVE IRELAND

The tradition is that the villagers overnight rebuilt the cottage following an eviction.

Lackan

The village of Lackan consists mainly of a delightful, long, low shop which sells everything. Just beyond it a signpost indicates St Boden's Well by way of a road which winds steeply down hill, past a neat church, to the lake shore. It is a lovely spot, with miles of white, sandy beach in both directions setting off a view back to Ballyknockan.

The Well was a spring, some distance down the hill from where the beach now lies, and therefore inundated in 1940. It was revealed again in 1978 when the lake level fell lower than ever before. This time the devotees were ready to act and sought help from the secular powers. To atone for its past sins in swallowing the well, the ESB laid a pipe from a point above high water mark down to the well, planted a village pump at the top and donated the land to the worshippers. Now you can pump the holy water into a rectangular font, hewn from a single granite block. The shrine stands, surmounted by a small cross and surrounded by concrete walls, to the west of the carpark.

The granite/sandstone boundary crosses the road just south of Lackan. As at Baltyboys, it is not conspicuous, but it may explain why the hill down to St Boden's Well is so very steep. After Lackan, the road rises to run around the great spur of Lugnagun. The underlying rock along the ridge of the spur is diorite, an igneous rock intruded about the same time as the granite. Its chemical composition is quite different, giving it an almost black colour in contrast to the pale granite.

Diorite intrusions cross the road at two points, west of Lackan, standing out above the sandstone and making the road rise steeply. It outcrops above the glacial till at Sroughan, to the east of a house with rounded windows. The second intrusion lies buried where a narrow road marked 'Cul de Sac' runs away up the hillside. This, the hamlet of Carrig, is an interesting place to stop and look across the lake - and a beautiful one anyway for those not committed to the more abstruse points of geomorphology.

'NEW' St. BODEN'S WELL

The gate posts opposite the side road are built of sandstone, not of granite nor, indeed, of diorite. Across the lake, the village of Blessington spreads along the edge of the valley. The long, low range of hills to the west and north are crucial elements in the development of the Liffey and the lakes. They have a core of sandstone which the Liffey, flowing down from the higher hills to the east, was unable to breach until she came to Pollaphuca. This forced her to embark on the long journey through Kildare instead of going direct to Dublin Bay.

The Blessington gap

There was a gap in the sandstone to the west of Blessington. Meltwater from the Midlandian ice sheet rushed through it and deposited enormous quantities of gravel. It was a very wide gap and is marked by the colossal quarrying operation where the gravels are being removed for building. The quarries can be seen to the right of the church tower. To its left is the long-established Forestry plantation of Glending and, immediately to its left, though not easy to distinguish, the deep valley of the same name cut by another torrent of meltwater.

A little way down the hill there is a picnic place beside a tiny stream crossed by a stone bridge with a square opening. The road formerly took a sharp turn to go over this bridge, but a new, straight road has been built over an embankment through which the stream now runs in a culvert. Diorite blocks have been used in the construction of the bridge.

The last picnic place on the circuit lies beside the Blessington Bridge. It serves also as a car park for the pavilion of the Dublin Metropolitan Regatta Council who hold their annual rowing festival there. There is a pleasant view of the northern end of the lake, with its backdrop formed by Seahan and Seefin, with brown or purple shades of moorland and across the lake to the green of the limestone pastures.

Woodend and Oldcourt

The road continues eastwards, keeping close to the edge of the lake and returning once more to the granite, again over an imperceptible border. An ESB bridge takes the road across the bay formed by a streamlet and then an old bridge crosses the Woodend Stream. On its left bank a grassy track through a pinewood goes down to the lake shore. The bridge is a very neat one, using both kinds of the local stone. The sides of its walls along the road are very neatly built, using the slatey sandstone, while the sides facing the stream are of granite, built into round arches.

That is very nearly the end of the tour. The road rises from the Woodend Stream and moves away from the lake, to go through the village of Oldcourt. This village, incidentally, is less than 4 km from the upper Liffey at Ballysmuttan, by way of a right turn for Sally Gap. Opposite this turn, a seldom-used track goes down to the river, meeting it a little way upstream of the lake. It is the old road which used to cross by a bridge and continue past Three Castles on the right bank. The modern way back to the castle leads over Ballyward Bridge and westwards above the Liffey under Golden Hill.

Fieldfare and Song-thrush

The Blessington Lakes

The Southern Circuit — Burgage

South of the Overflow, on the road from Blessington to Pollaphuca, a left turn with a signpost for Valleymount shows the way across the lake by Burgage Bridge towards Baltyboys. This is a land of hawthorn hedges, at its very best in May when the white flowers bloom and the beeches, oaks and lime trees of the demesnes are wearing fresh, green leaves.

The picnic place on the east side of the bridge is the good work of the Wicklow County Council. Behind it stands a beautiful cluster of trees: one oak, one beech and one lime, planted so close together that they give the impression of a single tree with three trunks.

The fence between the trees and the picnic tables, with its concrete posts and taut wire, extends all the way around the lake. It was built as close to the 189 metre (620 foot) contour as practible, according to the requirements of the Law (page 55). Just outside the fence, a row of squat concrete pillars with pointed tops and stamped with the letters ESB, mark the boundary of the ESB property. They follow the fence around the lake, which is kept to a level of 3 metres or more below them.

Across the lake the tower of Burgage stands out dramatically, conjuring lake-isles and maidens in durance vile but innocent of any such associations. Depending on the height of the lake it sometimes occupies an island and sometimes is attached to the shore, but always sheltered by the larch wood behind it. There are long sandbanks close by where wild duck and black-headed gulls like to assemble. Farther in the distance are the sandstone hills which confine the Liffey to her upper valley.

A path leads around the point below a line of beech trees with oak and even, in 1988, with a living elm which had survived the murderous Dutch elm disease. Elms are relatively few around the lake and the isolated specimens have a much better chance of avoiding infection than do those in more crowded situations. There are traces of an old road along the line of the beeches, but the path becomes difficult where it enters a jungle of nettles and elder.

The loneliest lake

Above the picnic place, the road leads on around the point of Baltyboys, passing a Youth Hostel and, a little way farther on, crossing the geological boundary from sandstone to granite. Then it proceeds through Valleymount, as on the main circuit, but you keep to the right instead of taking the left turn for Ballyknockan. This leads up a hill and then down into the valley of the King's River, through Lockstown, crossing by an old stone bridge.

The next turn to the right is the road to go on to continue the circuit of the lake. But there is a very tempting diversion to the enchanting glen of Hollywood with its little church whose neat slate roof conceals a stone vaulted one of great age. Hollywood Glen is another of the 'overflow channels' scoured out by the meltwaters.

However, the scenery on the way around the lake is every bit as exciting. The road is narrow and climbs high above the water. You can look down on its most remote point, far from roads, where the King's River enters. Shrouded by spruce and larch and tucked in by the Valleymount peninsula, the lake lies in peace. Visit it in October when the larches shine like gold.

Then the road goes steeply downhill, by a wonderfully winding cutting beneath old

beech trees. A little farther on is Coill Log na gCro, a Forestry car park with paths through the wood. The forest, as usual, is planted on the poorer, high ground. Below it roll the rich farms with cattle and expensive horses. The road thereafter runs on above the Pollaphuca lake, over the Dry Bridge and so to Blessington.

Taking the waters

Wild geese, wind surfers, the mountains mirrored on the calm surface: it is easy to forget that the Blessington lakes were conceived and born as a sound economic proposition. In the next chapter we interrupt our journey down the river and discover how the strength of the Liffey, as well as her beauty, has been enrolled for the benefit of the people of Dublin. •

The Bounty of Anna Liffey

 nna Liffey is rich and beautiful and generous, freely sharing her wealth and power with the people of Dublin. The citizens of a thousand years ago, to say nothing of their forbears and successors, sought her help in two directions. In the first place, the waters of the dark pool provided a well sheltered haven for ships, while the ford of the hurdles made for an important crossing by land. Dublin owes its very existence to the river.

Keeping Dublin pure

The second task which the citizens required of the lady was less savoury. While the splendid ships carried merchandise and people to the ends of the earth, the service of the waters was also demanded to remove the waste of the Dubliners. This they did discreetly and efficiently as long as the population remained small. But when it increased in the 18th and 19th centuries, the burden of ordure and excrement began to approach unpleasantly intolerable limits.

Fortunately, in the latter half of the 19th century, help was at hand. My great grandfather, George Spencer Harty, devised the main drainage scheme by which the River Liffey ceased to be the city's main sewer. This work allowed the waters to remain remarkably pure, when judged against the standards of the majority of European capital cities.

The acid test for the health and purity of a river is whether salmon can survive in it. Even in the worst years, the 1950s and 60s, salmon did continue to run. Although there have been setbacks, the general trend through the '70s and '80s has been for the sanitary state of the Liffey to improve, in spite of the greatly increased human population she serves.

Relieved of her squalid burden, Anna L. was free to inspire the people to accept her more wholesome gifts of drinking water and electric power. Dublin in the 19th century enjoyed a supply of excellent water from a number of sources. Both canals had been tapped since the 18th century. When these became inadequate, the Corporation looked towards the rivers on the eastern side of the Wicklow Mountains, the Vartry and later the Dodder. It was not until the 20th century that serious moves were made towards harnessing the Liffey on the grand scale.

Power for the people

The Water Power Resources Sub-Committee of the Board of Trade under the chairmanship of Sir John Purser Griffith in 1921 proposed the erection of a dam in the gorge of Pollaphuca to form a storage reservoir with a top water level at the 600 foot (182 metre) contour. This committee identified the Golden Falls and salmon leap sites and also recommended a dam at Cloghlea on the upper Liffey and one at Lockstown on the King's River.

A major, perhaps the major, step forward came from the Commission of Inquiry into the Resources and Industries of Ireland in their Report on Water Power published in January 1922. The Commissioners stated:

> 'The Liffey powers are of immediate national importance owing to their proximity to the city of Dublin, and should, therefore, be especially investigated at once.'

Investigations of the power of the Liffey did indeed begin at once, as the Commissioners advised. Two questions had to be answered: first, whether enough water was available and, second, whether the valleys could hold the water if a dam were to be built. The water supply would have to be measured over a long period and this was put in hand immediately. In 1922 a water level gauge was installed in the Pollaphuca gorge and daily records of the height of the river were maintained up to 1938 when the construction of the dam ended their usefulness. The average flow for the twelve years 1922 to 1934 was 9,459 litres per second. The river was described as 'flashy', a mild enough term considering that its extremes of flow were found to range from 1,000 in a drought to 300,000 litres per second in a high flood.

The flow calculations thus confirmed that the Liffey had more than enough water available both for generating and for water supply, provided it could be retained in the valleys by a dam at Pollaphuca. There was no problem concerning the impenetrable granite core of the mountains to the east. But the nature of the low range of hills to the west, with their superabundant gravel, was far from promising. In the words of the Commissioners:

> 'Unfortunately, it is doubtful if a considerable portion of the hill, which would form the northern side of this reservoir about half a mile above the dam, would be watertight. The surface indications all suggest that this portion of the hill is an old watercourse filled with gravel and sand. (*This refers to the Blessington gap, page 50, with its glacial gravels*). If so, it would not be watertight, and serious leakage would occur . . . This point cannot be decided until trial borings should be made.'

The Liffey Reservoir Act

In the event, a large number of borings, trial pits and trenches were made under the guidance of geologists, Dr J. Hug of Zürich and T H Hallissy, Director of the Geological Survey. These trials extended from Blessington to Golden Falls and the geologists expressed themselves satisfied with the results. The information provided by the water gauge and by the test drillings confirmed that the entire project was viable. The proposals for dams at Lockstown and Cloghlea were not pursued, but Pollaphuca, Golden Falls and Leixlip went ahead. Legislation was prepared and the Liffey Reservoir Bill became law in 1936. The Act contains an Agreement:

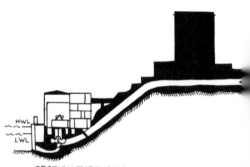

SECTION THROUGH POLLAPHUCA
GENERATING STATION

'made the 18th day of June 1936, between THE RIGHT HONOURABLE THE LORD MAYOR, ALDERMEN AND BURGESSES OF DUBLIN (Hereinafter called 'the Corporation' . . . of the one part and the ELECTRICITY SUPPLY BOARD . . .'

This Agreement set out the details of how the land was to be prepared, what water levels were to be maintained and how much water the Corporation was entitled to draw off. The ESB was required, among other provisions to:

'(i) Cut down and remove from the site of the Reservoir all growing timber and undergrowth to the satisfaction of the Corporation:

(ii) Remove all dwelling-houses, sheds, stables, cow-byres, and piggeries,' and shall render sanitary the sites of the same by sprinkling the site with chlorate of lime to the satisfaction of the Corporation:

(iii) Subject to obtaining all necessary ecclesiastical and other permissions, remove from any graveyard which may be flooded by the Reservoir the bodies buried therein and inter the same elsewhere . . . .

(iv) Remove and level down, or partly remove and level down as far as may be reasonably neccessary, all mounds, fences, ditches and obstructions upon that part of the Reservoir which shall lie over five hundred and seventy five feet . . . .'

The reservoir

The final scheme was more ambitious than the earlier proposals. Pollaphuca remained the chosen site for the dam, but the top level of the water was fixed at 618 feet (188.4 metres) rather than 600 feet. The low water level is 177 metres. Between the levels of 177 and 187.5 metres, the water storage capacity is 148 million cubic metres, equal to half the annual inflow to the reservoir.

In all, 2,268 hectares of land were acquired by the ESB below the 620 foot (189 metre) contour. There were 76 farm houses and labourers' cottages in this area for which compensation was paid to the owners. Besides the dwellings and farms which were completely destroyed, the rising waters occupied substantial portions of the farms whose actual buildings stood on dry land. Major works were undertaken to restore their fences and to replace water supplies where wells and boreholes had disappeared.

As the law required, the farmsteads were demolished and disinfected and the bodies were duly removed from Burgage cemetery to be left to rest in peace again at a more exalted site. Trees, shrubs and fences were cleared. In spite of the fact that there was plenty of saleable timber, no acceptable offers were made for the removal of the trees by contractors. So they stayed where they fell until the valley was flooded when the trees could be floated to suitable gathering places. Some of the timber was removed in this way, but by no means all. This I discovered in the 1950s when the nets I used in fishery research were repeatedly snagged on submerged branches.

The Agreement also required that the entire reservoir should be fenced in. The fence is 51 km in length. Concrete posts were used with barbed wire in places, but mainly with five strands of plain galvanised wire: a happy choice which facilitates entry to the forbidden ground. Furious notices, neatly printed on enamelled steel, were erected at all

The hydro-electric development of the River Liffey was begun in 1937 and the last stage was completed in 1949.

The construction of the Pollaphuca dam in particular was an enormous undertaking in its day. The number of dwelling houses actually submerged by the formation of the lake was small though up to 300 land-owners had some of their land taken or suffered other inconvenience. Relocation or compensation was, in general fairly amicably arrived at – though not always, as will be seen from an incensed (though probably tongue-in-cheek) letter from one local land-owner, some of whose land was 'borrowed' to give working space during the contruction.

27 Aug 1943

My dear Sir,

I am in receipt of a registered letter containing a map of the portion of **** land you have had as temporant acquired also a notice your Board proposed handing it back to me on the 23rd prox.

Your Board have kindly presented me with a large portion of your Rubbish Dump to have and to hold till death do us part. It is kind of the Board to offer me such a gift which I do not feel worthy of. I don't care to pay rates for a rubbish heap. May I suggest that they think over the matter and continue their tenancy during my life time, a lease for one life. They might offer it to The Trustees of the Lusitania Memorial Jerome Connors bronze figures of 2 weeping fishes then even without any dove of Peace might be a great improvement to the new wcrks and be symbolical of the sorrow generally felt for the poached trout in your new Reservoir also a sign of grief for those in Dublin who will have to drink the water.

Many good wishes,

convenient access points, telling the public that they were forbidden to enter, boat, bathe in or otherwise enjoy this, their property.

From the very start, these instructions were honoured in the breach. Even in those restrictive times, however, boating, fishing and shooting permits were issued. The fishing was managed by the Dublin Trout Anglers' Association and the shooting confined to members of the Blessington Gun Club. Membership of the latter was restricted to people resident within one mile of the lake. This measure gave the wildfowl a satisfactory degree of protection.

A change of heart on the part of the authorities began in the 1970s and visitors are now welcomed to the precincts. Curiously, the old, forbidding notices remain in place and have been updated. Nine 'amenity sites' have been provided for the general public. In addition, there are discreet, unsignposted points of access for board-sailers, yachting people, anglers and others. The reservoir of the eighties does much more than provide power and water.

In the submerged valley, two bridges had crossed the Liffey and one had carried the road from Valleymount to Humphrystown over the King's River. All three had to be replaced as well as two small bridges and 8 km of road. The new bridges were all made to the same design from reinforced concrete. Burgage is the longest and tallest, with 11 spans of 18 metres each and a height above the bed of the river of 22 metres. Humphrystown Bridge is next, with 8 spans and Blessington Bridge the smallest, also with 8 spans. Humphrystown, however, is the longest when the approach banks are included.

Burgage Bridge and old Cemetery just before the flooding of the valley around 1943. Trees have been felled, and remains from the old graveyard, which is seen at the top of the picture, have been re-interred in a new cemetery above the proposed water-line.

The three bridges were completed in 1940, up to a point because of one serious problem. The spans are laid on metal bearings and, because of the war, the correct alloy was unobtainable. So in due course the bearings had to be replaced and this took place between the early 1950s. It was a spectacular operation in which some of the spans were jacked up above the level of the bridge for the correcting procedures.

Pollaphuca

The Pollaphuca dam is 31 metres high and 79 metres wide at the crest. Nearly 10,000 cubic metres of rock were excavated for the foundations and 18,000 cubic metres of concrete were used in building the dam. There is a second, much smaller dam at Pollaphuca, over the hill from the main one. It closes off the Dry Valley, the prehistoric valley cut by the Liffey, but abandoned by her in favour of the Pooka's gorge. Until the lake was created, the valley hung incongruously, high above the river bed.

The dam was made in a narrow part of the gorge, at a point upstream of the waterfall. To get the greatest possible head of water, the power station with its two turbines was built about 400 metres away from the reservoir. The water is brought there under the road through a concrete-lined pressure tunnel, 5 metres in diameter. Tunnelling through the hard slate and sandstone was a formidable task and progress was limited to 8 or 9 metres a week. The upper end of the tunnel is protected by a screen and can be closed by a steel door, operated by a switch at the power station.

Power stations

When the water rushing down the length of this tunnel is shut off, its momentum makes it want to react violently, putting a tremendous strain on the system. Its energy is allowed to dissipate itself by surging into a special tank, built at the lower end of the tunnel.

This surge tank is the most impressive construction at the power station, a colossal tower, 36 metres high and 20 metres in diameter, made from riveted plates of steel. When the turbines are shut off, the water in the tank can surge to about 8 metres above the level of the lake within the tank. The top of the tank is 9 metres above the maximum lake level to allow a margin for safety.

Underneath the surge tank, the roof of the pressure tunnel is open so that the water can escape into the tank. The tunnel forks into two conduits which slant slightly downhill to a valve house where the water can be held or released by butterfly valves. These valves command the entrance to the two penstocks, steel pipes, 3.6 metres in diameter, through which the water makes its final descent to the turbines. The penstocks bring the water down a further 29 metres.

The turbines at Pollaphuca and at Leixlip are based on the principle developed by Viktor Kaplan in Austria in 1920. The water is led to the turbine through a snail-shaped tube. The axle is vertical and the pitch of the blades can be adjusted from within the hub. The turbines generate 15 megawatts each under a head of 47 metres. At full load each consumes 40,000 litres of water per second. They run at 300 revolutions per minute.

Pollaphuca began to generate electricity in 1944. The power is transmitted at 110 thousand volts to Inchicore where it joins the national network. The output is about 30 million kilowatt hours per year.

The Pollaphuca turbines normally run only at peak periods of electricity demand

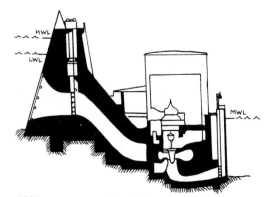

SECTION THROUGH LEIXLIP GENERATING UNIT

and then close down. The water driving them at full power flows so quickly that it would cause serious flooding downstream, if left to its own devices. This is prevented by the dam at Golden Falls, 1,500 metres down the river from the main power station. This dam is wider and lower than the dam at Pollaphuca: 15.5 metres high and 90 metres wide.

There is room in the little valley upstream of it to take all the water that rushes through Pollaphuca in three and a half hours. This is quite enough to give the desired safety margin. The water from Golden Falls is released much more slowly, through a propellor turbine which produces 4 megawatts and a smaller 'house generator' with an output of 250 kilowatts. It supplies the power needed to heat and light and control the machinery to operate both power stations. The Golden Falls generator uses 30,000 litres of water per second and this flow is acceptable in the river downstream.

The Liffey is left to traverse the 60 odd kilometres from Golden Falls to the Salmon Leap at Leixlip without major impediments. There, between Celbridge and Leixlip, the

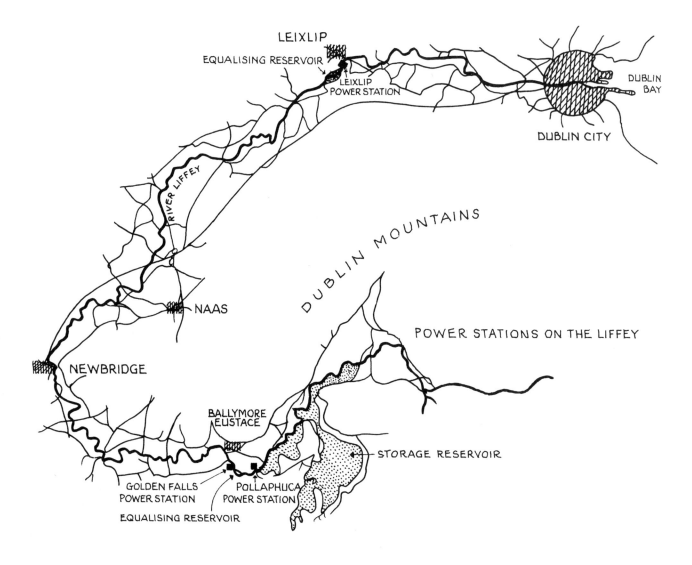

POWER STATIONS ON THE LIFFEY

The Bounty of Anna Liffey

river has a fall of 18 metres. In 1949, a dam was built just upstream of the Salmon Leap. This created a narrow reservoir about 3 km in length at a height of 45 metres above sea level, 142 metres lower than the surface of the Blessington Lakes. The head of water, of 17.4 metres, is almost exactly the same as at Golden Falls and the equipment is a single Kaplan turbine with the same rating, 4,000 kilowatts, as the main generator there.

The waters of the Liffey

The sparkling, clear water of the infant Anna Liffey is a pleasure to behold, and a delight to drink on a hot summer's day on the slopes of Kippure. A mountain stream is part of all that is pure and good in the wilderness. But there is an element of myth in the joys of the wilderness and in the purity of the proverbial stream. The wilderness is wonderful for people who have comfortable homes to go to and the water, though undeniably delightful and delicious, is far from pure.

The acidity imparted from the smoke of the city of Dublin and from more distant regions can scarcely be detected and is of little consequence. But when you cup your hands for a draught, you can see both the pale brown colour of the humic acids in solution and the dark brown specks of peat. If you are lucky, you may also see some minute insect or water flea darting about. The water flea, incidentally, is an innocuous crustacean, having nothing in common with the parasitic insect of the same name, apart from small size and saltatorial habits. Farther downstream, especially in times of flood, the water carries an added burden of silt.

And these are just the visible contaminants. Invisible are the bacteria. In the deep, slow-flowing stretches, microscopic plants of the plankton can multiply. They don't become really noticeable until you reach the lake where they can impart a green and hazy appearance to the water. The water fleas and a great variety of insects eat the plants. Fish eat the water fleas and insects. People and pike eat some of the fish, but most of them die and decay on the bottom. A great many of the smaller creatures die of old age and, to add to the quantity of decaying material, there are insects and leaves blown in from round about.

It sounds awful, but it isn't really - just a couple of paragraphs concentrating on the death and decay which is an essential part of life itself. Of more immediate concern is the fact that the waters of the wilderness are in no way fit for consumption by the citizens of Dublin on a regular basis - the chances of picking up anything dangerous from a casual drink from a stream are remote. The point is that it is not enough just to store the water and pipe it to the people. It must be purified on the way.

Once upon a time, water for drinking was purified simply by allowing it to percolate down through a sand filter. The principle is excellent and a sand filter does indeed remove most of the bacteria, along with all the solid particles in suspension. To this day, it is an essential part of the treatment process. However, the modern demand is for bacterially sterile, colourless water. There is also an economic problem: water which is as soft or acidic as that of the upper Liffey eats away the piping systems and needs to have lime added to correct this tendency.

Tapping the supply

The path of the water from reservoir to city tap begins at a point 100 metres along the lakeside from the dam at Pollaphuca. The Agreement in the 1936 Act stipulated that a

On tap!

minimum level of 177.1 metres above sea level would be maintained in the lake. The Corporation would be entitled to draw off not more than 20 million gallons (90 million litres) a day. Article 7 of the Agreement puts it this way:

> 'The Corporation shall be at liberty at all times to draw from the Reservoir the water supply of the Corporation through an intake which shall be erected by and at the expense of the Corporation upon a site at or in the Reservoir to be mutually agreed between the Corporation and the Board, which site shall be upstream and away from both the dam and the intake of the pressure tunnel to the power station.'

Two tunnels bring water from the reservoir, beneath the road, to the octagonal valve house 50 metres away from the shore. The first is 177.1 metres above sea level, a little higher than the lowest point to which the reservoir is allowed by law to fall. The second one is 8.5 metres lower down, directly underneath the first and 9 metres above the bed of the lake. The lower tunnel is 150 cm in diameter and lined with blue Staffordshire bricks. It runs for nearly 100 metres. The upper is shorter and lined with nothing more exotic than concrete.

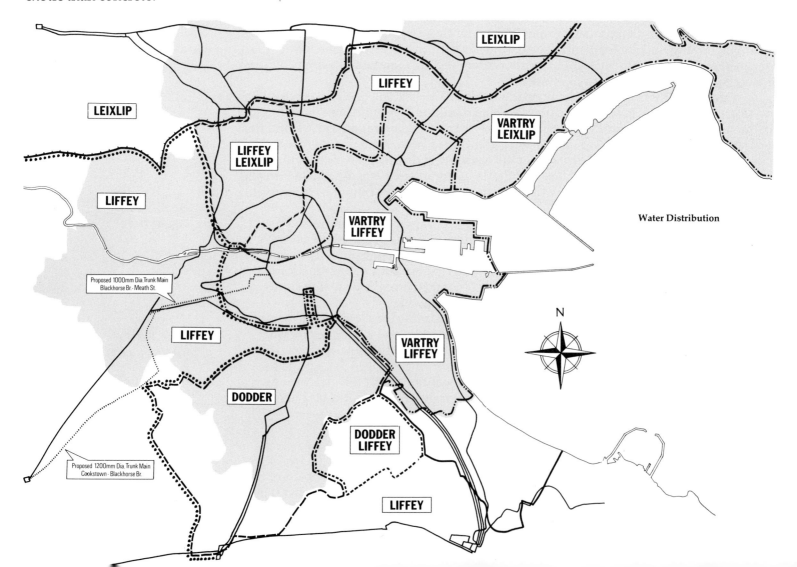

Water Distribution

The valve house stands on top of a vertical shaft going down to meet the lower intake tunnel, 21 metres underground. The upper intake runs horizontally to enter the valve shaft. From the bottom of the shaft, the water flows, first through a concrete-lined tunnel and then through a pipe 1.5 metres diameter for a distance of 500 metres to a valve chamber. There it enters two 914 mm pipes which go underground for 1 km to the intake tank at Ballymore Eustace. A third pipe, of pre-stressed concrete, 1,600 mm diameter was laid in 1987.

Purification

The first step in the purification process is the removal of the very finely divided particles of silt. These are so small that, although heavier than the water, they are held in suspension. The treatment aims to flocculate them, making so many particles cling together that they sink to the bottom.

In 1944, when the water treatment plant was brought into service, the chemical added to bring this about was aluminium sulphate, better known as alum. After the treatment the water is led into settling tanks where the floc sinks gently to the bottom. Subsequently, a polyelectrolyte flocculating aid has been used with the alum to assist the settlement process. It makes the particles about half as big again and speeds up the sedimentation.

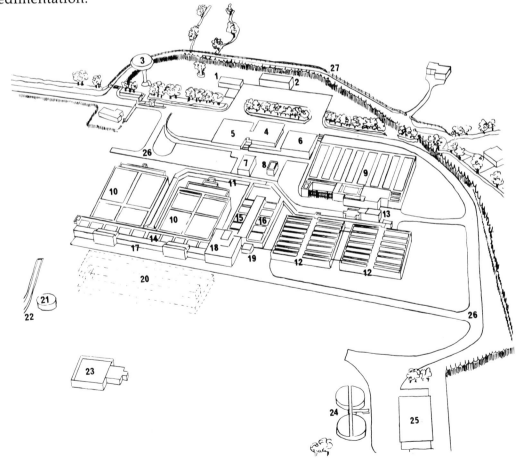

PROPOSED PLANT

1. Manifold Building.
2. Chemical Storage Building.
3. Service Water Tower.
4. Chemical Dosing Building.
5. Liquid Alum Tanks.
6. Maintenance Workshop.
7. Administration Building.
8. Pilot Plant.
9. Upward Flow Clarifier.
10. Horizontal Flow Clarifier.
11. Settled Water Channel.
12. Upward Flow Clarifier.
13. Meter House.
14. Filter Beds 1-10.
15. Filter Beds 11-15.
16. Filter Beds 16-20.
17. Filter Gallery.
18. Lime Dosing Building.
19. Compressor Building.
20. Contact tank.
21. Header Tank.
22. Overflow Channel.
23. Sludge Balancing Tank.
24. Sludge Thickeners.
25. Sludge Press Building.
26. Site Roads.
27. Private Access Road.

The clarified water flows into filter units where it percolates down, first through a 30 cm layer of anthracite, then through 30 cm of Leighton Buzzard sand which is supported by 45 cm of coarse aggregate. The filtered water is then thoroughly dosed with chemicals.

Lime is added as a hardener, raising the pH to 7.5, making it less liable to attack the piping system. Chlorine is used to kill any bacteria which have survived the filtration, its average dosage rate being 1 part per million. Finally, fluoride, in the form of hydrofluorosilicic acid, is supplied at a rate of between 0.8 and 1.0 parts per million. Fluoridation, to control tooth decay, became a legal requirement by an Act of 1960.

After the chemical treatment, the water is held in a Contact Tank for 20 minutes to allow the chemicals to diffuse evenly through the water. Then it goes into the supply. The greater part of the water is delivered to Dublin, but towns and villages from Ballymore Eustace downstream are also served.

The meeting of the waters

Thus are the living waters of Anna Liffey purified and encased in concrete, ready for their long journey from Ballymore to the city of Dublin. For the first 19 km the water runs through a concrete culvert amongst the western hills, close to Rathmore and Kilteel in a northerly direction as far as the Naas Road, 2.5 km west of Rathcoole. There it turns eastwards around the hill with the old windmill tower. To the south of Rathcoole the culvert opens into a pair of 838 mm pipes which feed into a reservoir at Saggart.

From Saggart, the water is piped downhill to the western parts of the city, passing on the way through a reservoir at Cookstown, a little to the west of Tallaght. Most of the water from Saggart is piped to the western part of the city and suburbs. Some of the Liffey water, however, can be directed to the east and fed to the 19th-century reservoirs at Ballyboden and Stillorgan. There it meets and mingles with the water from the older systems. Ballyboden is supplied by the Dodder from Bohernabreena and Stillorgan by the Vartry from Roundwood. Shortages from either of these, smaller, rivers can be made good by the bounty of the Liffey.

The original plant at Ballymore Eustace, completed in 1944, was designed to treat 22 million litres a day but was in fact capable of handling twice as much. This supply was adequate for Dublin at the time, but the city was growing and the story of the Liffey water supply has been one of continuing expansion. In 1953, nearly all the installations at Ballymore Eustace were duplicated to cope with the additional demand. It was at this time that the 19th-century reservoirs at Ballyboden and Stillorgan were joined to Saggart.

The next major development took place in 1965 when the Leixlip reservoir was tapped. This was the work of the Dublin County Council, faced with the expansion of

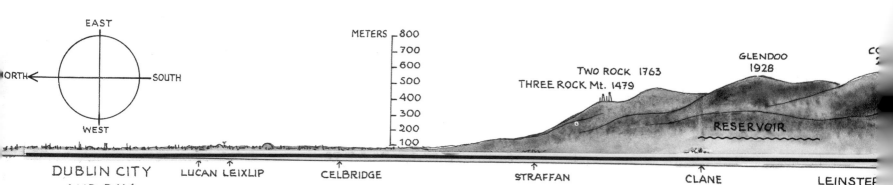

The Bounty of Anna Liffey

greater Dublin to the west, beyond the jurisdiction of the Corporation. The Leixlip water was piped to a temporary filtration plant on the right bank. Two years later, the permanent treatment works were completed and 20 million litres a day could be pumped to Ballycoolen, north of Blanchardstown.

In the late 1960s, Ballymore Eustace was once again being over-taxed and major new developments began. By 1973, five new filters had been installed, bringing the number from ten to fifteen. In 1976, two more sedimentation tanks were commissioned. These were an innovation, using a vertical rather than horizontal flow, allowing for much more rapid treatment. This work increased the capacity to 186 million litres per day. The throughput at the Leixlip treatment plant meanwhile was doubled, to 80 million litres a day.

In 1974 a main of 102 cm was installed to carry water from Leixlip to Ballycoolen and the Ballymore Eustace plant was extended yet again. It could now deliver 204 million litres a day. In the succeeding years, more pipelines were laid to cope with the additional flow and Ballymore Eustace continued to grow. The ultimate aim is to treat 270 million litres a day.

The daily flow of the Liffey in times of drought can be as little as 9 million litres, rather less than the 270 million which the people of Dublin require from it. The average daily flow, however, is 800 million litres a day and the Blessington Lakes should be well able to hold all the water that will be needed. There will also be a surplus to make sure that the Liffey downstream of Pollaphuca always has enough water for its fish.

One problem yet remains, however. The treatment relieves the water of its burden of animal, vegetable and mineral matter to the satisfaction of the consumer. But the impurities do not disappear: they accumulate, together with the flocculating chemicals to form what the engineers euphemistically call a blanket. Something has to be done about it. At Ballymore Eustace, the sludge is led into lagoons where it lies, dark and viscous, to be released slowly back to the Liffey. This can have a devastating effect on fish life for some distance downstream.

Help is at hand in the form of an alum sludge treatment plant. The sludge is concentrated in circular tanks and then led into filter presses which squeeze the water out and produce a dry cake which can be used safely as landfill. Sadly, owing to shortage of funds, the treatment plant, although completed, was still, in 1988, waiting to be brought into service.

Meanwhile, the citizens of Dublin enjoy one of the most reliable and purest supplies of water in the world. Dwellers in the eastern suburbs, such as myself, seldom enjoy a glass of pure Liffey water, our thirst being slaked by the product of the Dodder or the far-off Vartry. But they can fail the thirsty populace and then the bounteous Liffey supplies even the residents of Ballsbridge and Sandymount. ●

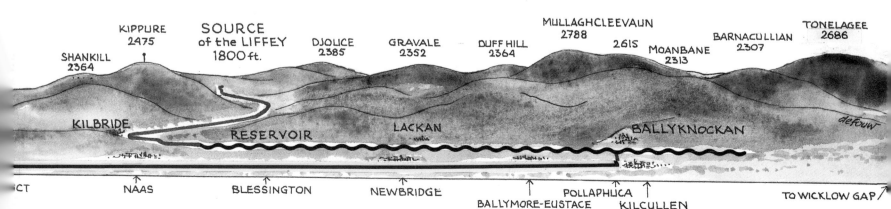

SHANKILL 2364 · KILPURE 2475 · SOURCE of the LIFFEY 1800 ft. · DJOUCE 2385 · GRAVALE 2352 · DUFF HILL 2364 · MULLAGHCLEEVAUN 2788 · 2615 · MOANBANE 2313 · BARNACULLIAN 2307 · TONELAGEE 2686

KILBRIDE · RESERVOIR · LACKAN · BALLYKNOCKAN · deFouw

CT · NAAS · BLESSINGTON · NEWBRIDGE · BALLYMORE-EUSTACE · POLLAPHUCA · KILCULLEN · TO WICKLOW GAP

A short course in watermilling

Anna Liffey is hardly seen as ever having been a great thoroughfare of commerce such as the Rhine or the Nile, nor has she the industrial associations of, say, the Clyde or the Ruhr. And yet a closer examination will show that the bounty of the Liffey has in the past supported a variety of industries on or close to the river and its tributaries. Typically paper mills and tanneries, breweries and distilleries added to the load of the City's effluent, whilst woollen mills and especially corn mills were a feature of the surrounding countryside.

Paper mills, woollen mills, corn mills were all typical examples of watermills, that is where the river powered a water-wheel which in turn drove the machinery inside. To a casual visitor there's little to show that there were many mills on the Liffey, but the reality is quite different.

A detailed survey and search has so far led to the identity of almost two hundred sites in the Liffey catchment, representing a couple of dozen different types of industry, ranging from sea level (only able to operate when the tide was low) to 1,400 feet above, and in time from before the Vikings to the present day. All were worked by the Liffey or her tributaries, and having employed goodness knows how many men and women over the centuries, the histories of these watermills have mostly all been lost to even local memory. However, traces of many can still be found and a handful are yet reasonably intact; every year the number of these grows less.

By scanning old maps – such as the 1838 copperplate edition of the Ordnance Survey, and Deeds, valuations and so forth, and by digging into textbooks on old industries and millwrighting (not so hard to find), much of the picture can be outlined; but this can be dull and dry stuff, and on its own truly not very scientific. Far better combine the paper-work with an expedition, leave the dust on the archives, get out and explore the banks of the river and streams, perhaps with a note pad or a camera. Even though the buildings themselves may have gone, there may still be a weir, or a millpond, or maybe an empty millrace.

To get a quick feel for the rich variety and extent of these mills, many of which were special industries linked to the City, let us start from Dublin and have a look at some of the mill sites before making a circle back.

Going up river between the walls of the quays, several low arches and holes can be seen at low tide, discharging water of varying hue, through gratings closing off the dark tunnels behind. These are not, at least not officially, sewers, many are just storm drains, but quite a few are in fact little rivers, tributaries of the Liffey now unknown to most Dubliners, and running forgotten under the streets and pavements above. When Dublin was young these would have been flowing between the crops towards the medieval city, just as similar streams still swell the river further west in Kildare and Wicklow. Just like rural streams anywhere else in Europe, these supported their share of watermills, before the coming of steam and later electricity. As the demands of Dublin grew and with better roads and new technology, these mills increased in number and size and variety; where there were originally only corn mills, by the eighteenth century the water of the Liffey and its tributaries was turning the wheels for such things as woollen cloth, cotton printing, paper making, sawing wood and others besides.

As we go up the Liffey, the first clear sign of a watermill must surely be the weir at Islandbridge. This is pretty big and impressive, and represents a late stage in the development of waterpower. The very first watermills, and primitive mills ever since, were worked directly off a stream, without the help of weir or millpond or millrace. Production was at the mercy of the weather – too dry and no power, heavy winter rain and a stream in spate meant that it would be too dangerous to operate. An early development was to slice a bit off the stream, i.e. build a millrace, and control the flow with sluices. A millpond guaranteed a supply in dry weather, and the combination of millpond, millrace and sluices allowed the miller to control waterlevels, i.e. the 'head' and volume of water could be kept fairly constant. The function of the weir was to take this 'cut' off a river or large stream; it acted as a dam in dry months, but when the river was swollen the excess flowed over the top.

At Islandbridge there were two quite large watermills; much of the buildings and a very pretty millpond are still there. This is an old site, much older than the weir or other structures that can be seen today. From the middle of the twelfth century and for the next four hundred years it and an associated salmon weir were owned by the powerful and wealthy Knights of St. John of Jerusalem, whose Priory was at Kilmainham on the site of an older monastery close to where the Royal Hospital is now. The salmon weir and possibly a mill were most probably first established by the monks of this monastery of St. Maighnenn, more than a thousand years ago. The Knights milled corn at Islandbridge until the dissolution of the religious houses by Henry VIII; after this the mills had a chequered history until 1741 when Dublin Corporation decided to purchase them for the purpose of supplying parts of the City with water.

Water-driven pumps were installed the following year, the Corporation leased these with an adjoining mill to various persons until eventually better arrangements for water supplies were negotiated with the new Canal companies. In 1811 one Alderman Manders took over the lease of 'the old engine house' and the mill; under the Manders family the mills

The Bounty of Anna Liffey

prospered, by 1838 there was a calico printing mill as well as a flour mill, and for many years the Manders' flour mills were well known in Dublin.

Flour milling is essentially no more than a refinement of corn milling. In a simple corn mill the grain, which was usually wheat or oats, was ground unscreened, and the relatively coarse grist was returned to the farmer or baker. As time went on the millers introduced vibrating screens before the millstones and then after grinding the grist was passed through mechanical sifters or 'bolters' to remove the finest flour. A further refinement was the introduction of an initial grinding stage where the stones are set far enough apart just to break or 'end' the wheat, allowing the husk (bran) to be separated. Before the 1700s there were many small corn mills, generally grinding other people's cereals. The flour mills, which developed in Ireland from about 1760 on, were much larger affairs, more like modern factories, with machines on several floors; the owners bought cereal from the local farmers and sold a uniform product to the people in the towns.

One of the earliest of the new flour mills in Ireland was at Naas, on a tributary of the Liffey. There is a good example of a flour mill nearby that is still almost intact; this is at Morristown Lattin, near Yeomanstown, where the road from Naas to Kilmeague crosses the Liffey. It never had a millpond, but the

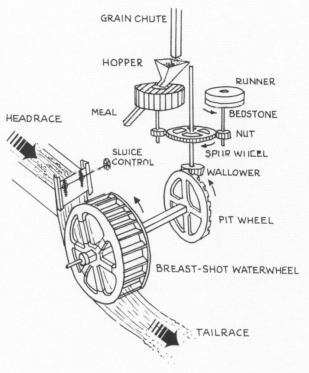

The framework of the great 14-foot breast-shot waterwheel at Morristown Lattin can still be seen, along with other machinery inside the building (see overleaf).

weir on the river, the millrace and the iron framing of a large breast-shot waterwheel (14 feet in diameter, 11 feet in width) are all there, alongside a solid mill building of several floors, complete with a kiln for drying the grain at the west end. Much of the machinery is in situ, including the stones and gearing.

The history of this site, like any other, can be traced from old maps and other records. It is clearly there in its present form back through the various editions of the Ordnance Survey, and the first O.S. 6" map describes it as a 'Flour mill' in 1838; it was there in 1783 (Taylor's map of Co. Kildare), and before that in 1752 Messrs. Noble and Keenan marked it 'present'.

We next step back to the seventeenth century, and check the Civil Survey of 1654. This most useful survey was a by-product of an unhappy time in our history, when Cromwell's 'Adventurers' put in their claims for land. The Survey recorded Yeomanstown as a watermill, but 'ruinated and wast', only too common a description in the period after the 1641 Rebellion. So this mill has certainly been in existence for over three hundred years, and very probably much longer. Of course it was only a corn mill in its earlier days, and like others that we know about, may have started as a mill for grinding the oats and wheat of the tenants of a local medieval Manor.

Travelling further up river, we pass the extensive remains of a large mill at Athgarvan (between Newbridge and Kilcullen), and there were others in Kilcullen and Ballymore Eustace. One of the most intriguing sites, and still quite complete, literally shows its head above water whenever the Pollaphuca Reservoir is low; this is – or was – worked by the Liffey just below Blessington. There is a fine photograph of the mill before the flooding of 1940, to be seen in the AIB's branch in the town (see also page 82).

The highest site that there can ever have been on the Liffey, or its tributaries, must surely be the water-wheel above the Army's shooting range at Shankill, and of all, this is the one that is most modern and is in daily use, providing power for a fish hatchery.

From near here we can look back towards Dublin, across Brittas ponds and down the Slade Valley. Brittas ponds, on

The mill building at Morristown Lattin is still almost intact, as can be seen from these photographs taken in May 1988.

the site of the old pre-ice age course of the Liffey, are not natural, they were built as millponds (strictly speaking, reservoirs, but it's the same thing) for the Saggart mills. Take the little and twisty road from the Ponds, down to Saggart. The skeleton of the principal mill building can be clearly seen on the left just before the village. Here, for over thirty generations was one of the main paper-making centres of Ireland, and boasted the largest diameter wheel in the land. The curve on the west end of the building gives a good idea of its size.

From Saggart it is a short run back to Clondalkin and the County Council's splendid new park at Corkagh. Now here, and available to the public and hopefully soon to be fully restored, are the remains of two very curious industries, both powered by water. The stream from Brittas (which lent its name to 'Swiftbrook Bond' paper), now is called the Camac. At Corkagh this little tributary of the Liffey powered no less than seven gunpowder mills. They were all small, and well separated – and for a good reason. If the inevitable happened and a powder mill blew up, only one seventh of the production was lost and hopefully an even smaller proportion of the staff. As an extra precaution the grinding stones (which ran on their edges) were made of limestone, far less likely to cause sparks than the usual French Burr or Millstone Grit. The other mill site worth visiting here was an 'oil mill', which extracted linseed oil from seeds. The present owner has done a lot to sort out the ruins, and it will someday soon be more fully restored.

The Camac flows on through Clondalkin, Inchicore and Kilmainham, to join the Liffey just under Heuston Station. On the way it used to turn many more waterwheels, more than a dozen after the oil mills. One of these was at Kilmainham, and the property of the Knights of St. John of Jerusalem, with whom we started this short tour.

This is only a tiny sample of the many water-mills supported over the centuries by Anna Liffey and her family of tributaries. The reader is again strongly urged to take a camera, or pencil and paper, or merely a weekend afternoon, and sample this veritable feast that lies waiting. ●

The Bounty of Anna Liffey

Christopher Moriarty

Fishes and Fishing — further bounty

Salmon

The capture of the first salmon of the new year in the Liffey is invariably greeted with front-page coverage in the press and an inordinately large sum paid to the angler whose skill and stamina are thus rewarded. The new year fish are always big and always elusive.

Although the season opens on 1st January, if conditions are not right, days can go by before any salmon get caught. It was not until 16th January that the first fish was landed in 1988. He was a twelve-pounder and Dunn's fish shop bought him for £1,000 from the captor, Mr. Harry Mason.

That salmon, like all the other 'spring fish' was a great traveller. He grew up from one of five thousand eggs laid by his mother in December 1983, high up in a tributary stream of the Liffey. The mother buried them in the gravel, choosing the spot very carefully so that the water would flow down over the eggs.

The following March, the infant salmon wriggled up into the stream to begin an active life, selecting a home where the current was slack and darting out from it to snap up any water flea or small creature that happened to come by. As well as being a proficient hunter, he was an aggressive little fish, keeping his brothers and sisters at a respectful distance.

As he grew bigger, he moved downstream to deeper and quieter, but still relatively fast water. And there he stayed until the spring of 1986, by which time forty-five thousand of his siblings had met with some kind of fatal accident. Most of them died in the first few months after hatching, crowded out by the more vigorous members of the family.

By that spring, he had reached a length of 35 cm and his colour had changed from speckled brown to silver, fitting him out for a journey to the sea. In April he reached the estuary and, in company first of other Liffey salmon and later with fish from many other rivers, he headed off to the rich feeding grounds around Greenland. There he feasted on small fish, sprat and capelin, and grew a great deal faster than had been possible in the stream. Then he headed back towards Europe and made his way to the Irish Sea where he scented the waters of Anna Liffey and returned to the river of his birth.

Having thus survived the aggression of his little brothers and sisters, and later in life the attentions of the hunger of trout, pike, herons and cormorants, whales and sharks and seals and the nets of fishermen, he finally succumbed to Mr. Mason's bait. What was particularly ironic was the fact that he wasn't even thinking seriously about a meal when he was caught. He had more than enough food stored away in his body and was incapable of digesting anything. But old habits of snapping at lively things had died a little too hard.

The other spring fish had much the same life-cycle. But the salmon which came into the Liffey later in the year from June to August, were smaller. They didn't travel as far away as Greenland and they came back to the river after only one winter at sea. The summer fish weigh about six pounds on average and are called 'grilse' or 'peal'.

Fortunately for the fishermen and all the other people and creatures who like salmon, there were many that got away. They swam up to Leixlip and then went through the strangest part of their odyssey, an adventure beyond the wildest dreams of their ancestors. Where the salmon of old had to leap over the waterfall, the ESB dam stands: impassable, but for a large tunnel at its base, leading to a shaft within the dam. The shaft has an outlet near the surface of the reservoir upstream. The salmon swim into the tunnel which is fed by water cascading down the shaft. Every so many hours, a gate at the bottom is closed so that the shaft fills with water. The salmon can swim effortlessly up the shaft and over the dam.

They are subjected to one last indignity before returning to the wild. They pass through an electronic fish counter which records the movement upstream of every large fish. In 1986 it recorded two thousand, three hundred and seventy-four. Some of these were subsequently caught by anglers, perhaps a few by otters and maybe some by poachers.

Those that survived made their way towards the headwaters of the tributaries, where the water flows clear over gravel. There they remained until the following January: often fighting, never feeding until the time came to pair and spawn. Few of them lived long after spawning: the year's fast, the energy of battling for a territory and the quantity of food reserves needed to provide each of the five thousand eggs with a generous supply of yolk, combined to leave the fish totally exhausted. In spite of all, a few did recover, to make their way back to the ocean and return to the Liffey to spawn once more.

In the 1930s Winifred Frost and Arthur Went made a study of trout and salmon in the Liffey. They found that, while the majority of Liffey salmon spend two years at sea, some grow faster: one salmon in every eight that they examined had gone to sea at one year old while one in forty took three years. The favourite food organisms of the young salmon were the larvae of small mayflies and caddis flies.

In spite of the salmon's legendary wisdom and undoubted strength and determination in surmounting obstacles, it was no match for the Pooka. So the headwaters of the Liffey, upstream of Pollaphuca, are devoid of salmon and always have been.

Eels

One other fish shares the salmon's propensity for travel and makes the Atlantic crossing. She, too, is frustrated by the waterfalls. That one is the eel and it is only she-eels which go all the way up to the Liffey. The he's are indolent and stay near Dublin. The eel, however, does the journey in reverse and never more than once in a lifetime. All the eels of Europe breed in the Sargasso Sea in spring and their young drift back across the ocean, reaching the continental shelf in autumn. In November or December, the first of the baby eels arrive in Dublin Bay, transparent creatures which look very like darning needles, only they wriggle.

Many of them spend their lives in the Liffey estuary, feeding on shrimps and crabs and worms. They grow to a good size. I fished for them under Butt Bridge where they measured up to 76 cm long. Other eels are much more adventurous and, when the water warms up in spring, make their way up over the weirs into the freshwater. The little ones don't like strong flows but prefer to wriggle up a weir through the moss where the water trickles down. Now and again they can be seen by the thousand. However, eels of all sizes generally prefer to travel at night time, so the small ones usually slip by unnoticed.

In the freshwater, the eels feed mostly on the larvae of insects of many kinds. They are also particularly fond of water lice, small crustaceans resembling woodlice. Some eels eat small fish, but they are the exceptions. Earthworms are a favourite food and the best bait.

Most of the baby eels settle down for a season when they reach the quiet waters upstream of Islandbridge weir. Some press on and over Lucan weir, and few travel farther than that in the course of their first year. The males always stay in the lower reaches, but adventurous females travel for miles and miles in the course of a lifetime. Therefore you may find eels in all of the tributaries and even in outlandish places like field drains and bogs.

When they have grown to a length of about 40 cm at an age of ten years, the males stop feeding, change their colour from brown to silver and head back to the ocean in autumn. The females live longer and grow bigger, to an age of fifteen years

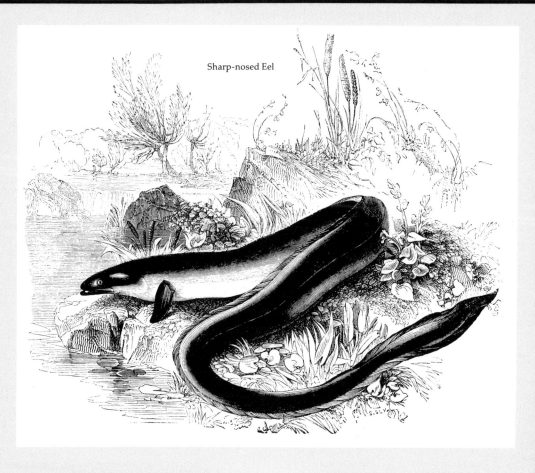

Sharp-nosed Eel

and a length of 50 to 60 cm. Those are the dimensions of average eels, but many of them live longer and grow much bigger: a lifespan of forty years is not unknown.

Eels shouldn't be able to get past Pollaphuca and into the Blessington lakes, but one did. She was caught in September 1987 when she tried to get out of the lake by swimming down a pipe which brought water to the ESB salmon rearing station at Pollaphuca. She was so big that she jammed the water supply and perished miserably. Most likely she was brought in by accident with a consignment of young salmon or trout from the Shannon.

Other Wanderers

Several other species make regular journeys up and down the Liffey, but none can equal the spectacular journeys of the salmon and eel. What they have in common is an ability to live in fresh or salt water, something very unusual in the world of fishes, most of which keep to one or the other.

The grey mullet is the finest of them, growing to the size of a summer salmon with a weight of 2 kg or more. In summer small shoals of mullet can be seen swimming near the surface along the inner edge of the South Wall. Usually they move in a leisurely way, but now and again get wildly excited, darting about and leaping into the air. Most of them go offshore in search of warmer water in winter, but a few remain in the Liffey, enjoying the warmth of the cooling water from the Poolbeg power station. Now and again you can see mullet at O'Connell St. Bridge and they will travel as far as Islandbridge weir.

The flounder, locally called the 'fluke', is a flatfish which spawns offshore in the sea but swims into estuaries and travels into rivers when it can. Weirs, however, are beyond the capabilities of the flounder so it is almost unknown in the

The Bounty of Anna Liffey

Grey Mullet

freshwater parts of the Liffey, even though plentiful into the estuary. With the flounder, a number of sea fish will move into the city of Dublin from time to time, especially when high spring tides bring the salt water a long way upstream.

Finally, there is the stickleback, a tiny fish with outlandish habits. It can live permanently in freshwater and does not have to change from one to the other in the course of its life. The male stickleback builds a nest, entices females to come into it and lay the eggs. Then he takes care of the young himself, leaving his wives to relax and enjoy life, the ultimate in feminist fish.

The Trout

In one respect, the trout of the Liffey succeeded where the salmon failed. They reached the waters upstream of Pollaphuca and can be found high in the hill streams. The life cycle of the trout resembles that of the salmon, insofar as

they lay their eggs in gravel in winter, as near the headwaters as they can travel. As they grow, they move downstream in search of more space and food, but they seek the streams of their birth again when they are old enough to breed. Some trout, called 'sea trout' or 'white trout' turn silvery and go to sea like the salmon, but they don't travel so far away or indulge in a long fast before spawning.

Winifred Frost, one of the great pioneers in freshwater fishery studies, spent many years in the 1930s and 40s in the Fisheries Branch of the Department of Agriculture, studying the life of trout and salmon in the Liffey. Her results were published in a series of papers by the Royal Irish Academy. She spent many happy days with rod and line, capturing her specimens at Ballysmuttan and at Straffan. The point was to compare the feeding and growth of the fish which lived in poor, acid waters close to the granite at Ballysmuttan with those which

lived an easier life in the rich, lime-charged stretches in the lowlands.

The upland trout were small, seldom growing to more than half a pound weight. They subsisted on a meagre diet of stoneflies and other not so nutritious creatures. The lowland trout grew large and quickly, reaching a weight of one pound after three years. They enjoyed a rich diet of the shrimps and the larvae of various kinds of mayflies.

The Trout of the Lakes

There is an element of tragedy in the tale of the trout of the Blessington Lakes. Irish trout reached their native land after the Ice Age, thanks to their ability to cross the sea. The only other fish in freshwater in Ireland at the time were those which could live in both fresh and salt water. The purely freshwater species, classed by trout and salmon lovers as 'coarse fish', had been expelled from the rivers and lakes by the ice. Throughout mainland Europe, the coarse fish were able to recolonise the freshwater as the ice receded. But the Irish Sea kept them out of Ireland.

So the trout were left, virtually free from competition, to enjoy the rich feeding of the lowland rivers and lakes. In the course of some thousands of years they developed breeding strains which grew fast and large. Their descendants still provide fabulous fishing. The traditional trout of the upper Liffey were able to respond to the new situation when the lakes were created and their living space was greatly expanded.

The trout multiplied and grew big and the fishing was excellent. A natural disaster took place in the 1940s when a severe infestation by tapeworms developed. Many trout died and the popularity of the survivors – not surprisingly – declined.

This problem would have run its course, since many trout did survive and their progeny would have developed a degree of immunity. It is more than likely that the wonderful trout fishery would have appeared again – and stayed. But a much greater and totally irreparable disaster was to follow. Early in the 1960s perch made their way into the lake. Nobody knows how or precisely when: it may have been an accidental escape from an ornamental pond.

The Book of the Liffey

Perch and Pike

Perch are much more prolific than trout and they eat the same sort of food. Within a few years, they had come to outnumber the trout by five or ten to one. What was worse, they crowded themselves out, too, so that they now live in the lake in enormous numbers but seldom grow to a good size. Like the trout, perch are very good to eat. But they are generally smaller and have very sharp spines and bones in all sorts of places so that they are very hard work to make a meal of.

But the abuse of the Blessington Lakes was not yet over. The final act of desecration was deliberate and utterly misguided. Certain trout anglers consider that, if there are pike in a lake or river, they make the trout feed at the surface so that the trout will be more inclined to rise to flies. There was also the idea that, if pike were introduced to the Lakes, they would eat up all the perch and leave lots of space for the trout which would also, of course, sacrifice themselves willingly to the fisherfolk. Even in the 1950s it was well known amongst fishery managers that all these theories were as credible as any angler's memory of the size of the fish that got away.

In or about 1960, a person or persons unknown put some pike in the lake. The result was that the pike completed the damage the perch had begun. Like people, pike prefer trout to perch so the lakes were transformed from a tolerable trout fishery to no trout fishery at all. The tragedy lies in the fact that there are thousands of lakes with good stocks of perch and pike, while as rich a trout lake as Blessington is almost unique.

Perhaps I should not weep too many tears. The fishing around the lakes is still excellent and many people get great pleasure from it without worrying about what it might have been.

The Crayfish

One very curious creature lives in the Blessington Lakes, though not a fish in the strict sense. It is the crayfish, a creature like a small lobster which likes to burrow in the mud. Crayfish used to be abundant all over Europe, but a fatal disease has been spreading over the continent since the turn of the century. It was originally brought when some

Perch

American crayfish were released. They can carry the disease, called 'crayfish plague' and spread it, but don't suffer from it themselves.

The plague finally reached Ireland in 1987, but it is possible that the Blessington crayfish may survive – because of their isolation from other waters. The crayfish made their way into the lakes from the Brittas River, though how they got there is anybody's guess. Big perch like to eat crayfish – so do Scandinavian people – but both these serious predators are scarce in the region. Eels can decimate crayfish populations and the absence of eels from the lake is the main reason why the crayfish thrive there. European crayfish get scarcer and scarcer and the Blessington Lakes stand a good chance of being amongst their most important refuges.

The Coarse Fish

Besides the perch and pike, already mentioned, one more species of fish, the minnow, lives upstream of the lakes and six, including the minnow, live downstream. The Coarse fish have all been introduced since the times of the Anglo-Normans. Some of the introductions were made without any notice being taken, others are reasonably well documented.

Three of the fish, the minnow, the loach and the gudgeon, are small and significant to the human race only in being used for bait for something bigger. The unpleasant, if effective, practice of impaling living small fish on a hook has been forbidden by law. Nobody knows for certain why anybody bothered to introduce the three: they might have come accidentally in a container used for something bigger. Minnows were first recorded in Dublin in the 17th century and were probably spread around the country when they were used for bait. That seems to be the only reasonable

The Bounty of Anna Liffey

Dace and Roach

explanation of how they made it to the upper Liffey.

Loach and gudgeon are confined to the lower reaches. The loach likes clear, stony streams where it can sniff around the bottom. It is usually active at night. Gudgeon are plentiful in the broad, slow reaches of the plains.

Perch, pike, roach, rudd and bream also live in the more tranquil parts. The pike is a particularly rugged individualist who eats those of his neighbours whom he cannot scare away. He occupies a fixed territory, preferably a spot where water plants blend with his green colouring and make him invisible. There he waits until hunger or claustrophobia overcome him and he darts out to grab some passing fish. Any kind of fish is acceptable, to say nothing of frogs, ducklings or just about anything which is neither too big nor too small and which moves.

Early in spring, pike relax their vow of solitude to the extent of tolerating the close proximity of a member of the opposite sex. But the eggs are laid one by one, each at a distance from the next, so that from earliest infancy the pike lives aloof.

Perch, roach, rudd and bream on the other hand are sociable creatures, depositing their spawn in great adhesive masses and living in shoals all the time. The bream grows to a fine size, the Irish angling record being over 5 kg. It is usually a placid, slow-moving creature, hunting on the bottom for small insects and things. Sometimes bream can be seen in clear water, swimming lazily here and there. All changes in May when they get together to mate and lay eggs, whipping themselves up into a frenzy of movement and splashing merrily at the surface.

Rudd and roach are rather small, silvery fish with red fins. Rudd have lived in Ireland for centuries and are usually called 'roach'. True roach escaped into the Munster Blackwater towards the end of the 19th century and stayed there for a long time. In the 1960s, particularly coarse fishermen began to distribute roach in other river systems. This is fine for roach specialists, but pretty dismal for other anglers since the roach displace the established species, above all the young of trout and salmon. They usually replace the rudd altogether, but nobody minds about that so much.

Roach appeared in the Liffey in or about 1978 and are plentiful now in the lower reaches. Not content with propagating themselves, they have also been forming illicit unions with bream as, indeed, have the rudd. The hybrids generally reach much larger sizes than the roach or rudd parents. Roach are fun to watch, as they move about in shoals, their bright red fins catching the light. But they are small and almost flavourless – in no way to be compared with trout, perch or pike. This does not worry the coarse fisherman whose aim is to catch as many as he can, put them in a keep net hanging in the water and let them depart in peace at the close of the day.

Fish rearing

The floating cages out on the lake near Pollaphuca are the home of thousands of brown trout. Their parents live in pens in the Shannon at Parteen in Co. Tipperary where they are hatched, to be moved to the cages during their first summer. When these trout have grown big enough to satisfy the anglers, between half a pound and a pound weight, they are released into the lake between Burage and Pollaphuca. Forty-five thousand of these fine fish are provided every year, but in small numbers at a time so that good stocks for fishing are available through the season.

Downstream of Pollaphuca, the ESB plants between 10,000 and 20,000 young salmon every year. They stay in the river and its tributaries for long enough to learn to consider the Liffey as their true home. So they return to it after their journey to the sea.

Finally, down at Islandbridge, the Liffey Salmon Anglers rear their own fish. These ones are released into the river when migration time comes and go to seek their fortunes in the sea along with their wild neighbours. ●

The Liffey of the Plains

fter her dramatic plunge through the gorge at Pollaphuca, Anna Liffey takes a sharp turn to the left and continues to make a rapid descent towards Ballymore Eustace. A little way upstream of that village, at Golden Falls, she hurtled down in days gone by and once more has been ensnared by the ESB with a small dam and power station (page 58). Thereafter she embarks on a more leisured journey, falling from 125 metres at Ballymore to 33 metres at the next dam, at Leixlip, 55 km farther down.

Following the Liffey closely from Pollaphuca presents difficulties because she makes frequent forays through private demesnes, along back gardens and even along the walls of houses. A legitimate descent can be made by canoe since the water and the bed of the river are not private property. But that belongs to another chapter and, moreover, many good citizens prefer to keep their feet on firm ground.

The plan of this chapter therefore is to go gently down the river by road all the way to Chapelizod. This journey of discovery is planned for dilettante motorists and cyclists: those, like me, who want to stop everywhere possible to take a pleasant walk or just sit and contemplate.

Golden Falls

Golden Falls reservoir can be seen from the Dry Bridge at Pollaphuca, after which there is a turn to the right for Ballymore Eustace. The road parts company from the river and climbs and twists amongst green hills of outwash gravel. The Midlandian ice sheet penetrated the lower ground between Ballymore and Pollaphuca, depositing great mounds of till. As the ice receded, the Pollaphuca gap, like the gap at Blessington, was a channel for melt water flowing into the prehistoric lake. Beneath the gravel, the bed rock is a continuation of the sandstone which forms the western boundary of the lakes and the upper valley.

The way to Ballymore and the Liffey is a right turn at the next crossroads, but a diversion must be made to see the Piper's Stones of Broadlea. They form a rather small, compact ring of oval boulders, lying on their sides. Two thorn trees grow on the west of the circle and an elderly ash on the east. An incongruous holly is rooted in a cleft between two stones to the south, looking as if it is overflowing after being squeezed out. Most of the stones are granite, some of them an unusual porphyritic form with big crystals of quartz. A few are massive blocks of sandstone.

Golden Falls dam can be glimpsed through the trees to the west of the road going down the hill towards Ballymore. The colourful buildings up on the hill are part of the water treatment plant, where the water from the lakes is cleaned and purified to a state fit for the citizens of Dublin (page 61).

Ballymore Eustace

A beautiful bridge with six arches crosses the Liffey, carrying the road into the ancient village of Ballymore Eustace which lay, or perhaps sprawled, on the right bank. On the upstream side of the bridge, a tall iron gate stands at the entrance to the old woollen mills which made Ballymore a prosperous place many years ago. The path to the ruined mill is a delightful, shaded walk. It sets off beneath a tall pine tree with a rookery, continues through a strip of woodland which grows on the edge of the flood plain and climbs the steep bank behind it.

There is a small stone circle there, but it has the air of a nineteenth century creation and is none the less charming for that. The stones are uncommonly large blocks of quartz, twelve on the circumference with a bigger one in the middle. The track passes them to go to the walls of the mill, 'a most flourishing business' under the ownership of Messrs Copeland (father and son) in the latter half of the nineteenth century.

The great iron axle of the mill wheel still lies in its position and the millrace, which ran along the base of the steep bank, still holds water. Its left bank makes a good footpath over most of its length.

A delightful row of mill-workers' cottages runs along the side of the road at the bridge. They are brightly painted and well kept, having enjoyed a much longer life than the mill. From the cottages, the road goes up hill and then branches off in all directions between houses of varying degrees of antiquity.

Ballymore is an interesting case in the history of town-planning. It is one of the villages which was not planned at all but which developed all over the hillside in a sort of organic growth. The 'Eustace' of the name goes back to the Anglo-Norman family who settled in the region and remained powerful for centuries.

The size and strength of the bridge testify silently to the importance of Ballymore and the highway through it towards the end of the eighteenth century. It was the main coach road between Blessington and Baltinglass. But the building of Nimmo's bridge at Pollaphuca in the 1820s shortened the journey and put paid to Ballymore's importance as a river crossing.

The old church of Ballymore stands amongst hoary trees on a hillside outside the village on the right bank, half a mile upstream. It is grey and slightly unkempt on the outside, an appearance which belies its beautiful interior. Within the churchyard there is an ancient cross and traces of an earlier church. The tall cross belongs to the same family as St Mark's, near Blessington: of granite, with a circle between the arms, but no trace of figure sculptures. This one has an intriguing inscription. On the left arm are the letters:

R

N   O

T   H

It might be the word 'north' or it might be somebody's initials. The right arm bears the date 1689, but the cross looks a great deal older. It was probably re-erected then. There is, indeed, an 'Erected by' legend, but by whom cannot be read.

A new road on the right, a little way past the church, leads to the Water Treatment Works (page 61). It is worth diverting to take a look at the settling tanks. All is concrete and cubic, but on a large enough scale to allow the water to sparkle and give an air of space and tranquillity amongst a formidable array of valves and pipes.

From the waterworks most of the way to the main road at Pollaphuca beech trees line the right hand side for a kilometre, bordering an estate called Bishopland and conjuring up the good old times when bishops were bishops with a goodly share of the temporalities.

Ballymore to Harristown

A signpost for Kilcullen shows the way out of the maze of roads in Ballymore Eustace and leads up a hill overlooking the valley. A screen of beech and ash trees keeps the river hidden from the road, but there is space to park at the top of the hill for a visit to the wood and to admire the great meanders down below. The wood is something of a rarity: such good stands of ash are very few, even though the tree is so common in Ireland.

The Liffey wanders merrily amidst the alluvium but the road forsakes it and begins a long journey through a region of affluent farms and classical houses. In the eighteenth and nineteenth centuries, most of the landowners planted fringes of beeches and other trees inside their demesne walls. Planting was not only fashionable, but attracted cash incentives administered by the Royal Dublin Society, provided the plantations were properly fenced and cared for.

Trees were also planted around the great houses themselves, so that in many cases the view from the road is of noble gateways, charming gate lodges and then nothing but timber where the mansions hide. The trees provided shade for horses and cattle, firewood for the houses and valuable hardwoods to sell.

At Carnalway Cross, a left turn leads back towards the river, passing the curious church of St Patrick. The tower and spire were built by John LaTouche about the year 1800, but the church was rebuilt in 1891. Instead of the prevailing gothic style of the 19th century, St Patrick's adopted the Irish romanesque tradition. The entrance arch to the cemetery on the right of the church was built nearly a century later as a memorial to another landlord, Thomas Tickell, who died in 1898.

Another beautiful, six-arched bridge crosses the Liffey nearby at Harristown. This one has an inscription, in delightfully uneven lettering. It was built in 1788 by 'Ino LaTouche'. There is a stile on the left bank on the upstream side of the bridge giving access to an angler's path beneath the beech trees by the water's edge. The stately home of Harristown looks over the river from the right bank, surrounded by immaculate pastures, studded with many great trees. Downstream of the bridge there is a pleasant walk of a few hundred metres by the edge of the water, past a long, bushy island, as far as the wood which grows on the steep bank where the river turns sharply to the right.

Harristown to Kilcullen

Over the bridge, the road goes through Brannockstown, a village of attractive small houses, spread along the roadsides and passes a tiny Baptist church before continuing

Continued on page 78

Some Liffey Valley Plants

The distinctive botanical character of the Liffey Valley derives from three principal sources – the aquatic plants of the river itself, the introduced species that have escaped from gardens and made its banks their home and the indigenous flora surviving in the well-developed deciduous woodlands that fringe its course. In a countryside where so much natural habitat has been lost through intensified farming, its margins, where even today agriculture is impracticable, provide a ribbon-like sanctuary in an increasingly undistinguished landscape. Its circular route, passing from mountain blanket bog to estuarine saltmarsh, through the lime-rich glacial soils of the Central Plain, past raised bog and fen, floodplains, cliffs and lakes, constitutes an elegant precis of most of Ireland's remaining habitat types.

To experience the variety of the flora one must begin in its upper reaches. Once the young river has freed itself from the mountainous bogs it cuts down into the granitic bedrock. Here, Water Crowfoots (*Ranunculus penicillatus*) – water buttercups enabled by their tassle-like leaves to endure the shearing effects of the torrent, gain a foothold. They grow in small quantity in the Liffey proper and in the King's River where the water is both rich in oxygen and poor in nutrients. To see them properly however, you must look over the bridge in Ballymore Eustace, just below the great lake of Blessington. Here their bright white flowers covering large stretches of the river's surface testify to its cleanliness. Downriver, the water becomes enriched by naturally-occurring nutrients, agricultural run-off and domestic pollution, and the water buttercups thin out gradually, surviving as a few sickly fragments as far down as Chapelizod. At their expense, perhaps, and certainly in their former niches, now grows the pollution-tolerant Fennel-leaved Pondweed (*Potamogeton pectinatus*) a plant with few redeeming features other than as a barometer of pollution.

The Lakes at Blessington though scenically attractive have not yet acquired a flora of their own. Here and there in bays around the shore, emergent vegetation of sorts has become estab-

lished in the shallower water but, as yet, the flora is only at a developing stage following the flooding of the valley in 1938/40. The gorge at Pollaphuca is a more spectacular affair, with several rare Hawkweeds growing on the boulders below the bridge. Anyone who descends to the bottom of the gorge will gain an impression of what the Irish countryside must have looked like prior to the arrival of man, despite the proximity of the hydro-electric dam and the planted nature of much of the woodland.

Below Ballymore Eustace the river both slows down and widens and a number of interesting plants appear, including the most distinctive species of the Liffey banks, a very uncommon Figwort called *Scrophularia umbrosa*. Though widespread along the banks of the middle and lower stretches of the river, it is almost unknown elsewhere in Ireland. It is a tall (1.5m) herbaceous plant with hundreds of tiny maroon flowers, much-visited by wasps.

In the floodplain of the river, where various tall species of grass thrive in the richer conditions, the Flowering Rush (*Butomus umbellatus*) may occasionally be encountered. It is widespread in the lower stretches of the river, but seldom flowers, despite its name – nor is it even a rush. It bears large heads of strong pink flowers and may occasionally be found growing with the equally-striking Arrowhead (*Sagittaria sagittifolia*). Both these species have suffered severely where river banks have been tidied, grazed or straightened.

Anyone who has ever looked at the bank of the Liffey between Kilcullen and Islandbridge can hardly have missed the tall (2m+) stems of the invasive species Policeman's Helmet (*Impatiens glandulifera*). A native of the Himalayas (it is also known as Himalayan balsam), it was introduced many years ago and has spread vigorously on river banks throughout Ireland. In late summer, if the fruits are removed carefully and squeezed gently, they will explode in the hand scattering the seed, an attribute which no doubt greatly assists dispersal. It has even managed to spread onto waste ground adjoining the Liffey in the centre of Dublin. Often growing with Police-

man's Helmet is another introduced species which has also escaped from gardens. This is Monkey Flower (*Mimulus guttatus*), a low-growing plant with very showy yellow flowers blotched with red which came originally from North America.

The survival of large stands of woodland along the banks of the river from Ballymore Eustace down to the Strawberry Beds has enabled many old woodland plants to maintain a presence in the greater Dublin area. Chief among these is Hairy St. John's Wort (*Hypericum hirsutum*) and Yellow Weasel-snout (*Lamiastrum galeobdolon*), both of which have their Irish headquarters in the lower Liffey valley, where they are occasionally joined by the sinister looking Toothwort (*Lathraea squamaria*), a pale pink plant which lacks chlorophyll, and parasites the roots of other plants. Their occurrence depends on shade and reduced levels of grazing, and despite the fact that much of the existing tree-canopy is now composed of introduced species such as Beech, the ground flora continues to thrive. Red Campion (*Silene dioica*), Wood violet (*Viola reichenbachiana*) and Ramsons or Wild Garlic (*Allium ursinum*) are present throughout the valley wherever such conditions prevail. Dutch Rush (*Equisetum hyemale*), which is actually a horsetail and seldom seen nowadays, occurs in patches between Chapelizod and Celbridge, as does Broad-leaved Helleborine (*Epipactis latifolia*), an inconspicuous woodland orchid, which unfortunately is soon likely to join the ranks of the East of Ireland rarities. ●

LIFFEY VALLEY PLANTS

1   *Lamiastrum galeobdolon.* Yellow Archangel or Weasel Snout.

2   *Lathraea squamaria.* Toothworth.

3   *Allium ursinum.* Wild Garlic.

4   *Ranunculus penicillatus.* Stream Water-crowfoot.

5   *Equisetum hyernale.* Rough Horsetail or Dutch Rush.

6   *Impatiens glandulifera.* Indian Balsam.

The selection of Liffey Valley Plants were painted especia for The Book of the Liffey by the celebrated botanical art Wendy Walsh. The flowers were painted from nature early summer of 1988 and are reproduced here actual si The plants, however, vary greatly in height: for instance, Indian Balsam (No. 6) may grow to more than 2 metres c ft. tall, while the Toothworth (2) rarely grows more than cm. Wild Garlic (3) is usually seen less than 25 cm. or 1 high, the Yellow Archangel (1) a bit taller.

2

3

5

6

4

W. Walsh.

Kilcullen Bridge in 1820, from a drawing by W. Petrie. It has since been widened on the upstream side, but has retained the old arches downstream.

through the rich land of stately homes and stately horses. The County Kildare boasts no less than 8,500 hectares of stud farm, the majority of them lying in the fertile lands of the Liffey valley.

At Kilcullen, the road rises high above the river which emerges from the horse country and sweeps through the village, below the church. It is the first limestone church in the valley, standing a few miles west of the geological boundary between limestone and sandstone.

Old Kilcullen and Dun Ailinne

Kilcullen owes much of its present day importance to its position on the river crossing on the Dublin to Carlow and Waterford route. It is also one of several towns servicing the bloodstock industry and the place where the finest saddles in the world are made by hand. A little way to the south, however, two thousand years and more of history lie.

So we must divert once more to take the road to Athy which runs between two grassy hills. The one on the left is signposted 'Old Kilcullen' and welcomes visitors. There once was a signpost on the right, to show the way up the great, green, flat-topped mound of Dun Ailinne, also known as Knockaulin.

The churchyard of Old Kilcullen contains, besides windswept trees, about half a round tower with a well-made granite doorway. Its greatest treasure is the shaft of a high cross decorated with bold figures in relief. This is the most northerly specimen and the only example in the Liffey valley of a group which includes the fabulous Cross of Moone, 16 km to the south.

Identification of most of the figures on the cross shaft has puzzled the experts. The top one on the north face is supposed to be the founder of the monastery, St Mac Tail, with his bell and his crozier, smiting some enemy who lies at his feet. At the bottom, the future King David attacks a lion. The figures on the west face are beautifully carved, but only the lowest of the three can be identified. It shows the flight into Egypt, with the Virgin and Child seated on a donkey whose ears are as long as his legs.

Across the way, to the west, is Dun Ailinne, a royal seat of the kings of Leinster in the Iron Age. Excavations showed that it had been occupied for very much longer, from the Bronze Age, through the Iron Age and as late as the eighteenth century. When times became more peaceful, there was no need to have dwellings on exposed hilltops commanding a view of the property. The landowners duly sought more comfortable and sheltered sites.

The Curragh of Kildare

Dun Ailinne looks out over one of the most remarkable landforms in Ireland, the Curragh of Kildare, known in the past, indeed, as *Cuirrech Lifé*, the Curragh of the Liffey. The Curragh extends over 3,500 hectares of green pasture on glacial outwash gravels, in

The Stone Cross in the churchyard at Old Kilcullen, sketched in 1805 by John Morris Jr. of Tankardstown. It has since been re-erected.

places no less than 70 metres deep. The gravel drains so easily that there is practically no surface water. The rain percolates down through it to reach the Liffey by seepage. As it is a limestone gravel, the soil is rich. But, because cattle need water to drink and sheep can get their moisture from the grass, it is given over to sheep grazing - and to the training of the finest race horses in creation. The exercising usually takes place in the morning and the only sign of life in the afternoons is of sheep munching the sward.

The Curragh (one meaning of the Irish word is 'a place for horse racing') was royal property. It has been used for horse racing and other sporting gatherings for centuries, perhaps for thousands of years. Grazing rights are leased to the surrounding landowners and therefore the area was not fenced at the time of the Enclosures of the eighteenth century.

Continued on page 85

The Curragh

*'Is the Curragh of Liffey in your land?
Are you a descendant of fifty highkings?'*

These rhetorical questions from a poem which was probably written in the seventh century AD reflect the prestige which attached in ancient times to the Curragh or *Cuirrech Lifé* as it was known. This broad limestone plain of 3,500 hectares lying between the towns of Kildare and Newbridge was a much sought after possession for which kings were once prepared to do battle.

Today, watching the peaceful progress of its Liffey or the sheep grazing its sheepwalks, it is difficult to imagine that battles once raged on the Curragh. In early times, warring tribes living on its boundary fought for the overlordship of Leinster. These battles took place in the shadow of the nearby prehistoric hill fort of Dún Ailinne (Knockaulin), symbol of the power of the Leinster kings.

One of the prizes for the victorious king was the privilege of presiding over one of the most significant fairs in ancient Ireland, the 'Fair of the Liffey' on the Curragh. This fair was held on important occasions near ancient burial grounds – potent symbols for a king since they established continuity with past glories and ensured prosperity. It consisted of an assembly of the king's tribe and featured horse-racing as one of its most important events. We do not know when it was first held. In the ninth century tale 'The Destruction of Dá Derga's Hostel' we read that the great mythological king Conaire Már travelled to celebrate games at the Curragh 'i Lifiu'. The son of Finn Mac

Cumhaill, another mythological figure, Oisín, in a poem ascribed to him in the Book of Leinster, regretted that old age prevented him from participating in the sports there as he did formerly.

As befits an area rich in ritual associations, the Curragh has many legends associated with it. Many of these relate to St. Brigid who established her monastery in the late fifth century on the site of a pagan sanctuary where the town of Kildare now stands. The saint was given possession of the Curragh when she cured a deformity afflicting the king. Before granting it he asked her to spread out her mantle. All the land which it covered, he told her, would be hers. Unfortunately for Brigid the mantle was torn and didn't cover the whole of Ireland. The grant was confined to the Curragh which became known as Brigid's Pasture.

Brigid not only grazed her own sheep on the Curragh but also allowed others to bring their flocks there. The plains were so fertile, we are told, that on one occasion she got so much milk from her cows that the surplus formed a lake, Loch Minnaun. We have no record of Brigid taking part in the races at the Curragh but we are told that she used to travel on the Curragh in her chariot drawn by two horses. (A poem written about 600 AD which mentions her custom of driving across the Curragh provides us with one of our earliest references to the plain.) Brigid's successors may have been more competitive in this respect than she was. The Abbot Cobhthach, for instance, was known as the 'racing Cobhthach'.

The origins of modern racing are traced, not to the chariot racing of the earliest times, but to practices in the middle of the seventeenth century. Then as now, the Curragh was the focal point for racing in Ireland. Competitors issued challenges to each other and horses were matched over a selected piece of country. In 1634, for example, Lord Digby and the Earl of Ormond matched each other's horses over four miles at the Curragh. More than a century later in 1751 the famous match between 'Black and All Black' and 'Bajazet' was held for the then princely sum of 1000 guineas and a further 10,000 guineas in side bets – an event which resulted in victory for 'Black and All Black's and a further challenge, this time to a duel. Later racing at the Curragh received encouragement from successive kings of England, it being the view of the royal court that 'The common where the race is held is a much finer turf than Newmarket.'

The Curragh in the mid seventeenth century was, according to one commentator, 'a place naturally adapted to pleasure; and its vicinity to Dublin – being but seventeen miles distant occasions that hither repairs the Lord Lieutenant, or Chief Governor . . .' Later the army established a camp there increasing the attractiveness of the Curragh as a social centre. (The Curragh Camp became the headquarters of the Irish Army in 1922.) Some of the most important races in the country became established there. The best known of these, the Irish Derby, first run in 1866 after many false starts, now has a foremost place in the international racing calendar.

With racing, in this rich limestone plain, has gone breeding and training activities. Stud farms are found at all points along the Liffey but when the river reaches the Curragh it has along its banks some of the best known and most successful breeding establishments in the country. Near the town of Kildare stands the Irish National Stud, perhaps the most famous stud of them all. In 1915 its founder Lord Wavertree presented it, together with its Japanese Gardens and valuable stock, to the Irish nation. It was fitting that he should do so for, like the Curragh as a whole, it continues to serve the country well. ● Brian Smith

This Stone Circle is to be found in the woods near the old woollen mills at Bally-more Eustace. It is not an ancient ritual site, however, but a Victorian 'folly'.

The small cross at Ballyknockan is much revered by the people of the locality.

The Book of the Liffey

(Left) Before the flooding: Blessington Bridge and the old cornmill, with the new road and bridge in the background. (Right) The new bridge under construction near Blessington. (Below) Foundations are laid for the Penstock pipes carrying the water to the generators at Golden Falls. (Below, right) At Pollaphuca, the pressure tunnel from the intake at the reservoir to the surge tank was cut through solid rock. Here is seen under construction.

Aerial view of the lakes (above) and (left) Golden Falls dam.

Looking up the great wall of the dam at Pollaphuca.

The Liffey of the Plains

Army headquarters lie on the south side of the Curragh and the race course, where most of the Irish classics are held, occupies the middle. The ground is fairly littered with ring forts, circular banks of earth which surrounded houses or served as pens for stock in the Iron Age.

At the western end is the cathedral town of Kildare, a holy place since the time of the almost mythical St Brigid, a near contemporary of St Patrick. Kildare isn't really a Liffey town, but there are so many interesting places in and around that it has to be mentioned. In the cathedral grounds stands one of the few round towers which has a stairway to the top. The view is fantastic. To the east of the town are the National Stud with its horse museum and the enthralling Japanese Gardens.

The Curragh of Kildare was in times gone by known as The Curragh of Lifé, or Liffey. Horses have been raced on this open plain since ancient times. Kildare is now the home of the National Stud, to which is adjoined the famous Japanese Gardens.

Kilcullen and Newabbey

Back in Kilcullen, the bridge is a busy one and has had to be widened to take the heavy traffic. The old bridge of gentler days can be seen on the downstream side, built of limestone with five arches. The widening was accomplished mainly in reinforced concrete, but the engineers did have the decency to keep their new piers in line with the old and to face the outside with cut stone.

There is a car park on the right bank upstream of the bridge and the first of a number of little inscriptions commemorating the good work done by many citizens of Kilcullen in the late 1970s. Some contributed substantial sums of money and others hard work to create a delightful park and riverside walk. That on the right bank is small and leads to a narrow approach to the canoe club and its little marina. It is worth going there to admire the club's poker work sign, a refreshing piece of local craft in a situation usually adorned by plastic.

The left bank, however, is where the riverside at Kilcullen really begins. The entrance to the park, with its planted poplars and well-tended lawns, is after the third house up the road from the bridge. Near the top of the hill is St Brigid's Well, with a relief sculpture by Father Flanagan of Newbridge College of the saint feeding the poor. Below this a stile marks the beginning of an ancient footpath across the alluvial plain.

The path leads to a cemetery which gives a first impression of a rather dull collection of not very ancient monuments. But there are small treasures lying unobtrusively amongst the celtic crosses. Fragments of three or four tombs have been fixed together, forming a low wall. The best of them dates to the first half of the 16th century and shows, on the left, St Catherine with her wheel, in the middle the Virgin with a sadly defaced Child and to the right another female saint. The group would be commonplace in a great cathedral. Here they have a special position beneath the sky, close to the gentle river.

Not far from them, and quite as inconspicuous, lies the recumbent effigy of Roland Eustace, Baron Portlester, a descendant of the Eustace who founded Ballymore two centuries before, and his lady. They lie peacefully, their features rather obscured by the patches of pale grey lichen which encrust the stone. A helpful little plaque at their feet gives the names of the couple and the date of death of the baron in 1495. He was the founder of the monastery on the site, still known as Newabbey.

Cemented into a wall of the cemetery are fragments of the abbey, a selection of carved stones which show that it once was a building of noble proportions. Beyond the abbey there is a wood of pines and beeches beside the river. Elsewhere sheep graze and the grass is short enough to allow a pleasant walk back by the river bank. There are reed beds in places. Dippers live nearby and fly up and down the stream and redpolls visit the alders by the bank. All in all, it is a lovely spot, encouraging a gentle and philosophical stroll with the music of bird and river.

Kilcullen to Athgarvan

From Kilcullen the road on the left bank to the next bridge, Athgarvan, climbs a wooded hill and passes the lovely eighteenth century gateway of Castlemartin, the home of Tony O'Reilly. There is a magnificent avenue of limes, already planted by the time of the Ordnance Survey in 1837.

A little way past the avenue, the road crosses the totally unobtrusive geological boundary from sandstone to limestone. It is unobtrusive because all the rock lies deeply buried by the glacial gravels. Many things happened between the times when the sandstone of the Ordovician and the limestone of the Carboniferous era were deposited. The two strata are separated in time by about one hundred million years. The Carboniferous was a pleasant time to be around in. The Wicklow Mountains stood by the shores of a warm, clear sea with coral reefs where the limestone now lies. The main influence that the geological change has on the scenery is that limestone rather than sandstone begins to appear in the buildings.

Athgarvan, the 'Ath' of the name meaning a ford, is a pleasant valley where the river widens, becoming shallow enough to make an easy crossing before the introduction of bridges. There is a tradition that one of the five great roads, which led to all points of Ireland from Tara, crossed the Liffey here.

The road to the ford takes a sharp turn and makes a steep descent, bringing it round the outer edge of the great earthworks called Rosetown Rath. Covered with trees and with ivy trailing over the ground, its man-made origin is far from obvious. The rath has not been excavated and its age is unknown. It is certain that the Anglo-Normans would have made a motte-and-bailey at such an important river crossing. But the rath looks older than that and could go far back towards the Iron Age.

The bridge has five broad arches of sandstone masonry with granite coping. Upstream there is a long weir which leads to a water mill on the left bank. The wheel remains, though it turns no longer, but the buildings are still in use. They have tall ventilation chimneys from past service as a malthouse.

On the left bank, downstream of the bridge, a footpath leads between the old tailrace from the watermill and the river. The easy walk by the bank is brought to a sudden end by the tailrace whose bridge is reduced to a sorry skeleton.

Athgarvan to Newbridge

The road along the right bank, towards Newbridge, stays away from the river. 5 km from Athgarvan, a turn to the left marked 'Cul de Sac', leads to the one remaining wall of a ruined church, a very large one in its day. Its name was Greatconnell Abbey and it was founded in 1202 for the Augustinians by Myler Fitzhenry. It is hard to believe that it was one of the greatest of the monasteries. Greatconnell now is little more than a neglected burial place, its sole distinction being the beautiful script on many of the early 19th century tombstones. Its state of neglect is equalled only by the much more recently ruined church in an overgrown churchyard by the main road nearby.

The next town is Newbridge, spreading on both sides of the river. The new bridge was built in 1308. Its successor is very much newer, having been built of reinforced concrete in 1936 with three wide arches. The Liffey runs shallow and was easily forded so that the town has had strategic importance at least since the times of the Anglo-Normans. They built a motte-and-bailey to defend the ford. A splendid remnant of this stands in the form of a tall, green mound in the grounds of Old Connell on the right bank.

In spite of its early importance, Newbridge failed to develop until 1816 when a cavalry barracks was built. As armies do in times of peace, this one brought prosperity to the town. The landlord, Thomas Eyre Powell, laid out new streets and in the course of time Newbridge College was built, in a beautiful setting on the left bank. It was a foundation of the Dominicans who already had a friary on the site.

The barracks, which once looked out over the main street, has been hidden away behind houses and shops and taken over by cutlers, rope-makers and Bord na Mona. The barrack buildings, in red brick with yellow stone, in a simple, classical style, can be seen behind the Post Office.

Down by the riverside, a pavement on the left bank has railings which keep you safe from the perils of the water. It leads down to the College, whose general architecture purports Victorian severity as a boys' boarding school. But the old architecture hides a thriving co-educational day school and an incomparable church. It is a simple, beautifully proportioned building, dedicated to St Eustace.

The church's crowning glory lies in the brilliant colours of the windows. My first visit was on a gloomy day in midwinter. Even then the interior was a place of warmth and light. On a bright day the glass throws a shower of colour on the altar and its surroundings. The windows are the work of John Murphy and the large ones on the south wall all relate to major visions of the Book of Revelation. The smaller windows are abstracts, but symbolical: all contain a stylised cross; the rectangular treatment of one may represent the earth-bound body; the blue with white shapes of another, the soul shaking off the fetters of earthly existence. The sculptures, in bog yew, limestone and concrete, are all the work of a member of the Dominican Order and former teacher at the College, Father Flanagan.

The Hill of Allen

Just downstream of Newbridge College there is a short walk by the bank, over rather neglected grass, looking across to a line of willows. The walkway ends in a thicket of elder and blackthorn, with ash and sycamore trees. The positive side of the unmown grass is that many wild flowers are left to bloom unmolested. Thereafter, the road keeps close to the riverside for a few miles.

Common Kingfisher.

Towards the west, 6 km away, stands the legendary Hill of Allen, made to look even more impressive by the 19th century tower at the summit. It is well worth diverting from the Liffeyside to enjoy the view from its slopes. The hill gives its name to the great bog which lies mainly to the west. This was the headquarters of Finn MacCumhail and the Fianna of legend, legend which was already ancient when the Christians came to Ireland. Indeed, the theme of a community of hunters, living in the forest and rejoicing in the song of wild birds, has overtones which could extend back to the Mesolithic people, before even the times of the Neolithic farmers and their buildings.

Whatever the period, it is easy to see why a warrior band should use the hill as a refuge. It is tall enough to command distant horizons. Most of the approaches are through bog, which was a great deal wetter and more treacherous than its modern, well-drained remnants. No stranger could have launched a surprise attack. Towards the east there was plenty of fertile land: abundant grazing for herds of deer. And there was the Liffey, teeming with salmon, especially in winter when other food was scarce.

The view from the hill, besides all the midland bog, includes the precious Fen of Pollardstown, one of the most important examples of a landform of increasing rarity. The peat bog is acid, but actually grew up to cover older fens which are alkaline. Pollardstown is fed by drainage water from the Curragh which is rich in lime.

In summer, many orchids and a great variety of unusual wild flowers make it a lovely spot to visit. The fen lies just to the right of a line from the hilltop to Newbridge. Far to the east are the Wicklow Mountains and the lower hills of sandstone which divide the Liffey Valley in two. The lakes are invisible, however, since the ridge which holds them back is higher than the Hill of Allen.

The Hill itself is formed from volcanic rock of the Ordovician period, more or less contemporaneous with the granite of the Wicklow Mountains, but formed as a lava flow rather than injected deep down at the roots of the mountains. To the northeast of the Hill the rock is of Old Red Sandstone age, to the southwest there are Ordovician sandstones and all around lies the very much younger limestone of the Carboniferous: younger than the hill, but still of respectable antiquity at three hundred million years.

Victoria Bridge and Carragh Bridge

Meanwhile, back at the river, the road leads past a little beech copse in a cemetery, where there are traces of a church and a rather modernised holy well, dedicated to St Patrick, whose plaster effigy stands nearby in a grotto. The well is lined with concrete but, in spite of this intrusion, yields crystal clear water.

Around the corner you come on one of the most enticing picnic spots of the lower Liffey. The banks are shaded by tall beeches and the water rushes through breaches in an old mill dam. There is an abundance of that most showy of the riverside flowers, the balsam. A native of the Himalayas, with tall stems, large leaves and bulbous pink flowers, it was introduced to Ireland in the nineteenth century. It has run wild and established itself by river banks and has lived by Victoria Bridge at least since the 1930s.

The mill stream ran beneath the road and turned a great mill wheel whose iron skeleton is still in place, supported by neat stone masonry. The four-storey mill is dilapidated, but the charming home of former millers nearby is very well preserved, lived in and loved.

Close to the mill is the graceful bridge, of two wide arches, all of quarried limestone blocks. Her Majesty would have been less than amused to observe the plaque from which her royal name has been pretty effectively expunged. The rest of the neat lettering survives, giving the date as that of her Coronation, 1837, and the builder's name as S R Mulleda. On the right bank, where enormous alders grow, there is relatively easy access to the pasture beside the river downstream.

The next crossing of the river, Carragh Bridge, is the narrowest and probably the oldest of all the Liffey crossings. It is supported by six stone piers with round-headed arches. The stone work is rather rough, making a charming rustic bridge contrasting with the sophistication of its 18th-century companions upstream and downstream.

The Leinster Aqueduct

At a T-junction, 4 km downstream of Carragh Bridge on the right bank, the right turn leads to Sallins while the left mounts the most splendid of all the 18th century works on the Liffey, the Leinster Aqueduct. Canal and road together march across the river, the road standing 8 metres above the river bed. The exact location of the aqueduct was that favoured by the Engineer in Ordinary in Ireland, General Charles Vallancey, in the face of some opposition. It necessitated a considerable diversion from the straight line of the canal. The engineer in charge of the building was Richard Evans and the work was completed in 1780. Evans subsequently became a major figure in the construction of the Grand Canal.

Canal and road are supported by five rather squat arches, with a high wall on each side. On the left bank of the Liffey, a lane leads down to the riverside, passing an old but well-tended, whitewashed house. The path goes to the other side of the aqueduct by a muddy track under a low, brick-lined arch. On the right bank of the river three pale blue pipes descend to a concrete pump house.

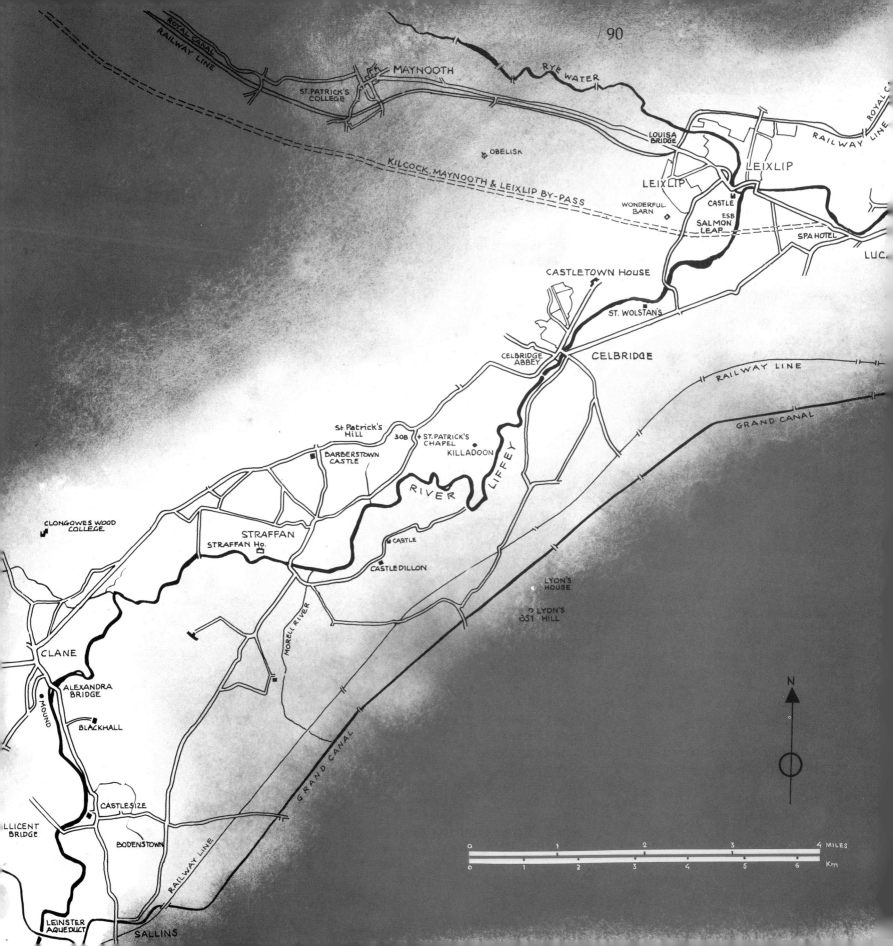

The pumps can be used to raise water from the Liffey to maintain the level of the canal. The ESB needed canal water for its cooling system at Allenwood peat-burning generating station. In wet weather there was more than enough for their needs, but the canal feeder streams were not able to maintain the level in a drought. So the Liffey serves once more, if indirectly, in the power supply.

The Leinster Aqueduct to Millicent Bridge

The road going eastwards over the Leinster Aqueduct leads into the one-time canal harbour of Sallins, still a very important flour milling centre. The mills were powered by quite small streams, but the advantage of a branch and harbour on the Grand Canal allowed a thriving industry to develop. When the railways came, a main line went through Sallins and so prosperity continued.

From Sallins, the Clane road heads towards the river and a left turn goes to the six-arched Millicent Bridge, recently rebuilt and repointed. Beside it on the right bank there are two enormous beech trees which are probably as old as the bridge itself. They stand by the wall of a pleasant green pasture sloping down to the river bank. Close by is a ruined farm cottage with a curious remnant of a hawthorn hedge which once bordered the cottage garden. The hawthorns have grown tall and leggy, no longer trimmed nor needed to keep the cattle out. Across the bridge you pass the entrance drive to Millicent House, with its polite notice to say that it is private.

Millicent Bridge to Alexandra Bridge and Clane

Close to Millicent crossroads there stands the Church of St Mary and All Angels, a large, italianate building. It has a lych gate, a roof over the entrance where the coffin could be placed before interment, a rare enough churchyard feature in Ireland.

The road from Sallins passes the gateway and avenue of Castlesize House on the left and on the right the road to Bodenstown Churchyard, where Wolfe Tone lies buried. Flagstaffs and a speaker's rostrum beside the ruined church in the cemetery cater for annual memorial meetings.

The bridge at Clane was built in 1864 and named in honour of Princess Alexandra who had been married the year before to the Prince of Wales, the future King Edward VII. A path on the left bank goes to the riverside, downstream of an abandoned weir beside a lovely old willow. The bridge has three main arches and a fourth, smaller one to take flood water.

A little way back from the river stands a small, round, flat-topped mound with a crown of four beech trees. Tradition tells that it is the burial place of Mesgegra, King of Leinster. And his burial place it well may be, even though the mound looks suspiciously like an Anglo-Norman motte, built a mere millennium later. Clane was an important strategic spot, standing beside a ford where the Liffey makes a boundary between fertile land to the east and bog, long since cut-away, to the west.

Weston Joyce's *The Neighbourhood of Dublin* contains a photograph of Clane Abbey, taken in 1906: a great, stark ruin standing on its own in a field. I often wondered why I had never noticed such a large building in passing. The reason is that, in the course of eighty years, yews and cypresses have grown. The abbey ruins still stand there, between the motte and the village, but now hidden by the trees in the cemetery. Building was begun in 1260 by Gerald Fitzmaurice, Lord of Offaly.

The church of the friary was a splendid one in its day, with the walls of the nave

The Mound of Clane

The story of Mesgegra and his Queen is told in the ancient tale 'The Siege of Howth' in the Book of Leinster.

Mesgegra was King of Leinster and resided at Naas (*Nás na Riogh*: Assembly-place of the kings) with Queen Buan, his wife. About the year AD 33, the chief poet of the Ulster court came to visit the Leinster king, as was the custom of the time. The laws of hospitality decreed that he be accorded all honour during his visit. The poet was arrogant and greedy, his behaviour and demands outrageous, but his privileged position made it impossible to refuse or offend him while in Mesgegra's territory. Once outside of it, however, he was no longer protected. The men of Leinster courteously escorted him, with his newly-acquired cattle, gold and women, to the borders of Leinster and handed him over to an Ulster bodyguard who awaited him there. No sooner had they done this, however, than they pursued him and his guard to Howth, where a siege ended in victory for the men of Ulster.

Mesgegra fled for home but was overtaken by the Ulster warrior, Conal Cernagh of the Red Branch Knights, who killed him in single combat. He then cut off the King's head, which he bore away with him in his chariot, heading for Ulster.

On his way he met Buan and her retinue. Flourishing her husband's head, he bade her to come with him to Ulster. But she 'lifted up her cry of lamentation, and it was heard even unto

The Book of the Liffey

extending for 40 metres. But they have been savagely attacked so that practically nothing remains but two arcades, covered in a dense growth of ivy. All the stone mouldings and tracery have been removed, except for the granite surrounds of one tomb niche in the south wall. Near to it, by the opposite wall, stands the stone midriff of a friar, all that survives of a medieval effigy.

The road back towards Millicent Bridge runs by the demesne of Blackhall, where trees have been planted with great care for generations. There are several mature beech avenues, together with much younger shelter belts of cypress, some flanking the road, others marching in straight lines across the fields.

Tara and to Allen, and she cast herself backwards and she was dead. On the road is her grave, called Buana, that is the hazel (coll) which grew through her grave.'

Mesgegra is buried beneath the mound at Clane. Buan's resting-place is marked by the mount at Mainham, 2 km to the north, near Clongowes Wood College.

There is a long poem by Sir Samuel Ferguson called 'Mesgegra, King of Leinster'. It begins:

When glades were green
  where Dublin stands today
And limpid Liffey,
  fresh from wood and wold,
Bridgeless and fordless,
  in the lonely Bay,
Sank to her rest
  on sands of stainless gold . . .

and ends:

And let the earth-heaped,
  grass-renewing tomb
A time-long token eloquent remain
Of Pity and of Love for all who come
By murmuring Liffey
  and the banks of Clane.

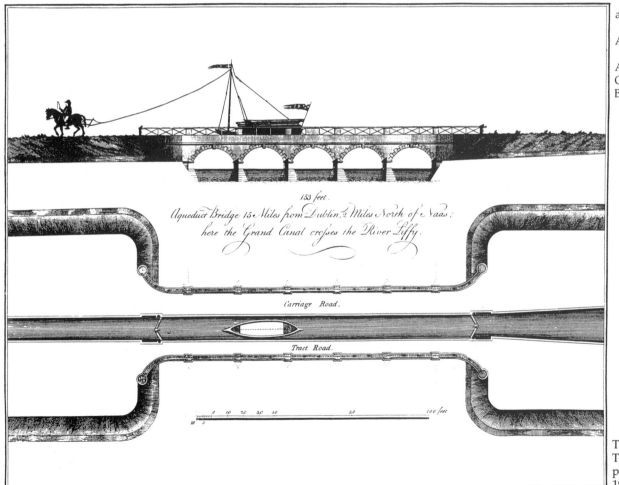

The Leinster Aqueduct: detail from Taylor's Map of County Kildare, published in 1783 and republished in 1983 by the Royal Irish Academy.

Alexandra Bridge to Straffan and ArdCloc

The road into Clane passes a pleasant little park, set by the banks of the Butterstream. The main street is wide and straight and leads to a long, level, straight road in the direction of Straffan. To the left of the road, in the distance and appropriately hidden by trees is Clongowes Wood College whose chapel, like that of Newbridge, contains outstanding stained glass. Two artists, Michael Healy and Evie Hone designed the windows and both of them died before they could complete their work. The Liffey stays away from the road, running first amongst the open fields of the plain, then going to hide from public view in the demesne of Straffan House.

A narrow road skirts the demesne and goes between two churches into the tiny, old world village of Straffan. The church on the left has long lain in ruins, replaced in the 19th century by its tall-spired neighbour. The ruined church is well worth a visit for a walk around its extraordinary tower. Four storeys high, it has tiny windows and a 14th or 15th century look. The only present day entrance is an inaccessible wooden door on the first floor, high above the walls of the rest of the church. There is a turret at one corner, forming a fifth floor beside a double arch where bells once hung. It seems to have been a dual-purpose building, serving to summon the prayerful in times of peace and offering a stout defence and lookout place on other occasions.

The road through Straffan crosses the Liffey by a graceful, three-arched bridge. There is room to park on the left bank to get out and admire the river and a distant prospect of the white-painted Straffan House.

The house stands opposite to a pair of islands. From these to the bridge, the left bank is beautifully landscaped with a row of alternating cypresses and willows. An old weir crosses the river just upstream of the bridge, so that the water between it and the islands forms a calm, deep pool. The water at the weir drives a turbine and beside it cascades over a five-stepped salmon ladder.

Across the bridge, about 50 metres down the road on the left, a path leads through a laurel brake to the riverside. To the left of the path are traces of a millstream and a pathetic piece of masonry where once a mill wheel turned. It is called 'Straffan Corn Mill' on the old maps.

To the right a partly silted-up ditch runs parallel to the main river. It may have been the tail race of a mill. A curious line of sycamores grows on the right bank of the ditch. Their trunks start horizontally from near the bottom of the ditch and then curve gracefully upwards, but without ever managing to stand up straight. The sycamores began by growing away from the shade of the laurels, towards the brightness of the river bank, and then continued to grow out over the river.

A little way after Straffan Railway Station, on the Dublin to Cork line, stands the very new and rather lonely church of ArdCloc, well worth a brief visit. It is white-painted, tall and angular with a simple and dignified interior and some fine sculpture in wood. It was built in 1984 to a plan inspired by the shape of a St Brigid's Cross.

Lyons Hill and Celbridge

Beyond the village, the Grand Canal goes by on the right, high on an embankment over the low-lying ground, with boats seeming to sail up above the fields. The green hill towards the south has a curved ridge near the summit, with a distinctly artificial look

Continued on page 97

Vanessa and Swift

'I ever feared the tattle of this nasty town, and told you so, and that is the reason I said to you long ago that I would see you seldom while you were in Ireland.' So wrote Jonathan Swift to Esther van Homrigh, his 'Vanessa', in 1720.

They had met in London, this turbulent Dean and she, the daughter of a rich Dutch merchant who became a Lord Mayor of Dublin. After the merchant's death, his wife and four children moved to London, where Vanessa's strange relationship with the author of *Gulliver's Travels*, a man more than twice her age, began:

'Vanessa not in years a score
Dreams of a gown of forty four,
Imaginary charms can find
In eyes with reading almost blind.'

When Swift moved to Dublin to take up the Deanship of St. Patrick's they continued to correspond, in very loving terms. When Esther inherited the house called Celbridge Abbey, she moved to Ireland to be near him. Despite his words above, he came often to walk with her by the river, and share a lover's bower by its murmuring banks.

But his attentions were by now ambivalent. There was 'Stella', Esther Johnson, whom he had known since she was a child, and who was a close if not constant companion. The nature of their relationship may never be known. Vanessa, in a fit of jealousy, wrote and asked her. Stella showed Swift the letter. The story goes that Swift, infuriated, rode straightaway to Celbridge, stormed into the house and flung the letter on the table before the unhappy Vanessa, and stormed out again without uttering a word.

Vanessa, to whom he had once written 'you are the only person on earth who has ever been loved, honoured, esteemed, adored by your friend,' died three weeks later, it is said of a broken heart, at the age of 34. She is buried in St. Andrew's Church, Dublin.

The Book of the Liffey   Con Costello

Living by the Liffey

Castlelyons House.

The fertile lands of the Liffey valley, secure within the Pale, have been a favourite residential area for landed or wealthy families since the coming of the Anglo-Normans. Within easy distance of the capital, and on the main road to the south of the country, Kildare has always been a relatively prosperous county. The powerful Geraldines, and lesser families such as the Eustaces and Luttrells, had strong castles which, in more peaceful times, were replaced with fine mansions. *Carton*, the ducal residence of the Fitzgeralds, situated on the Rye Water, tributary to the Liffey, remains as the most important surviving 18th-century estate. But there were lesser people, with less important houses, many of which are lived in to the present.

When Col. and Mrs. Smith inherited their lands in the early 19th century they set about building 'a convenient mansion' on a circle of the King's river which in her *Journal* Elizabeth Smith described as being considerably larger than the Liffey, 'a very significant streamlet'. From her comfortable home at *Baltyboys* Mrs. Smith observed and recorded life around her. She sought to improve the lives of the local poor people, and during the grim famine years she despaired of the relief works, and worked valiantly in the neighbourhood. Sometimes she and the colonel would walk across the valley to visit the Milltowns at *Russborough*, to enjoy the high life there amidst the great rooms decorated with classical statues and fine paintings. When the Earl of Milltown returned the call, with his numerous family, they came to Baltyboys in a

procession; his lordship with his lady in a pony phaeton, one child on horseback, another on a donkey, and three in a little fairy machine, a little bigger than a wheel-barrow drawn by a shetland pony the size of a dog. The German architect Richard Castle had designed Russborough for Joseph Leeson, of the Dublin brewing family, in 1741; he was created Lord Russborough in 1756, and Earl of Milltown seven years later. Russborough has been described as 'the most beautiful house in Ireland', and now enhanced by its situation above the lake, and filled with the marvellous pictures collected by Sir Alfred Beit, it is indeed a magical place.

Elizabeth Smith also visited her less important neighbours at *Kilbride Manor*, *Tulfarris*, *Ardenode* and elsewhere. These three houses survive, and guests are welcomed to the hotel and golf course at Tulfarris. Ardenode too is now an hotel; it was after a lunch there when it was the home of the West family, to meet the protestant archbishop, that Mrs. Smith noted in her journal that *catholics* were included in the party, but she found that the archbishop was worth the drive! What Mrs. Smith did not know was that Baltyboys was to become famous as the birth place of one of her great-great-grand-children, Dame Ninette de Valois.

The first important house down river from the lake is *Harristown*, situated high above a bend with gardens sloping down to the water. On former Eustace lands, it was the home of the LaTouche banking family; in their improvements of the estate the old castle was demolished, an artificial lake was made and the main

road was taken outside the walls, leaving a fine arched bridge over the river within the demesne. John LaTouche built the Baptist church at Brannockstown, and his daughter Rose, a delicate child, was adored by the poet Ruskin who cried:

'Rosie, Posie, Rosie rare,
Rocks and woods, and clouds and air,
And Yet, and yet, and yet, and yet,
She is not here, but where?'

Ruskin is credited with the design of the Brannockstown gates to Harristown, across the road from which is the Georgian house *Sallymount*. When William Makepeace Thackeray dined at Naas in 1824 he joined in a toast to the Sallymount Beagles.

Near to Kilcullen, close to the site of the medieval Franciscan friary, is *Newabbey*, a mid 18th-century house remembered as the home of one George Brereton who, in 1786, was killed in a duel, with swords, in an hotel in Cork. The poet Edmund Spenser lived for a time in the friary and is believed to have written part of the *Faerie Queene* there. Now the only reminder of that great religious house is the double-effigy of the Eustace lord and lady Portlester, eroded by decades of wind and rain.

On the western side of Kilcullen, again high above the river and encased in the 18th-century *Castlemartin*, is another castle of the Eustaces. Built by a Dublin banker and used as headquarters by Lt. Gen. Dundas in 1798, the house has been splendidly restored and the 15th-century chapel re-roofed for worship. The present Earl of Gowrie inherited the house, and while he lived there penned these lines:

> Behind me, also rooted
>   raptured to a corner
> of earth and Ireland, the
>   eighteenth-century house
> Grey face, dummy windows
>   alternating with true
> were in the northern dawn
>   succinct at 6 a.m.

It is now the Irish home of business tycoon Tony O'Reilly.

North of Newbridge three houses, until recently owned by the Mansfield family, adjoin each other. *Barretstown*, a 19th-century spired and turreted house, has gables and bargeboards, while the great house of *Morristown Lattin* is a Tudor revival building, recently damaged by fire. It is built around a late 17th-century house. The filming of the television series *The Irish R.M.* at Morristown made the house familiar to many. The very charming *Yeomanstown*, an early 18th-century double gable-ended house, also belonged to the Eustaces.

Castlemartin House in the 18th century.

There the Naas Dominicans were sheltered when they were expelled from the town at the end of the 17th century, and before they settled in Newbridge a century later.

Near Sallins are three good houses, *Millicent*, *Castlesize* and *Osberstown*. The latter was the home of Dr. John Esmonde, the United Irishman, who was hanged in Dublin in 1798. His neighbour at Millicent, Richard Griffith was commander of the Sallins Yeoman Cavalry, and his evidence at Esmonde's trial did not help that man. Millicent was attacked and damaged by the rebels. Sir Richard Griffith, compiler of the Valuation Books, was a son of the house. Castlesize, meaning Cashen's fields or gardens, a two storey late 18th-century house, was in recent years for a time the home of novelist Evelyn Anthony.

Lost in beech trees south of Clane is *Blackhall*, an 18th-century house and a stud farm. The Rev. Charles Wolfe, remembered for his poem *The burial of Sir John Moore*, was born there and the Tone family were freehold tenants. Wolfe Tone

was named after the family, and he is buried at nearby Bodenstown. North of Clane and north of the river is the Jesuit *Clongowes College*, famed for its association with James Joyce, who came there at the age of six. Formerly *Castle Browne* it, and the nearby *Rathcoffey*, were the homes of the catholic Browne and Wogan families, the last of whom, Lieut. Wogan-Browne was murdered in Kildare town in 1922. Sir Charles Wogan's adventures in rescuing the future bride of the Old Pretender, the Princess Clementina Sobieski, at Innsbruck in 1719 have been the subject of several books. The United Irish Leader, Archibald Hamilton Rowan demolished the old castle of the Wogans to build himself a house on the site. It is now a ruin.

Two houses which had strong family connections in the 18th century are *Straffan* and nearby *Lodge Park*. The Henrys lived in both houses and Hugh Henry, who built the five-block-long Lodge Park in 1777 was said to be trying to rival the size of his father-in-law's mansion of Russborough. The architect is believed to have been Nathaniel Clements from nearby *Killadoon*. It was he who designed that other great house whose park once swept down to the Liffey, *Áras an Uachtaráin*. The chateau-like Straffan was also the home of the Bartons, a family which, since the early 18th century, has produced fine wines on their vineyards at Bordeaux.

From the river east of Straffan can be glimpsed the tower of *Barberstown* across the river, a tower house with additions, now an hotel. To the south, under *Lyons Hill*, is the mansion built by Lord Cloncurry, and since 1962 part of University College, Dublin. It was the home of the poet Emily Lawless.

The Celbridge run of the river is embellished with many good houses such as *Kildrought* on the main street, with its garden to the water, and the stately *Castletown*. Built in 1722 for the Speaker of the House of Commons, William Conolly, Castletown is regarded as the best of our Palladian mansions. With its well proportioned arcades and steps, its impressive hall and staircase, print room and long gallery, it was saved and restored by Mr. and Mrs. Desmond Guinness and the Irish Georgian Society twenty years ago. Much of the original decoration of Castletown was the work of Lady Louisa Conolly whose sisters lived nearby in two other important houses, Emily, Duchess of Leinster, at Carton, and Lady Sarah Napier at *Oakley Park*. Three of the five sons of Colonel and Lady Napier, who were educated in Celbridge, were famous generals in the British army. An earlier owner of Oakley Park had been Arthur Price, Vicar of Celbridge, and afterwards archbishop of Cashel. For a time he had been suitor to his neighbour at the *Abbey* across the road, the wealthy Esther Van Homrigh. She was the loved Vanessa of Swift, who often came to the Abbey, and their bower by the river is still known.

Across the river from Castletown is the early 19th-century Tudor-revival house of *Donacomper*, formerly the home of the British diplomat Sir Ivone Kirkpatrick. Next door to it is the much altered 17th-century *St. Wolstan's*, now a school. It takes its name from the ruined medieval abbey of the Augustinian Canons which stands close by.

At Leixlip the oldest and continuously inhabited house on the river rises above

∧ Morristown Lattin before its redesign and reconstruction in Tudor Revival style. Sadly, this fine house has suffered a very damaging fire in recent times.

St. Woolstons, or Wolstans, near Celbridge, is now run as a girls' school by the Sisters of the Holy Faith. It has been much altered since this view by Wheatley in 1792. The design on the plate is based on Wheatley's. If the building among the trees to the right is Castletown House, you can see that it has been 'corrected' on the plate by the addition of several ∨ windows in the facade.

the confluence of the Liffey and the Rye Water. The great towers of *Leixlip Castle* have watched over the waters for eight hundred years, inspiring artists and writers including Emolibie de Celtis who, in 1883 wrote: 'Leixlip castle raising high its crested head and embattled towers above the rich amphitheatre of woods that emboss the sloping terrace . . . as the forking rivers take their turbulent course along its base.' It is the home of the Hon. Desmond Guinness, pillar of the Irish Georgian Society.

Beside Lucan village, within the old estate of Patrick Sarsfield, the hero of the Siege of Limerick, is the beautiful late 18th-century Palladian house which is now the *Italian Embassy*. It was built by Agmondisham Vesey MP, whose family had succeeded to the Sarsfield estate. He is said to have designed the house himself, with some advice from Sir William Chambers. The last great house on the river before it reaches the environs of Dublin is *Luttrellstown*, a gothicised mansion of that ancient family of Luttrell. They are remembered by two sad stories. In 1717 Col. Henry Luttrell was murdered in his sedan chair in Dublin; he had made himself hated on account of his betrayal of the Jacobites at the battle of Aughrim. His sister Elizabeth was said to have committed suicide at Augsburg when she was accused of picking pockets and sentenced to sweeping the streets, chained to a wheel-barrow.

Of the thirty-five houses mentioned in this chapter it is salutary to know that today only one of them remains in the ownership of the original family, Mr. and Miss Clements at Killadoon, a couple of miles up-river from Celbridge, have the distinction of being the oldest county family still in occupation of their ancestral home. ●

The Liffey of the Plains

about it. This is a trace of the earthworks which go back at least to the Iron Age. Its name is Liamhuin or Lyon's Hill, one of the royal seats of the kings of Leinster. Like Dun Ailinne, Lyon's Hill stands in the midst of exceptionally fertile land, a property well worth defending.

Further fame was achieved by Lyon's Hill as one of the places claiming to be the site of Daniel O'Connell's duel with John d'Esterre in February, 1815. The mansion on the hillside is Lyon's House, built in 1797 for Lord Cloncurry and, since 1962, part of the Faculty of Agriculture of University College, Dublin. From ArdCloc the road approaches the Liffey once more, but in these regions she is modestly concealed from the gaze of the populace by the impenetrable high walls which enflank the environs of Celbridge.

Admirers of these adornments of the rural roadside will rejoice in the length, the height and the variety to be seen here. Some have neatly pointed, clean blocks, some have delightfully damp surfaces bright green with moss and algae, others flaunt decaying plaster. Fortunately, they come to an end just before the village, by the side of the Abbey National School, built in 1845. At the time it, too, was concealed behind the walls within the grounds of Celbridge Abbey. A charming, classical building of one storey, the school was divided in two by a solid wall to separate the boys from the girls. In those chaste times, even the entrances were independent. In 1988 a major refurbishing job was completed, giving the old building a delightfully fresh and cared-for appearance the better to fit it for its new role as a community centre.

Three 'records' were declared for the Liffey in the vicinity of St. Wolstan's when the house was owned by Richard Cane, who bought it in 1822. They were: the longest stone to be taken from the river, the longest bone, and the deepest water. The stone, an impressed 20-ft. granite needle, was erected on the river-bank, and can best be admired from the river. The whereabouts of the bone have been forgotten.

View of the river, near Luttrellstown Park.

Celbridge Abbey

Opposite to the entrance of the school is a gateway to the Abbey grounds. From the gate, a rather ill-defined path leads upstream, between the river and the demesne wall which shuts out the noise of 20th-century traffic. Across the river, partly hidden by magnificent trees, are the gardens and buildings. The great house was redesigned towards the end of the 18th century by Dr Richard Marley, uncle of Henry Grattan who wrote of his love for this same riverside walk. The main house had fallen into decay in the 1960's and was restored with great devotion by the present owners, the St John of God Brothers.

A narrow stone footbridge joins the two parts of the demesne. Upstream of the bridge an outcrop of limestone forms a small cliff. Above it the roots of beech trees intertwine and wander in all directions, trying to find a little soil for anchorage. Between the beeches and the weir a summer house with a stone seat occupies the 'quiet romantic spot overlooking the weir' where Vanessa made her bower. Vanessa, Esther Van Homrigh, after the death of her father, had come to live in Celbridge Abbey and there she pursued her passionate and tragic romance with Swift.

The original bower was destroyed when the bridge was built some time after Vanessa's death. The lack of originality in the newer bower matters little. The Liffey still runs over the weir, shaded by old trees and the spot remains quiet and romantic.

An extraordinary lime tree grows by the side of the weir. It fell across the water in a storm a long time ago, but remained securely rooted to the bank and very much alive. Since that time, three shoots from the horizontal trunk have grown straight up to form healthy new trees standing on a natural bridge.

Castletown

Although the walls are uninviting, and the roads of Celbridge narrow, it is well worth driving down to the gate of Castletown, first to look at the neat little church within the demesne and then to walk back along the village street. It is lined with a number of beautiful town houses which face the street with their backs to the river. By this arrangement the owners could parade their affluence before the people and retire to the back rooms to enjoy in seclusion the scenery of the riverside.

Then there is Castletown, not only the most noble dwelling of the Liffey Valley, but the biggest house in Ireland. It belongs to another chapter and deserves a special visit when it is open to the public. The gates are open every day and visitors can walk or drive beneath the magnificent lime trees of the avenue to see the outside of the house and wander at will in the parkland. Or you can stop at the gate and walk all the way to Leixlip Reservoir along the Liffeyside.

The ground for some distance in front of Castletown was raised and levelled artificially as part of the landscaping and the pond was also specially created. From this terrace the land slopes down to the riverside and the weir. Lime, oak and beech trees of a great age spread their branches and add to the wonderful feeling of space. The way downstream by the riverside passes the ruin of a Doric temple and a stone summerhouse, both the work of Lady Louisa Conolly in the 1760s. A little way up the hill from the river bank there is the ice house, a stone-lined and vaulted cylindrical pit, approached through a tunnel. Snow was packed in during the winter and would remain frozen for many months.

Across the river, amongst green pastures and cow byres, stand the remnants of St Wolstan's Abbey: one fine stone tower and two gateways. St Wolstan's was founded in

OPEN TO THE PUBLIC

**Castletown House
Celbridge, Co. Kildare**

To visit Castletown House is to see one of the finest houses in Ireland – and the largest. No less than eighty windows face the visitor as he stands before it. There are nearly three hundred in all.

Inside, a noble staircase curves up from a wide hallway with superb plasterwork. The small room whose walls were covered with prints by Lady Louisa Conolly herself has been carefully preserved, as has the 'Long Hall' upstairs. Here the walls are covered with intricate coloured designs in the Pompeian manner, by a more sophisticated hand, and the room is further adorned with statuary and extraordinary Venetian chandeliers.

Some of the original furnishing of the house has been retrieved, and more of the same period added, along with portraits and other paintings.

There is a restaurant, and banqueting facilities. For visitors, teas are served at weekends. At time of going to press, the house is open to the public every afternoon except Saturday, but as this is subject to change, better check it in advance (Tel. 01-288252). Bus No. 67 goes by the gates.

See page 103.

The Placenames

As the Irish usually named their settlements in relation to the physical features of their location, the names of the towns along the Liffey reflect their positions. There is of course **Dublin** itself – the Black Pool and the Town of the Hurdle-Ford. **Leixlip** was named by the Viking settlers, from their *lax*, salmon, and *hlaup*, leap – and so, in Irish, *Léim an Bhradáin*. It was the salmon's river long before man set foot there.

Scholars argue about **Kilcullen**. *Cill Chuilinn* could be, simply, the Church of

Esther Van Homrigh (above, left), Dean Swift's one-time beloved 'Vanessa' and her Irish home, Celbridge Abbey.

1202 by Adam de Hereford and flourished as a great monastery until the supression in 1536. The Alen family then lived there for more than two hundred years, ultimately building the existing classical house with stones from the medieval foundation. On the left bank, a lane leads up the hill, away from the river to one of the gateways of Castletown and the Batty Langley lodge, with its gothic ornamentation. The laneway from this gate leads to the Leixlip Reservoir.

The park at Castletown is the property of the Honourable Desmond Guinness who bought the estate from its last private owners in 1967, saving an irreplaceable treasure for the people of Ireland. The house and its immediate surroundings are owned and maintained by the Castletown Foundation. The history of Celbridge has been thoroughly chronicled by Tony Doohan in a delightful book published locally in the 1980s.

The Conolly Folly

At Celbridge, the road downstream on the left bank goes a long way from the Liffey, heading off in the direction of Maynooth which should perhaps be considered a Liffey town. It lies close to one of the main tributaries, the Rye Water, and certainly belongs to the region of fertile land on the limestone till of the Liffey valley. But Maynooth, with its centuries as headquarters of the Fitzgeralds and its subsequent life as a religious and academic citadel, merits more than a passing glance in our journey down the river. Somebody else must write that book.

We will therefore resist the temptation to divert and keep to the narrow lane which climbs the hill beside the marvellous obelisk. It was built by Mrs Conolly in 1740 and provided much-needed work for the poor, following a harsh winter. The obelisk appears

St. Cuileann. But equally it could be the Church of the holly, or of the slope, which would suit the lie of the ground.

Sallins is *na Solláin*, the willow groves, which so often overhang rivers. **Clane** is *Claonadh*, the sloping ford. It was an important crossing-place on the unbridged river. **Castlesize** nearby – *Casán Soillse* – is from a lighted path down to the ford. The Rev. Canon Sherlock (1891) maintained that even in his time many fords, now spanned by bridges in different parts of the country, still went by the name of *Ath Solais* or Assolas, the Ford of the Light.

Celbridge, the Church of the Bridge, is half alliteration, half translation. In former times it was known as Kildrought, a more straightforward rendering of *Cill Droichead*. **Blessington** is another matter. The old Irish name was *Baile Coimin* – Comyn's Townland. The English name apparently derived from a misunderstanding of *Coimin*, which was thought to mean a favour or blessing. If the usual pattern had been followed, we would be calling it Ballycummin.

in all the best books on Georgian architecture, but the grandeur of the work doesn't really make itself felt until you stand beneath the great central arch.

The view, even from the ground, is delightful, over Castletown itself and the Liffey valley and away to the mountains. The memorial tablets in the great arch were placed there by Mrs Rose Saul Zalles, an American lady who bought the obelisk in 1968 and presented it to Castletown. Curiously, the land on which it was built had not been a part of the old estate.

Louisa Bridge

The road circles back to the Liffey, passing first between a succession of stud farms and then entering a housing estate. A left turn on the main road from Leixlip to Maynooth, which runs close by, leads to Louisa Bridge, named in honour of Lady Louisa Conolly. It was built to cross the Royal Canal and extended in due course to provide for the railway. To the north, the canal flows over the Rye Water on a massive embankment, pierced at the bottom by a stone arch. The river valley on the right bank is terraced near the embankment and the terrace is fairly strewn with stone-bordered ponds and an ancient swimming pool.

The water entering the highest pool comes from a thermal spring, always a few degrees above the temperature of normal ground water. This water is also highly charged with iron and other minerals and was the basis of the 18th-century spa which made Leixlip a rich and important village. The bed of the warm pool and the pond nearby are pale brown, coated with ochre from the spring water.

Besides the remnants of the watering place, the terraces support a small fen, bright with wild orchids in June and July and also with a bank of lime-rich pasture, a mass of colour in summer: yellow lady's bedstraw, blue and purple vetches and wild marjoram, the delicate quaking grass and many others. It is not so much that any of these are rare, more that pastures of this kind are usually so thoroughly grazed that the flowers seldom appear in such profusion.

The Wonderful Barn

The Liffeyside road, found by going back through the housing estate, passes next the Wonderful Barn and its two satellites. The bottle-shaped tower was built in 1743 by John Glin for Katherine Conolly, widow of the Speaker. Tradition and many of the books explain the conception and shape of the barn as a relief measure to provide work for the poor. This was undoubtedly part of the motivation, but the fact is that quite as much relief could have been afforded by building a perfectly ordinary barn. The Conollys loved large and beautiful buildings and it seems likely that Katherine was seeking to introduce an element of art to an essential farm outhouse.

Finally, the lane crosses the Liffey at the upper end of the Leixlip Reservoir, a delightful lake, inhabited by anglers and canoeists and storing water for the generating station at Salmon Leap. Access to the left bank is possible just downstream of the new bridge whose stones were cut in 1308 by direction of John leDecer, Mayor of Dublin. Unfortunately, the hydro-scheme required the demolition of the no longer new structure. In rebuilding, the old stones were used and the present bridge is a partial copy of its predecessor. The new one, however, has three arches in place of the original four.

Spring sunshine blows a willow tree to flame on the river near Kilcullen.

Fragments of tombs reward inspection in the graveyard near Kilcullen.

In Kilcullen cemetery, Baron Portlester and his lady lie beneath the open skies.

AND EUS A BARON POR
ORD CHANCELLOR WHO DIED 4
MARGARET D'ARTOIS HIS WIFE
UNDERS OF THE ABBEY ON THIS

HERE ARE ALSO BURIED
HIS DAUGHTER ALISON
OUNTESS OF KILDARE WHO DIED
AND HIS NEPHEW THOMAS EUSTA
VISCOUNT BALTINGLASS WHO DIED 154

Castletown house. See page 98.

Russborough House. See page 39.

Celbridge Abbey now belongs to the Brothers of St. John of God. Dean Swift was a regular visitor when it was the home of Esther Van Homrigh, whom he knew and loved as 'Vanessa'.

There are ten weirs between Straffan and Islandbridge — some gentle, some fierce.

Leixlip

The high road at Louisa Bridge looks across the valley to Leixlip Castle, on equally high ground, but protected from assailants and visitors by the Rye Water on one hand and the Liffey on the other. They join at the foot of the cliff beneath it. The main road takes a steep descent to the village in the valley, tucked in between the river and a cliff of glacial till, with some outcrops of limestone which have been quarried for building.

In the village you can reach the river bank by going through the secluded churchyard on the right. The tower of the church is ancient, the rest of the building a 19th century restoration. The Rye Water flows in just to the east of the church, rushing over the bare limestone in places. The Liffey at the base of the dam runs deep, but not silent. A little way upstream of the dam, deep down in the reservoir, was the Salmon Leap. Since the times of the Vikings, leaping salmon have been a feature of the Liffey at this point. 'Lax' still means salmon in the Scandinavian languages. The salmon leap no more. By courtesy of the ESB they swim effortlessly through the dam in the fish lift.

Across the road from the river, an alley leads up to a disused quarry. The greater part of the rock is massive limestone, sadly deficient in fossils. It was deposited in calm, deep sea water, not far from a seashore formed by the Wicklow Mountains. It took many thousands of years to build up the thickness of rock exposed there and, not surprisingly, the sequence of events was interrupted from time to time. This is shown by the presence of black, shaley bands in the limestone. The shale is derived from clay particles, carried out into the sea beyond the edge of a delta, in much the same way as the lake muds were deposited 300 million years later in Glacial Lake Blessington. By only a small stretch of the imagination, you might say that the shales represent the deposits of an ancestral Liffey, but it was a Liffey without birds or flowers or people.

Leixlip to Lucan

The main road towards Dublin from Leixlip rises high above the Liffey, giving only occasional glances into the valley through gaps or gateways in the stone walls. Then it passes the Spa Hotel and plunges downwards to the floor of the valley. The name of the hotel commemorates more warm and allegedly healthy springs of mineral water of the kind found at Louisa Bridge. A left turn at the traffic lights enters the older part of the village through which the road makes its way, by devious turnings, to the riverside.

The bridge is a splendid one, crossing the river in a single span of 34 metres and decorated with an iron balustrade. Neither its exact date nor its designer are known. Upstream of the bridge, a long weir crosses the river at a low angle, once providing power for Lucan Iron Works on the left bank. About half way along the weir, the water rushes from pool to pool of a salmon pass.

A footpath goes upstream on the right bank between road and river, in front of a neat row of houses, tucked in at the foot of the cliff. The most spectacular rock outcrop in the entire valley appears behind the last house in the row, between back gardens and a garage. The limestone has been savagely folded so that the beds, which once lay horizontally, stand upright in places and folded over at the top.

This structure represents a sort of final shudder of the Hercynian upheavals which occurred towards the end of the Carboniferous era, three hundred million years ago. The European and African plates of the earth's crust were moving against each other, forcing the rock strata to crumple. Many mountain ranges were formed, including the parallel hills of west Cork and Kerry. The forces were dying out towards the north, as at Lucan,

A Song for Anna Liffey House

Anna Liffey drowses beside the shining weir
The merry river passes, singing all the day.
The beeches bend to catch her. "Why must you go, my dear?
You gleaming, lovely Liffey, so beryl-bright and clear."
But still they never hold her. She always slides away,
Singing, singing, singing as she turns the wheel,
"God be with the miller, God be with the mill,
God be with the people who have their bins to fill,
And God be with the sorry folk who hunger for a meal."

Anna Liffey drowses with windows open wide,
Great beeches stand as sentries on guard at either side.
The heron is watching where the shallows run,
The kingfisher passes, a jewel in the sun.
All day the river murmurs – "Peace within the hall,
Peace upon the threshold, peace inside the house,
Peace upon the sunning cat and on the busy mouse.
Peace upon the garden and on the basking wall,
The heavy-laden fruit trees, the low humming hives,
Peace upon the barnyard, the red cock and his wives.
That God may smile upon you here and give His peace to all."

Winifred Letts

but still were capable of causing dramatic upheavals, to be revealed in recent millennia as the Liffey cut its way downwards. From Lucan downstream, further traces of the folding can be seen on the left bank. In the stream the outcrops formed rapids, to be used in the course of the past few hundred years as the foundations of a series of mill dams.

Upstream of the rock fold, the footpath ends at a private house called Bleach Green. There were linen spinning mills at Chapelizod, and perhaps also at Lucan. The linen was spread out on the grass to bleach in the sun. Across the river lies the lovely parkland of Lucan Demesne, now the Residence of the Italian Ambassador, once the ancestral home of Patrick Sarsfield.

The Strawberry Beds, Chapelizod and Palmerston

The final road by the rural river begins at Lucan Bridge where the limestone, covered by a great depth of glacial till, curtailed the wayward Anna Liffey by forbidding her to meander northwards and forcing her to follow a narrow path at the bottom of a steep hill. She did succeed in a trifle of dalliance so that a narrow alluvial plain has been built up along the way. Mills and houses have been tucked in wherever possible and quarrying has long been in progress on the left, downstream of Lucan.

On the right bank, the slopes are less steep and the grounds of a succession of great estates run gently down to the riverside. Few of them remain in private hands: hospitals, schools and Hermitage golf links have replaced the landlords. The sad thing about the narrowness of the valley is that there is scarcely room for the road and even less for a footpath most of the way from Lucan to Chapelizod. Nonetheless, it is a pleasant spot, especially at weekends or of a summer evening when the traffic is relatively light.

The well-drained, rich soil on the south-facing left bank provided a favourable spot for the cultivation of strawberries and this stretch has long been known as the 'Strawberry Beds'. Alas, the delectable fruits have passed away and the sole reminder of more spacious times is a pub called the Strawberry Hall. The roadside, with its cottages, was one of the most popular spots for Dublin's fair citizens to walk to in the 19th century.

Downstream of the mill at Lucan and its rows of workers' dwellings, there is half a mile of footpath beside the river, ending at the next weir. Beech trees grow on the steeper slopes across the river and the hospital of St Edmundsbury House is perched above them at the top of the hill, serenaded by the inhabitants of a large rookery. The footpath ends at a gate lodge, the entrance to the residence of the owners of Shackleton's Mills, whose derelict weir begins just opposite. Thereafter runs about a mile of forbidding walls, relieved on the right by the gateway to Luttrellstown Castle, hidden away in one of the finest of the private demesnes of the Liffeyside.

Generally speaking, the road is too narrow for parking to be safe or advisable except at any of the three hostelries: the Wren's Nest, the Strawberry Hall or the Anglers' Rest. The latter is a good spot to stop for a walk upstream, giving a view of the V-shaped weir where canoeists cluster and leading to the great, cast-iron bridge which seems to begin nowhere and end by plunging into the hillside. It connected the two parts of Knockmaroon Estate which were separated by the river. The wooden pavement of the bridge has long gone and, more recently, an attempt was made to demolish the fine ironwork. Fortunately, a vigilant resident summoned the police and rescued the bridge.

One more relic of affluent idealism remains about half way between the bridge and the Anglers' Rest, across the road from the river. It is a tiny funicular railway, built to carry the infirm, or perhaps the merely lazy, all of 10 metres and more of steep slope from roadside to house.

The Strawberry Beds

The Dublin Penny Journal of 1833 states that 'of the various pleasant drives around the metropolis, that through the Phoenix Park, by the side of the Liffey, and the Strawberry Beds to Lucan, Leixlip and the Salmon Leap appears to be the most esteemed by the citizens.'

Strawberries thrived on the well-drained south-facing slopes between Knockmaroon Hill and Lucan. In times gone by, an expedition to The Strawberry Beds was a popular weekend outing, especially with 'the artisan class'. Strawberries were served on cabbage leaves, and a portion, with cream, cost one penny.

The strawberries are gone, but the drive is still to be recommended.

The Liffey of the Plains

Finally, the road leaves the Liffeyside to climb steeply up Knockmaroon Hill and plunge down again for Chapelizod, passing beneath another iron bridge. This one connects two parts of Glenmaroon House.

Chapelizod and Palmerston

Chapelizod, of romantic memory, the chapel of the fair Isolde, is squeezed in between the Liffey and the steep side of the valley. Old mills, turned into factories, narrow roads and small houses all nestle together. A sharp right turn at the traffic lights leads to the bridge and again to a narrow road below a steep bank. Houses keep the road away from the river, but the first turn to the right, labelled Belgrove Lawn, really does go to a lawn, and a very pretty riverside one, too. You can look across the river from it to the splendid gardens of Glenmaroon House.

The next turn to the right, about a kilometre farther on, leads the way to a wonderfully secluded part of the Liffey, unbelievable amongst its surroundings of housing estates and institutions, almost within walking distance of the city centre. The approach is through the village of Palmerston, not too long ago a sort of irritating landmark with traffic congestion on the main road to the west, but now, happily, a village once more. The bypass road has allowed the villagers to come to life and cross their main street without peril to life or limb.

Tristan and Isolde – The Liffey Connection

Wagner's operatic masterpiece had its first public performance in Munich in the year 1865, and the world rediscovered the ancient story of Tristan and Isolde, the ill-fated Norman knight and his Gaelic lady.

But it hadn't been forgotten along the banks of the Liffey. Isolde, or Iseult, was the daughter of King Aengus, whose chapel-royal stood where the old Church of St. Mary stands now in Palmerston. Chapelizod is 'the Chapel of Isolde'. Part of the original 6th-century chapel from which the village took its name is built into the fabric of St. Laurence's, the

Sir Tristan asks for Isolde's hand on behalf of King Mark of Cornwall: fresco in the City Hall, Dublin.

A little way east of the church, Mill Lane goes wandering down the hillside, through Stewart's Hospital to a terrace of mill-workers' houses overlooking the river. Some of them have been there since the 18th century when the church-like scutch mill was built. A wicket gate at the end of the terrace gives access to the mill stream and a broad, green, sometimes damp pasture between the stream and Anna Liffey herself.

The pasture is a little overgrown, with big clumps of bramble and a swamp with reeds at one point. It is waiting until the County Council completes its scheme of acquiring a strip of land along the right bank. Then it will be possible, wonderful thought, to walk all the way to Lucan. Meanwhile, in spite of forbidding notices and a rubbish tip (closed at the end of 1987), stalwart folk with wellies can walk at will. Alder and willow grow by the riverside, moorhen and mallard, cormorant and heron scuttle about or rise protesting from the water. Kingfishers live on the mill stream and there are otters, too. Across the river, the bank is almost precipitous, in most places too steep for houses and therefore pleasantly wooded except where the cliffs are sheer and display the yellow glacial till.

The Lucan to Chapelizod road marks the end of this chapter. The Liffey remains a river of the plains for two thousand metres downstream of Chapelizod, but for this part she is confined by the ancient bounds of Phoenix Park which has a special chapter of its own.

Under the shade of sycamore and willow, Anna Liffey hurls herself passionately over Islandbridge Weir, to abandon herself to the embraces of the tide. But the citizens of Dublin were not prepared to surrender their benefactress so soon. With limestone from the lowlands and granite from the hills, they built seven long miles of walls to keep her from her pleasure. You may read of her fate in the ensuing chapters. ●

present parish church. The mound on which the Magazine Fort stands in Phoenix Park, not far away, was originally known as Isolde's Fort, and a spring there was also named for the princess.

Come far down-river now to Capel Street Bridge. Look at the street-name on Exchange Street Upr., and you will see that in Irish it is still Sráid Iosoilde: it was the street leading to Isolde's Tower, one of a number of defensive forts built by Aengus. This one, which he named for 'la Beale Isoud,' was for a period, after an earth tremor, left standing isolated on a rock outcrop. Historians hold that the tower is still embedded in the buildings which have grown there since.

Legend or history? It is difficult to unravel the two, and there are several versions of the old romance. But Aengus and his daughter Isolde are generally accepted as real people by historians, and early chronicles write of the arrival of Sir Tristan in Dublin.

In Dublin's City Hall there are a number of frescoes high on the walls of the Rotunda room depicting incidents in Irish history. One is described as taking place in the forecourt of King Aengus's residence on Palmerston Green. It shows Tristan asking King Aengus for the hand of Isolde on behalf of King Mark of Cornwall. Isn't that proof enough?

(*For those who have forgotten the story, King Mark sends Sir Tristan to ask for Isolde's hand on his behalf, and to bring her back to Cornwall. Inevitably, and with the help of a love potion administered by Isolde's maid, Tristan and Isolde fall passionately in love. The wedding with the king takes place, but the two lovers meet in secret, and are found out. Tristan is mortally wounded; Isolde's heart breaks. As in all tragic love-stories, they are reunited in death.*)

The Strawberry Beds around 1900: a portion, with cream, for 1p.

Mature and Stately, Through Dublin City

 lthough the tidal stretch of the Liffey starts below the weir at Longmeadows Park, the river continues its meandering rural way until it reaches the quays at Sean Heuston Bridge. Then it suddenly becomes both mature and stately as it curves gently through the city of Dublin to the sea. Here there is no sign of why it bore the ancient Gaelic name of Ruirtheach, which implies flash floods and torrents. Here is James Joyce's Anna Livia Plurabelle, placid and old, full of wisdom and experience as she flows to meet her father, Neptune, in the sea beyond the Kish lighthouse.

It was not always like this. Long before the Celts, Vikings or Normans sailed her waters, this stretch of the river was subject to sudden floods from the Wicklow mountains which were brought under control only this century when the hydro-electric dam was built at Pollaphuca. The old shore line ran on the north from what is still called Great Strand Street, along Amiens Street and the North Strand, and on the south by way of the present Fleet Street, Trinity College, Fenian Street and Beggar's Bush to the marsh at the mouth of the Dodder. Near the estuary it was a wide, shallow river which broke into a few branches as it ran quietly over mud flats. These branches came together near the confluence with the Dodder and the river joined the sea at Ringsend.

There were three fords over this stretch of river. The first was Kilmohavoc, roughly at the weir above Island Bridge, which could usually be crossed on foot and is said to have been used by Brian Boru before the Battle of Clontarf. Ath Cliath - the Hurdle Ford - was a little up river from the site of Fr Mathew Bridge. The third ford was near the mouth of the Poddle and crossed the river on a ridge of rock known as Standfast Dick. Both this and Ath Cliath could be crossed only on horseback. Below the first ford, Kilmohavoc, the Liffey was joined by a number of rivers and streams; the main ones are, from the north, the Bradogue and the Tolka and, from the south, the Camac, the Poddle, the Stein and the Dodder.

In the second century AD, Ptolemy, the geographer from Alexandria, marked Eblana or Dublin on his map. At this time, too, there was a small Gaelic settlement on the ridge above Ath Cliath where Cornmarket is today. This settlement was important because it was at the junction of four of the ancient roads of Ireland, the

'No city neglects its river as Dublin does. There is not a pleasure-boat on the Liffey from Butt Bridge to Lucan. If the river and town were in England there would be water-gardens and boat-houses and people delighting themselves in the lovely amenities of the water.'

'And drowning themselves' said Tim (Healy) . . . . '

St John Gogarty in As I was going down Sackville Street'.

Continued on p. 114.

Map of Liffey in Dublin: detail taken from Rocque's Map of Dublin 1756-1770.

the North of

RICHARDSON'S LANE

BARRACK
HAY YARD

PALATI
SQUA

THE
ROYAL SQUARE
BARRACKS

THE
HORSE SQUARE

LI
SQ

MONTPELIER HILL

TEMPLE STREET

BARRACK. STREET

PARK GATE

LONG MEADOWS

PART OF T

LORD GALLWAYS WALK

DOG

Slighe Mór coming from Galway, the Slighe Midhluachra from Derry and Water-ford, the Slighe Dála from Limerick and the Slighe Chualann, which crossed the Liffey at Ath Cliath, from Tara and from Glendalough. In the year 291 the name Dubhlinn first occurs in the *Annals of the Four Masters* where it refers to the estuary of the Liffey. The name Ath Cliath does not occur until 765 when the refer-ence is to the ford over the Liffey.

The Vikings arrive

In 837 a fleet of sixty Viking ships sailed up the Liffey to raid the settlement of Ath Cliath. In 841, realising that they had found a central and convenient position from which to raid Britain, they returned and, as was their custom, set up their Long Stone where they landed and established a fortified anchorage on the hill above the Dark Pool (Dubh Linn) on the Poddle. The Long Stone, which was about fourteen feet high, stood close to the junction of Hawkins Street and Pearse Street survived well into the seventeenth century, when Petty showed it on one of his maps for the Down Survey.

About the year 1000 a wooden bridge was built at Ath Cliath, the first ever over the Liffey, to encourage settlement on the northern bank of the river. In the rout after the Battle of Clontarf in 1014 many of the Vikings were slain at this bridge which in the *Annals* is called Droichet Dubhgall - The Bridge of the Norsemen. During the Wood Quay excavations in the 1970s, part of a stone wall was discovered which the Vikings had built in the late eleventh century to defend their town. This wall was dismantled with a view to its being re-erected at some future date. The first Viking quay was below Christ Church and on a line with what is now West Essex Street, but as there was no depth of water here. Wooden barriers were built towards the centre of the river and the land reclaimed behind them, hence the name Wood Quay.

About the year 1200 the monks of St Mary's Abbey, which was just north of the site of Grattan Bridge, developed the Pill or estuary of the Bradogue River which later became known as the Little Harbour of St Mary's Abbey. About this time ferries began to operate on the river. Many of the routes they used are shown on John Rocque's map of 1756 and they continued to operate further and further down the Liffey until 1984 when the East Link Toll Bridge was opened.

The first stone bridge

In 1215 King John gave permission for a new stone bridge to be built on the site of the Bridge of the Norsemen. A dam, which gave its name to Dame Street, was also built at this time across the mouth of the Poddle. This caused the dark pool on the Poddle, the original Dubhlinn, to silt up and facilitated the eastward expansion of the city. The Liffey at this time was about 200 yards across, but the banks were being filled in and extended to the central channel at Wood Quay and Merchant's Quay to enable the small merchant ships of the time to come up river to unload. In 1300 the first Custom House was built at the end of Winetavern Street. It was not until 1620 that a wharf was built at Essex Quay. This was enlarged in 1638 when a new Custom House was built here. The congestion was so bad in 1652 that Gerard Boate wrote: 'What the ordinary tide you cannot go to the quay in Dublin with a ship that draws five feet of water; those of greater draught cannot come nearer than Ringsend, three miles from Dublin Bay and one mile from Dublin.'

A dramatic moment in 1534 at St. Mary's Abbey, where meetings of Parliament and the Privy Council were held. Young Silken Thomas, son of the Earl of Kildare who was Lord Deputy of Ireland, throws down the Sword of State and launches the rebellion which will end in the death of himself, his father and his five uncles.

Mature and Stately, through Dublin City

The fishing rights of the Liffey were shared between the city, St Mary's Abbey, Holy Trinity Priory, which was attached to Christ Church, and the Hospital at Kilmainham. The fact that St Mary's and Holy Trinity held that the centre of the river was the limit of their respective rights gave rise to numerous disputes. River pollution was a problem even in medieval times when tanners were forbidden to wash their leather in the Liffey in case the lime, with which the hides had been treated, should injure the fish stocks.

Sir Henry Sidney built a bridge at the ford of Kilmohavoc in 1580 which lasted until the eighteenth century when it collapsed and was replaced in 1791 some distance down river by Sarah Bridge. In 1674 Bloody Bridge was constructed, and soon after that, came Essex Bridge in 1676, and both Arran Bridge and Ormonde Bridge in 1683.

The Growth of Dublin

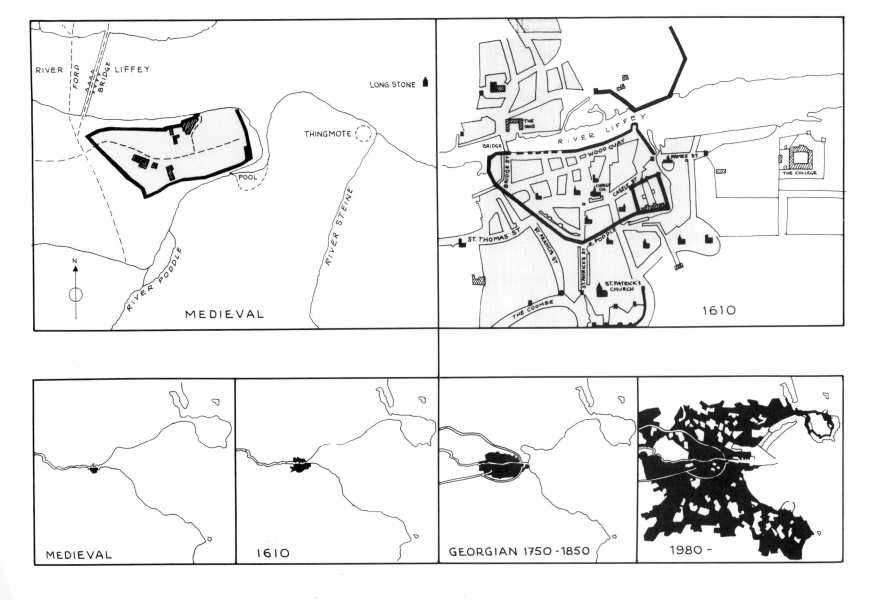

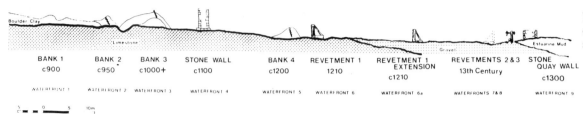

Diagram showing nine successive embankments of the river at Wood Quay – see page 119.

Building the quays

Quays were also being built at this time. From the mid-seventeenth century the Corporation of Dublin insisted that the backs of the houses should not run down to the river but that a quay should be built there. This set the pattern for the quays as they exist today. By 1700 the Poddle, the Stein and the Bradogue had been put underground, the markets had been moved to the north side of the city and the Liffey was lined on the north by stone quays from Arran Quay to Bachelor's Walk and on the south from Usher's Island to the old Custom House Quay, and from Aston's Quay to City Quay. This policy was actively encouraged by the Duke of Ormonde who wished to have a broad highway running from the city directly to the Phoenix Park.

The development of the Liffey in the eighteenth century was controlled by the Ballast Office which was established by an Act of Parliament in 1708 to conserve the river and to raise ballast. The Ballast Board decided that its first priority should be to deepen and straighten the bed of the Liffey and to lower the harbour bar in order to make the port more accessible and attractive for shipping.

In 1713 Sir John Rogerson had a wall built on the south side of the river as far as Ringsend but there was a gap between this wall and George's Quay which was filled by the Corporation in 1715, hence the name City Quay. By 1735 the Pigeon House Road had been built and in 1792 the Poolbeg Lighthouse and the wall leading to it were completed. In 1796 the Grand Canal Docks were completed and the Dodder, was confined within new banks. The diversion into the new channel of the branch of the Dodder, which ran between Tritonville and Irishtown, completed the reclamation of the land between the North Wall and Beggar's Bush.

With the great expansion of the city in the eighteenth century, foreign trade had grown and the old Custom House at Essex Bridge was acknowledged to be inadequate. There were always considerable delays in getting up river to the old Custom House quay and as many as seventy ships, eight deep, might be moored there at any one time. Nevertheless, the move to the new Custom House in 1791 met with a storm of opposition, both from the dockers and the merchants who either lived in the Liberties or had their businesses there, and also from those wealthy people who lived in the Georgian houses around Gardiner Street.

In this period, too, bridge construction went ahead with Queen's Bridge being built in 1776, Sarah Bridge in 1791 and Carlisle Bridge in 1794. James Malton's *Views of the City of Dublin*, which were published in 1799, show some of the Liffey quays as we know them today.

Mains and drains

Waste disposal had always been a problem in Dublin. In the eighteenth century in the poorer quarters of the city domestic waste, including human excreta, was dumped either in middens behind the houses or directly into nearby rivers or streams. Even in the more affluent districts, through lack of sewers, all types of domestic sewage were disposed of in cesspools which were usually excavated in front of the houses; these had to emptied periodically, which was a filthy and expensive business. Surface water was carried by open drains to the various waterways in the city. During the first half of the nineteenth century most of the existing cesspools were fitted with overflows to the street drainage system. This led the City Engineer to state in 1853 that the bed of the Liffey was foul and 'at low water, excessively disagreeable to the inhabitants of the Quays and to the public generally passing over the bridges'.

By this time more than thirty-five miles of sewers had been constructed in the city but none of this was in the poorer quarters, with the result that the Poddle was described as 'an immense sewer, carrying off the filth in its current and putrifying the streets under which it passes'. In 1868 the Vartry Waterworks enabled householders all over the city to install water closets and this led to an immense amount of raw sewage going directly into the Liffey which became a huge open sewer. In that same year there were fifty-four openings, including the Poddle and the Camac, discharging raw sewage into the Liffey and the stench, particularly in warm weather, was sickening. It was not until 1896 that the existing sewerage system was intercepted by new trunk sewers laid along the north and south quays and linked at Burgh Quay. These conveyed the flow of sewage to a treatment works at Ringsend. From 1906 the treated effluent was discharged to the Liffey estuary and the settled sludge was dumped in a fast moving current off the Baily lighthouse. In the 1980s the Dublin local authorities eliminated the deficiencies in their drainage system and controlled the polluting effects of the Camac on the Liffey.

The developments in road transport in the nineteenth century made it necessary for Wellington, Burgh, Wolfe Tone and Victoria Quays to be constructed. In 1816 Wellington Bridge was built, Butt Bridge in 1879, and the Loop Line Bridge in 1891.

This century has brought out its share of strange schemes for the Liffey. In 1913 Sir Edwin Lutyens designed an art gallery to span the river where the Liffey Bridge now stands; in 1930 it was seriously suggested that the river could be roofed over between O'Connell and Liffey Bridges to provide parking space in the city centre; and on two occasions this century plans have been put forward for the building of a barrage near Butt Bridge. All of these schemes have come to nothing.

Within the last ten years three new bridges have been built over the Liffey, the Matt Talbot Memorial Bridge in 1978, the Frank Sherwin Memorial Bridge in 1982 and the East Link Toll Bridge in 1984.

(Continued on page 125)

Lane's Liffey Gallery

This was Sir Edwin Lutyens' proposal for an Art Gallery spanning the Liffey, to house the European Painting Collection of Sir Hugh Lane. Lane had offered the collection to Dublin, on condition that a gallery would be built to house it properly. Lutyens' design comprised two main galleries, one on either quay, connected by a minor gallery surmounted by a colonnaded footbridge. In the event, Dublin Corporation didn't take to the idea, and Lane willed the collection to London instead. But he later changed his mind. An unwitnessed codicil to his will bequeathed the pictures to Dublin's Municipal Gallery. The codicil was deemed invalid. After lengthy negotiations, an arrangement was arrived at whereby the pictures were shared between London and Dublin, and exchanged at regular intervals. Instead of a kind of Ponte Vecchio, Dublin has the Ha'penny Bridge.

Wood Quay Today
Dublin's new Civic Offices dominate the quays, with Christ Chursh Cathedral dwarfed in the background. The Offices were built on the foundations of Viking Dublin, amid much public controversy.

Centre left:
The Viking Adventure
The streets and houses of Viking days have been re-created in the crypt of St. Audoen's Church (close to Christ Church Cathedral) in the heart of old Dublin, through the generosity of Irish Life Assurance plc. You can meet the people – the builder, comb-maker, leather-worker, along with their wives and children, to talk to them and learn from them about their way of life. Viking Dublin may be entered any day between 9 am and 4 pm, for a small fee.

Bottom left:
A replica of the craft in which the Viking founders of Dublin arrived, was built in Dublin for its Millennium celebrations (1988).

Bottom right:
Artist's impression of Dublin housing a thousand years ago, based on excavations at Fishamble Street/Wood Quay. Note that each house had its own plot of ground – more than we have today!

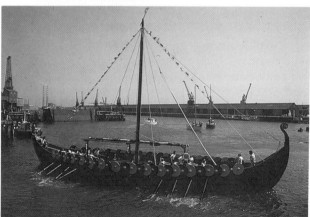

A thousand years ago, every Dublin family had a home and plot of its own. In some instances, the outlines of the individual properties survived for centuries after the Viking Age.

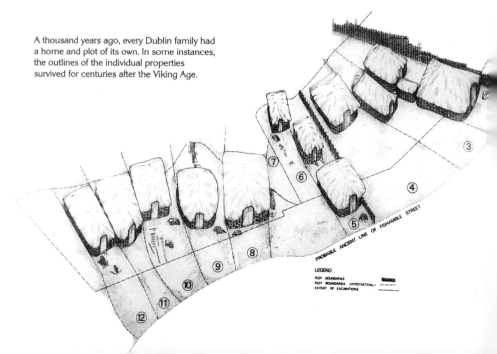

Nine Successive Stages of Wood Quay

The story of Wood Quay stretches from Viking times to the present day; never did it capture public imagination as much as in the 1970s when the very name became synonymous with public protest, 'taking on City Hall', legal cases and newspaper headlines. The public, alas, lost.

The modern day annals of Wood Quay began in 1956 when the area was designated appropriate for a proposed civic office complex and property acquisition commenced. By 1968 the 4.5 acre (1.8 hectares) site bounded by Wood Quay, Winetavern Street, Christ Church Cathedral and Fishamble Street was in the ownership of Dublin Corporation. As it was known to be the site of Dublin's beginnings, archaeological excavations commenced in 1969. Despite many serious interruptions, including periods when bulldozers were used on prime archaeological material, scientific excavations continued until March 1981. The site presented a remarkable opportunity to view the origins of Dublin by peeling back the layers of time.

The richness of the site can be gleaned from the following statement by Pat Wallace, director of the main excavations at Wood Quay:

'A whole townscape was uncovered and not just of one period but of as many as a dozen successive levels within the tenth- to eleventh-century period. The floors of the houses and the yards outside became higher all the time according as buildings became rewalled and freshly thatched, as pathways were renewed and as rubbish and occupation debris were trampled underfoot.'

These layers not only allowed identification of house and street layouts but also enabled the archaeologists to paint an accurate portrait of life in old Dublin. The occupations and crafts of the inhabitants can be determined by wood, amber, bone, horn and metal artifacts together with exposed craftsmen's workshops. Leather, cloth and jewellery indicate much about dress styles while shells, seeds, animal bones and other organic materials allow for a description of the diet of the first Dubliners. More exotic discoveries confirm Dublin's economic importance in the late Viking period and the trade links which flourished at that time.

The waterlogged nature of the Wood Quay site ensured that features and artifacts were remarkably well preserved and thus could contribute in a uniquely important way to our knowledge of early Dublin. The waterlogging was due to the location the original settlers picked; an area between the long narrow ridge at a height in excess of 16 metres and the River Liffey. The ridge is now, as it has been for many centuries, dominated by Christ Church Cathedral.

The River Liffey which the Vikings sailed up in the first half of the ninth century was tidal, broad and shallow. The Wood Quay excavations have provided evidence of nine successive stages by which the river was embanked over a period of 400 years. This involved reclamation of some 80 metres from the river bed. The initial structure of c.900 was built above the high water mark and is believed to have been a flood bank designed to protect the tenth-century town. The inhabitants later constructed a defensive mud embankment which encircled the town and was topped by a post-and-wattle palisade. By the start of the eleventh-century a larger embankment with a stave-built palisade was in situ and by about 1100 Dublin's first stone wall was in place. This may also have encircled the town but it fell into disuse with the arrival of the Normans who, in expanding the port, initially built a breakwater and then a wooden revetment wall. This was the original wooden quayside and it was followed by two others and eventually, c.1300, by a stone quay wall. The infill behind the embanking structures consisted of mud, gravel and town refuse.

Wood Quay, together with the adjacent Merchant's Quay, remained the major port area for centuries. Ongoing dumping contributed to serious silting up of the Liffey – public records of 1590 note that the depth of the river at the quays ranged from three to six-and-a-half feet (i.e. 1-2 metres). The congestion was eased with the building of the Custom House downstream, and the removal of the commercial pressure resulted in Wood Quay becoming one of the most fashionable addresses of the 17th century – adjacent leisure facilities included bowling and racquet alleys.

The buildings on the quayside were initially of wooden construction and it was only after 1640 that brick was introduced. This was followed by the brick and stone combination that has come to typify the Georgian city of Dublin. Despite the great variety of buildings and uses during the period from the introduction of brick to the site clearance in the 1970s there was one thread of continuity; all the constructions were of a human scale nestling in the shadow of the medieval Cathedral which had been established on the site of the 1037 Church of the Holy Trinity. Perhaps the best and most fondly remembered building on Wood Quay in recent times was The Irish House located at the junction of Wood Quay and Winetavern Street and demolished during the clearance for the Civic Offices. Its unashamed patriotism expressed in brick, stone, wood and Portland cement provide a total contrast to the massive concrete blocks which now occupy the site dominating the Cathedral, and the little that is left to connect us with the past. ●

The Secret Tributaries

Why not find your way some day to Ship Street and stand on the large manhole cover in the footpath and listen to the roar of mighty waters? You are now astride Dublin's most historic river, the Poddle. You can do the same on the other side of the Liffey for another river, the Bradogue, except there is no clear indication of the river's presence. I saw it myself in 1977 when Chancery Street was being repaired and the Bradogue getting a new culvert, which is the only way you would be able to see it nowadays. But the Poddle is not entirely covered: you can see small stretches of it here and there.

You may be surprised to hear that there are only two of the more than nineteen rivers flowing into the Liffey that most Dubliners traverse in their daily travels, and that there are more than fifty hidden rivers in all in Dublin. These one-time pleasant streams, though shorn of light and beauty, still chatter Liffey-wards through rock, pipe and culvert. Samuel Lewis, writing in 1837 says, 'Numerous small streams which supply many mills

descend into the Liffey'. Today it is both difficult and tantalizing to visualise them but some idea may be gained from a coloured one-inch map of 1898. Contrasting this with the present map of Dublin you will notice the main changes, of course, but on the earlier one you will see all the faint blue lines tracing their way towards the Liffey, or towards other larger streams still visible, (e.g. the Santry), or towards the Bay. Even on that old map you could see them already beginning to disappear where the city is edging out to meet them, and then swallowing them up or gulping them underground.

The Poddle, which helped to give Dublin its name, rises in Tallaght and, fairly visible until it meets the Grand Canal at Harold's Cross, goes underground from here on as far as Wellington Quay where it may be seen finally dropping into the Liffey through its culvert in the quay wall, exposing, as Joyce (more or less) says in *Ulysses*, its tongue, in yellow fealty to the Liffey.

However, if you see a tongue, yellow or otherwise, protruding nowadays, you cannot strictly call it the Poddle, because several years ago, on the completion of the large new sewer running alongside the Canal all the way down to the Bay, the Main Drainage Department of the Dublin Corporation decided to turn the Poddle into it, to avoid flooding downstream within the city after heavy rainfalls. So if anything is seen when the tide is low, it is surface water now being carried along the old Poddle bed. At this opening in the quay wall can be seen a grating placed there during the time of the Invincibles to prevent sabotage of Dublin Castle: the Poddle was the original moat around the Castle. Lately there was an attempt to use it by criminal elements trying to reach the vaults of the Allied Irish Bank in Dame Street. Bury it though they may, the Poddle is always making its presence felt.

You will not see it on the map, but between Warrenmount, Mill Street and Sweeney's Lane is a small portion of the Poddle still overground, hidden behind a high wall, sheds, rank grass and rubbish, about ten yards square, at most.

The earliest authentic map we have of

Dublin's hidden rivers
There are more than 50 rivers and streams flowing through and under the streets of Dublin, 19 of them directly into the Liffey. They may be hidden from our view, but their behaviour has to be regulated and controlled, which poses quite a challenge for Dublin Corporation.

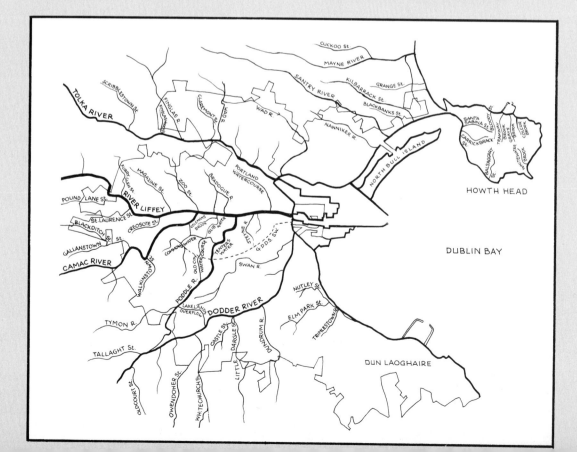

Opposite:
The Magazine Fort hill at Phoenix Park was a popular viewpoint for the city. This early view by Francis Place shows a Brewery and Mill which stood by the bridge. The infirmary of the Royal Hospital at Kilmainham stands in the centre distance flanked on the skyline by the towers of St. Michan's and St. Patrick's Cathedral.

The bridge was swept away in a great flood in 1784, one of the Liffey's many 'flash' torrents.

See also page 140 for a later view.

Mature and Stately, through Dublin City

Dublin's rivers is that of Speed, 1610. He did not mark them all in, nor their channels or cut-offs. But clearly shown are the three most important, the Bradogue, the Poddle, the Stein (or Steyne). The Bradogue, about which there is sufficient topographical data to fill a small book, is clearly drawn with its inlets or tentacles, its harbour or Pill, and part of its course. It rises at Cabra quite close to the Royal Canal; the highest crest of land visible here to the walker on the Ratoath Road, just outside the Dominican Convent gate, after which the ground falls away again to the valley of the Tolka. It is to the east, or right of the road, on the Broombridge Estate, that the Bradogue rises – a watershed, for the water is carried downhill towards the Liffey, all underground now, by way of Faussagh Avenue, Charleville Avenue, across the North Circular Road, down Grangegorman, east under North Brunswick Street, down East Arran Street and into the Liffey at Ormond Quay.

Also shown on Speed's map is St. Mary's Abbey, almost coeval with the foundation of the city itself. The Abbey is situated close to the Bradogue and must have been the reason for its foundation at this spot; all Cistercian monasteries were founded by flowing water and here on a bend of the Bradogue were two supplies – the second from the Liffey if need arose. At any rate the little harbour was sheltered, as the map shows, and further out in the Liffey there were fish in plenty. In the following century the Cistercians donated or rented that part of their land nearest to the original ford (at a spot where the first bridge was built) to the Dominicans or Friars Preachers, who came there in 1224. There is an indication as to the quality of the Liffey water in the petition that the Friars made to Prior and Brethren of Holy Trinity Priory, i.e. the monastery attached to Christ Church Cathedral; they asked for a supply of drinking water. This was granted to them from the city cistern, then situated where the Synod Hall of Christ Church stands today, at the top of the hill. The water was carried across the Bridge in hand-made pipes rolled from a sheet of lead, the Holy Trinity Prior stipulating to the Dominican Prior that the pipe was to be the width of a goose quill where it entered the Dominican priory.

So the Poddle crossed the Liffey. Both it and the Dodder supplied the Cistern – which makes us enquire why the Dominicans did not try to get water from the Bradogue. Well, for lack of evidence to the contrary, we may presume they did. But it is clear that they did not have enough or that the water from the Bradogue was polluted not so much by their landlords, the Cistercians, or by its long journey from Cabra, as by the delta-like terrain on which they found themselves where the water would have been very brackish.

Now St. Mary's Abbey also had land stretching right back as far as Clonliffe and the Tolka, but across the river Liffey they had other parcels of land donated to them by the Normans. One such was Theobald Walter, ancestor of the Butlers, future Dukes of Ormond. In 1349 this man made a donation of 2 acres or more to St. Mary's Abbey, which he called 'part of my land of Stein' and was the land around and to the east of Trinity College (then known as the Church of All Hallows). The name of Stein needs explanation. The Vikings had tied up their boats at two points; one at the Dubh Linn where the Poddle met the Liffey and the other at the Long Stone clearly shown in a map in Haliday's *Scandinavian Antiquities of Dublin*, roughly where Hawkins Street is today. This map of Petty is dated 1655, a map drawn 300 years after Theobald's gift, and the stone still standing evidently – more than 700 years since the Norsemen set it there.

The Stone gave its name to the whole district stretching from there for 40 acres and more; and from it came the name for the river which flowed south to meet the Liffey from the area anywhere between the present St. Stephen's Green and the Canal, and downstream by way of Grafton Street and Nassau Street, in front of Trinity College and into the Liffey near the present Hawkins Street. When the mouth of this river was accidentally stopped during flooding in the nineteenth century, the river backed up and drowned a servant in a basement cellar in Grafton Street.

Well, buried they all may be, but still alive. After all, dead things do not continue to menace, as the Poddle is capable of (in spite of the new culverting by the Corporation). It endeavoured to swallow whole gardens, near Harold's Cross, in 1987. ●

The Book of the Liffey

Can you name the bridges?

There are 13 bridges from Islandbridge to the sea, not counting the railway bridge near Islandbridge, or the Loop Line Bridge. Most of them have been rebuilt and/or undergone several changes of name over the centuries: few of them are known to Dubliners by their official names. They are, from west to east:

1. **Sarah Bridge**
Built 1791, (popularly known as Island Bridge).

2. **Sean Heuston Bridge**
Built 1827. (still generally known as Kings Kingsbridge).

3. **Frank Sherwin Bridge**
Built 1982.

4. **Rory O'More Bridge**
First built in wood, 1670, later in stone. Known at different periods as Bloody B., Barrack B., Victoria B., Emancipation B. (popularly known as Watling Street Bridge)

5. **Liam Mellowes Bridge**
First built in 1683. Known at different periods as Arran B., Bridewell B., Ellis's B., Queen's B., Queen Maeve B. (popularly known as Queen Street Bridge).

6. **Fr. Mathew Bridge**
Successor to King John's Bridge, built 1215. Later Friar's Bridge. (To Dubliners, Church Street Bridge).

7. **O'Donovan Rossa Bridge**
Built as Ormond Bridge 1683, rebuilt 1813, then named Richmond B. (To Dubliners, Winetavern Street Bridge).

8. **Grattan Bridge**
Built 1875. Originally Essex Bridge built 1676, rebuilt 1753. (To Dubliners, Capel Street Bridge).

9. **Liffey Bridge**
(Sometime Wellington B. or Iron B. (Now Ha'penny B. or Metal B. to all).

10. **O'Connell Bridge**, first built 1794 as Carlisle Bridge.

11. **Butt Bridge**, first built in 1878 and rebuilt in 1932, is officially Congress Bridge.

12. **Talbot Memorial Bridge**, built 1978.

13. **East Link Toll Bridge**, 1984.

This wash drawing of 'Islandbridge after the flood' by the Rev. Henry Barnard is signed May 19, 1788. It shows the bridge wrecked by the flood of 1784, with an attempt at temporary repair. The single-arched Sarah Bridge replaced it in 1791, a little downriver from this one. The large building in the left background is probably Mander's Flour Mill.

Compare this view with that of Place, of a slightly earlier date (page 120) and Ashford's lovely painting of Dublin from Chapelizod c.1800 showing the new bridge (page 140).

Mature and Stately, through Dublin City

'The King's Bridge' (Heuston Bridge), built in 1828, looking towards the Royal (now Collins) Barracks. (Petrie, 1834).

Frank Sherwin Bridge, built 1982.

Heuston Bridge with Heuston Station. It was originally named King's Bridge in honour of George IV's visit to Dublin in 1821. It was renamed in 1955 for Sean Heuston, executed in 1916.

WALKING THE QUAYS

Island Bridge to Heuston Station

Let us now walk down the river from the weir in the Longmeadows Park, beyond Island Bridge, which marks the tidal limit of the River Liffey. It can be reached through a potholed road opposite Clancy Barracks on the South Circular Road. This is an area of wide skies and broad horizons and the sense of tranquillity which gently flowing water can evoke. By the footpath at the water's edge is the Trinity College Boat House and on the slopes of the meadow the Memorial Park is half hidden by the ranks of elm, poplar and weeping birch. This twenty acre park was designed as a Garden of Remembrance by Sir Edwin Lutyens for the 49,400 Irishmen who are known to have died while serving with the British forces during the 1914 - 1918 war. In it a monolithic cross overlooks a war stone which is flanked by two fountains. Looking at these massive blocks of granite, one of which weighs more than eight tons, it is difficult to imagine how the park was built by hand without the aid of mechanical diggers or cranes, which it was. The rubble stone walls in the sunken gardens and around the lawns are works of great craft and beauty and are a lasting tribute to the craftsman who built them. The park was completed in 1939 and was recently refurbished by the Office of Public Works.

The swans that may sometimes be seen on the river here are a reminder of how, in 1922, Senator Oliver St John Gogarty, having been kidnapped, was brought here by his Republican captors but escaped being shot by swimming across the Liffey. Later in gratitude for his deliverance he presented two swans to the Liffey and released them here in the presence of President W. T. Cosgrave and the poet W .B. Yeats.

Directly across the river in the Phoenix Park, and occupying a commanding view of the city from Thomas' Hill, is the Magazine Fort. This is on the site of Phoenix House which, in the seventeenth century, was the summer residence of the Viceroys.

The Fort was raided twice; on Easter Monday 1916 a party of about thirty Irish Volunteers, under cover of playing a football match near the gate of the Fort, got near enough to surprise and overpower the sentry. They commandeered a number of rifles and set fuses to the ammunition in the stores. However, the fuses failed to detonate and the car carrying the rifles into the city centre was intercepted and the occupants arrested.

The Fort was again raided on 23rd December 1939, this time by the IRA. But by the end of the year the forty lorry loads of rifles, machine guns and ammunition that were seized had been recovered from various dumps around the country.

On the south bank of the river and immediately upriver from the bridge is the island from which Island Bridge gets its name. This was formed by a loop in the river which was later harnessed as a millrace. The island is reached though an unobtrusive road beside the bridge leading to a square which opens on to the river and is backed by the original mill buildings. Only from here can the elegance of Island Bridge be properly appreciated. Officially called Sarah Bridge, since the foundation stone was laid in 1791 by Sarah, Countess of Westmoreland, it is universally known as Island Bridge. It is on this stretch of water that the first salmon of the season is usually caught on 1st January each year. The houses on the north bank of the river have attractive, if quaintly ramshackle, jetties as back entrances.

When the Royal Hospital was built in Kilmainham the present boundaries of the Phoenix Park had already been established but, since the high road to Lucan ran through the Park, the deer there were constantly being injured or stolen. In the 1670s, Sir John Temple, who lived in Palmerstown, undertook to build an eight feet high wall on what is today Conyngham Road and the Chapelizod Road. He was rewarded with a grant of £200 and all the land between his wall and the river from Island Bridge to Chapelizod.

A few hundred yards east of the turnstile gates to the Park at Island Bridge there is a blind arch in this wall. This marks the position of the railway tunnel which runs under the Park to the North Wall and connects Heuston and Connolly stations. The bridge carrying the railway over the river is usually forgotten when the Liffey bridges are being enumerated.

The Wellington Testimonial, to give it its proper if rather pompous title, looms over Conyngham Road and looks, as George IV remarked, very like an overgrown milestone. It was designed by Sir Robert Smirke and the foundation stone was laid in 1817 by Lord Whitworth, the Lord Lieutenant. In 1820, however, the money ran out when only the granite obelisk had been built. It remained unfinished until 1855 when the Earl of Carlisle, who had been a close friend of Wellington, undertook to see it to completion. The monument was put on view to the public on 18th June 1861, the forty-fourth anniversary of the laying of the foundation stone.

In 1679 Charles II authorised the establishment of a hospital for disabled soldiers similar to the Hôtel des Invalides in Paris and so opposite the Wellington Testimonial, the Royal Hospital stands superbly sited on rising ground above the south bank of the Liffey. It was designed by William Robinson, the state surveyor-general, who also designed Marsh's Library. It was built at a cost of £24,000 and was completed within six years. The steeple was added in 1704. Recently restored at a cost of about £20m, this is the most important seventeenth-century building in Ireland and now serves as a national centre for culture and the arts.

Over the tops of the trees at the north-east corner of the Phoenix Park the cupola of what used to be the Royal Military Infirmary can just be seen. It is built of Portland stone and was completed in 1793 to the design of James Gandon. It is the subject of one of James Malton's views of Dublin and today it houses the Army Headquarters. Padraic Pearse was brought here to sign the surrender of the Republican forces in 1916.

A little way past the junction with Infirmary Road is Ryan's, which is one of the few genuine Victorian public houses in the city. Inside, the layout and the solid mahogany counter and fittings are unchanged since the 1890s, when they were originally installed.

Sean Heuston Bridge is the most westerly bridge on the Liffey quays. This undistinguished iron structure was designed by George Papworth and erected as King's Bridge in 1827 to commemorate the visit of George IV to Dublin in 1821. In 1955 it was renamed in honour of Sean Heuston who was executed in 1916. The two crowns which originally adorned the balustrades have been crudely removed and at close quarters this serves only to emphasise the forlorn appearance of the structure and makes it a poor memorial to a national patriot.

In 1945, the bronze head of Field-Marshal Lord Gough was retrieved from the riverbed nearby, having been sawn off the equestrian statue in the Phoenix Park on Christmas Eve, 1944. The head was replaced amid a hot debate on the artistic merits of the statue. The debate was brought to an abrupt end in June 1957 when, after an earlier unsuccessful attempt, an explosion blew the statue from its base. What remained of it was stored in the grounds of the Royal Hospital and was sold in 1987.

On the south side of the bridge is Sean Heuston Station. This was built as

In June 1988 it was announced that 'an imaginative development' incorporating hotel, studio offices, apartment blocks, sports complex and marina was being planned for Islandbridge, on the 5-acre site between that bridge and the Railway Bridge.

Lord Gough astride his horse in Phoenix Park. This fine equestrian statue was blown to pieces in 1957.

(Continued on page 132)

'A Gift of Swans'. The photograph shows Oliver St. John Gogarty (second from left) releasing a pair of swans into the Liffey, in gratitude to the river for helping him to escape from his kidnappers in 1922. The group includes President W. T. Cosgrave, W. B. Yeats and Mrs. Gogarty. Tradition has it that there were no swans on the Liffey before that, and that all the swans there since are descended from this pair.

To the Liffey with the Swans

Keep you these calm and lovely things,
And float them on your clearest water;
For one would not disgrace a King's
Transformed beloved and buoyant daughter.

And with her goes this sprightly swan,
A bird of more than royal feather
With alban beauty clothed upon:
O keep them fair and well together!

As fair as was that doubled Bird
By love of Leda so besotten,
That she was all with wonder stirred:
And the Twin Sportsmen were begotten!

Oliver St. John Gogarty

Rory O'More Bridge at Watling Street was preceded by Bloody Bridge, shown here. It got its name from the riots at its opening in 1674. Note the elaborate gateway which stood at this point on the quays. It was dismantled brick by brick in the 1840s and re-erected to form the west gate of the Royal Hospital at Kilmainham. The odd appearance of the Wellington Testimonial in the background suggests that it was a later or last-minute addition, probably before that monument was completed.

The Phoenix Park

The Phoenix Park has a fascinating physical, social and political history. The first official mention of it occurs in a letter of King Charles dated 1st December 1662, ratifying the purchase of 441 acres adjoining the Phoenix Demesne at Chapelizod. The nucleus of the Park was formed by the lands of the Knights Hospitallers of Kilmainham, which had reverted to the Crown on the dissolution of the monasteries by Henry the Eighth. It was extended by purchasing lands to the north and west. The Park, as initially envisaged, was to be no more than 1000 acres. However, later land acquisitions extended the area to 2000 acres, lying on both sides of the River Liffey, before it was reduced again to its present size of 1,750 acres (708 hectares) when the Royal Hospital was built at Kilmainham in 1684.

The establishment of the Phoenix Park as a Royal Hunting Park was the work of one of Ireland's most illustrious Viceroys, James Butler, Duke of Ormond. It was opened to the public of Dublin in 1747 by Lord Chesterfield. He was responsible for constructing new paths and roadways, including the main avenue through the park, Chesterfield Avenue. He was also responsible for erecting the Phoenix Column – known to some as the Eagle Monument.

The Park was initially stocked with pheasant and a herd of deer. Because of the deer it was necessary to enclose the Park lands on both sides of the Liffey with a wall. The straightening of some parts of the wall subsequently excluded six acres. When the building of the Royal Hospital began, this, coupled with the inconvenience caused by the Chapelizod road running through the Park, led to the erection of a new boundary wall along the Chapelizod road from Parkgate Street, excluding the road and some further acres.

The original boundary wall had been erected by a building contractor named Dodson. His workmanship was most unsatisfactory and the poor construction led to frequent escape, injury and loss of deer. The 'new' stretch of wall replacing it was built in 1682 by Sir John Temple, Solicitor-General, for the sum of £200.

The total cost of acquiring the lands in the first place was over £40,000, and Dodson's useless wall cost a further £6,000.

The origin of the Park's name is still a matter of conjecture. A manor house named Phoenix House originally stood on Thomas's Hill where the Magazine Fort now stands. Most scholars assume that the name was a derivation of the Irish *Fionn Uisce*, 'fair' or 'clear' water, in association with one of two spa wells there, one located near the Phoenix Column, the other in the grounds of the Zoological Gardens. The popular association with the legendary bird, the Phoenix, 'rising from the ashes', has no real basis.

A ranger and two keepers were appointed to manage the Park in 1668, but the intended higher appointment of Lieutenant of the Park was never made.

Control of the Park, as a Royal Park, was handed over to the Commissioners of Woods and Forests in 1830, who managed it until 1850. During their last decade of stewardship major landscape improvements were brought into being by the renowned landscape designer, Decimus Burton. He was responsible for improvements in roads and footpaths, the building of new gate lodges and extension of existing ones. Many of the existing woodlands and tree plantations are the inspiration of Decimus Burton.

Nowadays control and management is under the care of the Office of Public Works. In June 1986 the Park was designated a National Historic Park. Future developments will be in line with this designation, and with the historic aspects of the Park. Policy includes the development of Heritage Trails, Horse-drawn transport, and the reinstatement of traditional elements such as gas lighting, railings, bollards and signposting. Tree planting too will reflect traditional landscape groupings.

A Walk with a River View

In order to keep within 'viewing' distance of the River Liffey while at the same time discovering some of the delights of the Park, it is suggested that you take a 2 km walk, entering at the Knockmaroon Gate and exiting via Islandbridge Gate.

The Knockmaroon Gate is a handsome entrance, a double pair of Georgian gates separated by an attractive granite lodge. Just inside the gates, to your right, stands the Knockmaroon Information and Nature Centre.

This area of the Phoenix Park is zoned as a Wildlife area, and the aim is to maximise food sources and shelter. You will notice, for instance, how the vegetation is allowed to develop naturally; fallen trees and branches are left to decay to encourage insect and other forms of life. Fifty species of birds have been recorded in the Phoenix Park, including long-eared owls and sparrowhawks.

A Nature Trail commences close to the Information Centre, where a Nature Trail booklet can be purchased.

As you emerge from the Lower Glen Road to meet the Upper Glen Road you will see the broad expanse of the so-called 'Fifteen Acres' – in reality over 300 acres – to your left. You can usually get a glimpse of the herd of 350 Fallow Deer from here. There are three colours of deer – black, brown and menil, the latter very much in the minority. In the distance across the 'acres' you will see the soaring steel Cross erected to commemorate the visit of His Holiness, Pope John Paul II, in September 1979.

As you proceed towards Chapelizod Gate, the view of the Fifteen Acres gives way to a lofty tree-clad embankment on top of which stands Knockmary Lodge. This is occupied by one of the Park's Constable force. A short distance from here is an ancient burial site which, when excavated in 1838, revealed a stone chamber containing the remains of two adult males and an animal bone believed to be that of a dog, a large number of small shells which formed a necklace, and other artefacts. Another burial was found close to the old village of Chapelizod, and was re-erected in the Zoological Gardens.

Close by Knockmary Lodge is a park enclosure, inside of which is the Cara Cheshire Home. Next comes St. Mary's Hospital. This was originally the Royal

Mature and Stately, through Dublin City

Hibernian Military School, built in 1766 for the education and training of orphans and children of soldiers.

Continuing towards the Islandbridge Gate along the 'Corkscrew' road, you leave Chapelizod Gate and Lodge on the right. Along this road fine vistas appear, rolling down to the grassy slopes of the river. There are Gaelic and Soccer Pavilions to the left, as well as two Park staff residences, one of them traditionally known as Deerkeeper Lodge.

As you descend towards Islandbridge,

the Magazine Fort looms high on Thomas's Hill where the original Phoenix House stood. Work commenced on the Magazine Fort in 1735 and it was eventually finished in 1801. It is surrounded by a dry ditch and once had a drawbridge. Nowadays it is used only as a store but there are plans to make it into a Military Museum.

The Magazine Fort was traditionally a viewing point for the city and environs of Dublin, as can be seen from many old prints and paintings, including one of

James Malton's celebrated Views. From here also you can see the 205-ft Wellington Testimonial in the distance, a monument to the military exploits of the Duke of Wellington.

Just below the lofty heights of the Magazine Fort you come to a crossroads. The road ahead leads to the Wellington monument. The turn to the right leads you down to Islandbridge Gate and Lodge, on to the Chapelizod Road, and returns you to the banks of our River Liffey. ●

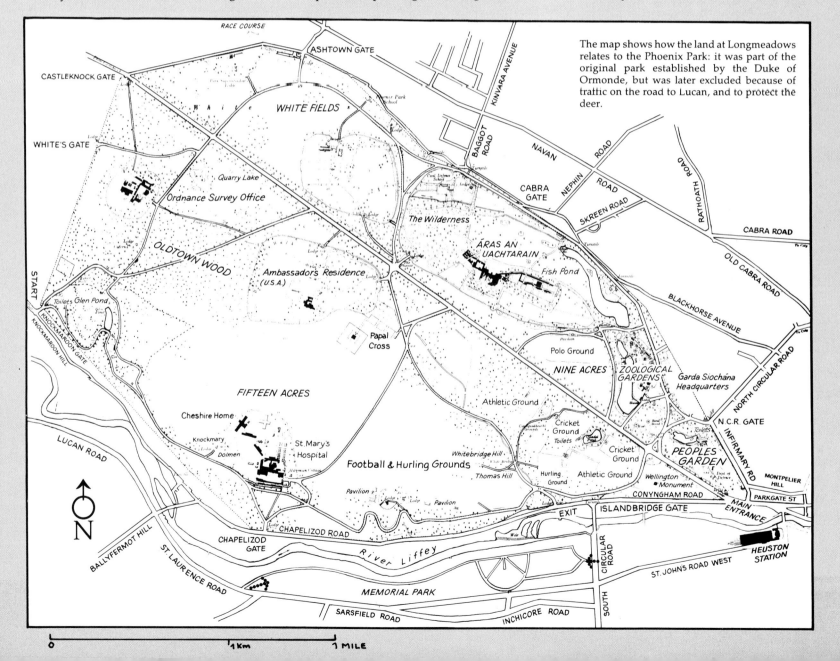

The map shows how the land at Longmeadows relates to the Phoenix Park: it was part of the original park established by the Duke of Ormonde, but was later excluded because of traffic on the road to Lucan, and to protect the deer.

Waterway to the World — The Liffey and Guinness

St. James's Gate Brewery, founded in 1759 on four acres, today extends over some 60 acres.

The first Arthur Guinness brewed ale for a short time, then porter (a drink which originated in London and was so called because of its popularity with the porters of Covent Garden and Billingsgate), and later, a stronger brew called extra stout which, in the course of time, was shortened to 'Stout'.

The brewing process has remained fundamentally unchanged in over 200 years, although full use is made today of modern scientific techniques. The same yeast strain which was introduced by the first Arthur Guinness is still in use.

In the closing years of the last century the St. James's Gate Brewery became the largest in the world. It is still the largest in Europe and exports more beer than any other single brewery anywhere.

The River Liffey has been one of the Brewery's main traffic arteries and, down the years, has supplied the very life-blood of its trade and commerce with the world.

The Link with Guinness
The Guinness connection with the River Liffey goes back to 1769, when the first export order of six and a half barrels left for England under sail from the Old Custom House below Essex Bridge. Today's Guinness fleet, comprising the tanker ships *Lady Patricia* and *Miranda Guinness*, depart with the bulk cargoes from the City Quay berth between Matt Talbot Bridge and the East Link, close to the Liffey mouth.

Arthur Guinness moved to Dublin from Leixlip in 1759 and on the last day of that year signed his famous lease for 9000 years on the derelict St. James's Gate brewery which in turn had been around since about 1600 or so in the hands of the Mees, Rainsfords, Espinasses and others.

History has shown that only a man of Mr. Guinness's determination and gritty work ethic could make it prosper.

By 1868 Extra Stout Porter for export to Britain was being transported by Grand Canal lighter along the Circular Road route from the Brewery to the Port of Dublin. Five years later, when the Cooperage and Racking Shed were transferred across James's Street to the riverside, a jetty was built on Victoria Quay, between Kingsbridge and Watling Street. And from 1875 onwards the full casks were taken by locomotive from the Racking Room to the jetty where they were loaded onto steam barges. Over the years the fleet was gradually enlarged until by 1920 (and allowing for replacements since the beginning) there were twelve vessels in service, including a 'dumb' barge which had to be towed by one of the others. These early Guinness barges were cumbersome and difficult to manoeuvre. All were given the names of Irish rivers, the oldest of them being the Lagan, built in 1877 by Harland & Wolff. Some of these were the barges that greeted Queen Victoria on her last visit to Dublin as the century dawned and with which she expressed herself greatly pleased.

Towards the end of 1927 the first of the 'Farmleigh' type of Guinness Liffey barge was launched. Others soon followed bearing such local names as 'Castleknock', 'Clonsilla', 'Fairyhouse', and 'Killiney'. They were built for Guinness by Vickers at the Liffey Dockyard and the old fleet was phased out by 1930.

These new ones were very different barges from their predecessors; well equipped, easily manoeuvred and ideally suited to the work. Each carried close on 100 tons of casks, was steam driven, and was equipped with jib cranes.

With a full load they could develop a speed of seven-and-a-half knots. Each boat had a Skipper, a Mate, three Bargemen and an Engine Driver. Small boys in the city used to shout down from

the Liffey bridges 'Hey mister! Bring us back a parrot!'

Barges sailed from the jetty any time after 3.30 in the morning, and these could be seen returning from the Port as late as midnight. This was due to dependence on the rise and ebb of the tide. Sailings were only possible at approximately two hours before and two hours after high water. This was to allow for headroom at the low Liffey bridges even though the barges had retractable funnels, and sufficient draught for sailing.

On reaching the port the clang of hooks on the quayside signalled that discharging had commenced. Fog was one of the chief enemies and barges were often fog bound at the port. Excessive rain and draught also affected sailings.

The Cross Channel Fleet
The Liffey barges discontinued service at the end of June 1961 due to the introduction of bulk packaging and transportation techniques. The traffic is now carried by road on the short journey from Brewery to Port, where in 1913 the first Guinness-owned cross-channel steamer, the *S.S. William Barkley*, came into service. She was torpedoed during the Great War on her way to England from Dublin.

During 1914-5 three ships – the *S.S. Carrowdore, Clareisland* and *Clarecastle* – built in Glasgow as self-trimming colliers, were added to the Guinness fleet. All three were commandeered by the British Government during the 1914/18 war and were used mostly in coaling battleships and carrying hay. The trio had all returned to Guinness service by July 1919.

During the Second World War the *Carrowdore* had a very narrow escape from sinking when a bomb came very close, tearing through the deck fittings only to explode in the water alongside, just fifteen miles out of Dublin on a bright July morning.

The *Clareisland* was replaced by the *S.S. Guinness* in 1931. Both the *Carrowdore* and *Clarecastle* remained in service until 1953.

The first two ships in the world to be built for the carriage of beer in bulk were launched in 1952. They were m.v. *The Lady Grania* and M.V. *The Lady Gwendolen*, both named after members of the Guinness family. Both identical, they were designed for carrying Guinness in

Guinness in the days of the barges, off to Dublin port. 'Bring us back a parrot' the children used to call after them.

transportable tanks between Dublin and the ports of Manchester and Liverpool. When the tanks arrived in England they were placed on platform lorries which in effect became road tankers. The empties were returned to the ship.

These two 'thoroughbred Ayreshires', as they were dubbed at their launching, were sold in the 1970s to make way for the world's first beer tanker ships, m.v. *The Lady Patricia* and m.v. *Miranda Guinness*, which makes up today's cross-channel fleet.

James Joyce's immortal washerwomen of 'the hither-and-thithering waters' would have seen the fateful departure from Custom House Quay in 1917 of the Barkley as she steamed away to her last encounter on the deep. For Joyce even the Guinness barges were 'stout ships', and in *Finnegans Wake* he records accurately the sound of the 'porteryark's chiggen-chugger'.

The rolling river bore silent witness to the demolition of the Irish House in 1968. This old pub, built in 1870 on Wood Quay, carried the last flourish of the Dublin plasterer's art, with tableaux of Grattan's Parliament, Daniel O'Connell and Erin weeping on a stringless harp.

The Stuccodores were Burnett and Comerford and the whole concoction capped with round towers, glowed in the light of the slanting evening sun like a Byzantine casket. 'O tell me all' runs the conversation by the river-wall. '. . . I want to hear all about Anna Livia.' 'Genghis is ghoon for you!' answers the exiled Dubliner, 'export stout fellow that you are.'

And so Guinness goes on past Liffey mouth into its third century. ●

Kingsbridge Station, the terminus and headquarters of the Great Southern and Western Railway Company, in which, later, Sean Heuston was to be a minor employee. Sir John Macneill, who was engineer to the railway company, designed the iron and glass passenger sheds which cover the platform area of more than two-and-a-half acres. This was one of the first such structures to be erected in Dublin and the immense glass roof is supported by seventy-two slim iron columns. Although the main building bears the date 1844, this is the date of the incorporation of the company. It was not until 1845 that a design by Sancton Wood for the terminus was unanimously selected, by a London Committee, from the designs submitted. The building, which is in the form of a renaissance palace, is the most impressive of the railway termini in the city. It is seen best from the northern side of the river.

The River Camac, which rises beyond Saggart in County Dublin and flows through Rathcoole, Ballyfermot, Drimnagh and Kilmainham, runs under Sean Heuston Station to the Liffey. The Camac was the principal pollutor of the Liffey until the 1980s when the Greater Dublin Drainage Scheme relieved the foul and surface sewers in the west of the city. Beyond Heuston Station on Steevens' Lane is Dr. Steevens' Hospital but the view from the Liffey is spoiled by the red brick nurses' home which was built in the late nineteenth century. Steevens' was, until its closure in 1987, the oldest hospital in Ireland still occupying its original site. Dr Richard Steevens, who was Regius Professor of Physics in Trinity College when he died in 1710, left his property in trust to his sister, Grizel, for her lifetime. After her death it was to be put towards the establishment of a general hospital in the city. Grizel Steevens was determined to have the hospital set up and, keeping a yearly income of £150 for herself, she gave the remainder to a Board of Governors to build the hospital immediately. The architect was Thomas Burgh, who also designed Trinity College Library, and the hospital opened in 1733. It is a reflection, on a very modest scale, of the Royal Hospital, as it is basically in the form of a courtyard surrounded by piazzas. The clock tower was added in 1736. Jonathan Swift was made a trustee of the hospital in 1721 and Esther Johnson (Stella) contributed £1,000 for the support of the hospital's chaplain. A trustee and governor, Dr Edward Worth, died in 1732 and bequeathed to the hospital his library of more than four thousand volumes and £100 to shelve them properly. These were housed in the Board Room and formed one of the most notable libraries in the city. Most of the books were subsequently moved to Trinity College, Dublin.

Heuston Bridge to Queen Street

A short distance below Heuston Bridge is the Frank Sherwin Memorial Bridge. This was built in 1982 and is named after a late alderman of the city.

To the south below Heuston Bridge is Victoria Quay. This most depressing quay is entirely occupied by Guinness's wall. In 1873 the brewery built a wharf here for their barges which ferried the barrels of export stout to the Guinness ships on Custom House Quay. The wharf was served by the brewery's own miniature railway and was equipped with cranes which lifted the barrels, two at a time, in and out of the barges. From 1961 the stout was brought to the docks by road and some of the barges were sold off to transport sand in Northern Ireland.

Dominating the north side of the river at this point is Collins Barracks. Because it was the first building of its type to be erected in Britain or Ireland it was called simply 'The Barracks'. It was built of granite, between 1701 and 1760, on what was part of Oxmantown Green, to enforce the new British policy of non-fraternization of the army

Mature and Stately, through Dublin City

with the native Irish. Heretofore, the soldiers had been billetted on the local householders. The architect was Thomas Burgh, who also designed Dr Steevens' Hospital. Later it was called the Royal Barracks and had accommodation for three regiments of infantry and one of cavalry, which made up nearly 5000 men. In December 1922, the Free State army, under General Richard Mulachy, took over the barracks from the British authorities and it was immediately renamed Collins Barracks after General Michael Collins who had been shot at Beal na Blath, County Cork, in August of that year.

The Croppies Memorial Park occupies the triangular space at the junction of Parkgate Street and Wolfe Tone Quay. On the footpath outside is an attractive fountain which commemorates the bicentenary of the Dublin Chamber of Commerce (1783 - 1983). Prior to its present use this small area was called Crimea Park and in it were displayed some of the cannon and mortars captured in the Crimean War. These artillery pieces have been moved to Collins Barracks but a few of the cannon balls may still be seen inside the gates of the army garage across the road.

The Croppys Acre , originally known as the Croppies' Hole, formed part of the ground which ran down to the Liffey in front of the Barracks. In 1798 the government was warned of possible attacks on the city by members of the United Irishmen. The Yeoman Infantry and Cavalry were put on alert and skirmishes occurred at places as far apart as Tallaght and Kilcock. Many of the rebels were killed and their mutilated bodies were put on display in the city. Some of those taken prisoner were killed in the Provost Prison behind the Barracks or hanged from Liffey bridges. Their bodies were buried in an unmarked common grave on waste ground on the south side of what is now Benburb

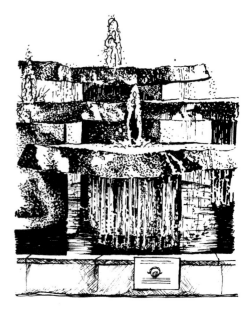

Parkgate Street Fountain.

'A Prospect of the Barracks of Dublin from St. James's Church Yard' (Tudor).

Street. Among those who were interred here was Matthew Tone, a brother of Wolfe Tone. The Liffey has been walled in since that time and the site altered considerably. This quay was first called Albert Quay to complement Victoria Quay across the river. In 1847 a Model Soup Kitchen was set up here to relieve the victims of the Famine in Dublin. Alexis Soyer, the chef of the Reform Club in London, came to Dublin to supervise the use of his recipe for nourishing soup for the poor. Hardly appropriately, the Kitchen was decorated with flags and bunting and equipped with a 300 gallon soup boiler. Thousands of starving people queued for the soup which they ate with spoons that were chained to the tables.

Ellis Street, formerly called Silver Street, runs from Benburb Street to Rory O'More Bridge has achieved fame through 'Belts', which is one of Rudyard Kipling's Barrack Room Ballads. This narrates how soldiers were involved in a fierce fight in the neighbourhood of the Barracks:

> There was a row in Silver Street
> That's near to Dublin Quay
> Between the Irish Regiment
> And the English Cavalree;
> It started at revelly
> And it lasted until dark,
> The first men fell at Harrisons
> And the last forn'st the Park.

Rory O'More Bridge, at the eastern end of Victoria and Wolfe Tone Quays, is on the site of Bloody Bridge which was built as a wooden structure in 1670. In 1671, the owners of the ferry which had been superseded by the bridge, incited some young apprentices to try to demolish it. This caused a riot between soldiers and the apprentices, twenty of whom were captured and brought to Dublin Castle. While they were being conveyed from the Castle to the Bridewell an attempt was made to rescue them and four were killed. This incident gave rise to the name Bloody Bridge. This was replaced in 1704 by Barrack Bridge, a humpbacked bridge with four semicircular arches, which was designed to enable troops and their equipment to enter the city quickly. This narrow bridge was, in turn, replaced in 1863 by the present utilitarian structure which was opened by Queen Victoria and was named after her. In 1929 it was renamed Emancipation Bridge and subsequently called Rory O'More Bridge. However, through all these changes Dubliners have always called it Watling Street Bridge.

Above and below:

15 Usher's Island. This is where James Joyce's story 'The Dead' is located.

Looking up Watling Street the vista is dominated by a windmill tower which is known locally, for obvious reasons, as the Onion Tower. In the early eighteenth century this was attached to a corn mill and the wind-power was used to drive the grinders. In 1757 it became part of Roe's Distillery which, in turn, was absorbed by the Dublin Distilleries Company. In the 1940s the premises were acquired by the Guinness company who restored the building and replaced the weather vane which is a depiction of St Patrick. It has been claimed that this is the largest windmill tower in Britain or Ireland.

Number 15 Usher's Island, which is one of the last surviving houses of its type on the quay, is the principal location of James Joyce's short story 'The Dead'. The house was the home of Joyce's great-aunts, Mrs Lyons and Mrs Callanan and of her daughter Mary Ellen. Members of the Joyce family, as they became old enough, went each Christmas to this house and Joyce's father carved the goose and made a speech. Gabriel and Gretta

Mature and Stately, through Dublin City

Conroy in the story have a lot of the characters of James and Nora Joyce. Michael Furey was, in real life, Sonny/Michael Bodkin, Nora's consumptive lover in Galway who, when he heard that she was going to Dublin, came from his sick bed and stood under an apple tree in the rain to sing his good-bye to her. He died a short time later. Through the story we learn a great deal about Joyce's relationship with his wife and his attitudes to Ireland. The story was filmed by John Houston in 1987.

Only the green cupola of the Incorporated Law Society building can be seen from Rory O'More Bridge. This is better known to Dubliners as the Blue Coat School or King's Hospital. Charles II granted a royal charter to the school in 1670 when it stood in Queen Street. When this original building became delapidated it was decided to erect a new school a short distance away on the corner of Oxmantown Green. The new building was designed by Thomas Ivory and was started in 1773 but, because it proved so expensive, building work ceased ten years later. Ivory's design was for a stately Palladian building with two wings. The tall central cupola shown in the architect's drawings was left unfinished for one hundred and fifty years. Then, in 1904, the present one was added. Until 1923 the pupils at the school wore blue coats with brass buttons and yellow waistcoats. The playing field at the back of the school was the last remaining **vestige** of Oxmantown Green. In 1970 the school moved to Palmerstown and the building is now occupied by the Incorporated Law Society.

A bridge was first erected on the site of Liam Mellowes Bridge in 1683. In 1728 it was named Arran Bridge and in 1756 it became Bridewell Bridge, from the Bridewell which was in nearby Smithfield. In 1766 it was Ellis's Bridge and in 1768 it was rebuilt to the design of General Charles Vallancey who was attached to the Ordnance Office. It was then called Queen's Bridge after Queen Charlotte, wife of George III. The bridge consists of a triple arched granite structure with a balustrade and it is the oldest and one of the finest bridges over the Liffey. When the Free State was set up it was renamed Queen Maeve Bridge and in 1942 it was given its present name to commemorate the Liam Mellowes who was executed in Mountjoy Prison on 8th December 1922. Dubliners in their own fashion know it as Queen Street Bridge.

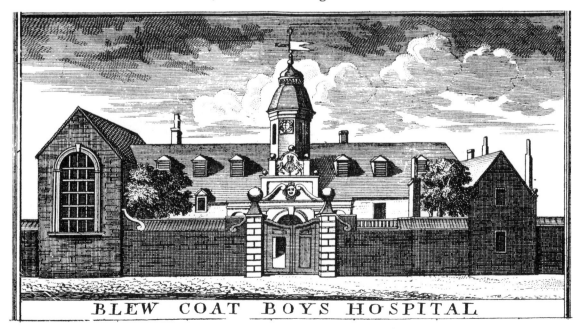

BLEW COAT BOYS HOSPITAL

The original Blue Coat School, or King's Hospital, from Brooking's Map of 1728. It was rebuilt magnificently to the design of Thomas Ivory in 1777. It is now the property of the Incorporated Law Society.

Queen Street to the Four Courts

On Arran Quay there is an unobtrusive turning which leads to Smithfield. In 1664 this part of Oxmantown Green was, by order of the City Assembly, set out as a market place for the sale of cattle, sheep, pigs, hay and straw. The cattle market was held here until 1886 when it moved to a new site on the North Circular Road. Today Smithfield is the widest expanse of cobblestones in the city and is dominated by the redbrick chimney, dated 1895, of what was the John Jameson Distillery. This company was absorbed into Irish Distillers who have built a fine office block in Smithfield, which blends in well with its surroundings.

St Paul's Church on Arran Quay was built on the site of a small chapel which dated from 1785. It was designed by Patrick Byrne, who was also the architect for St Audoen's, High Street. The portico is in the form of a Greek Ionic Temple above which are a tower and cupola. On the pediment are the figures of SS Peter, Paul and Patrick to whose dramatic attitudes the children of the locality have attached the following dialogue:

> St Peter: I have the keys of Heaven!
> St Paul: Give them to me.
> St Patrick: No, throw them into the Liffey.

The Bow Street Distillery

It sloweth age
and brighteneth the mind.
It keepeth head from whirling,
teeth from chattering,
Tongue from lisping
and throte from rattling,
It keepeth heart from swelling,
guts from rumbling,
The hands from shivering
and the bones from crumbling.
– Theoricus

Fifteen hundred years or so ago, some Irish missionary monks in the Middle East became intrigued with the way perfume was distilled there, using an apparatus called an alembic. With their fertile Celtic imaginations they came up with what they considered a better use for the alembic. They discovered that if, instead of a mash of flowers and herbs, they used a mash of barley fermented with yeast, the alembic separated out not perfume, but an alcohol of wondrous powers. They adapted the alembic and called it a pot still, and called the resultant liquor the Water of Life.

Not surprisingly, it fast became popular. Henry II's soldiers became

Jameson's Bow Street Distillery. Circa 1880   *Continued page 141*

Mature and Stately, through Dublin City

Lucan House and Demesne, painted by Thomas Roberts, c. 1770.

The Leinster Aqueduct, where the road and the Grand Canal together cross over the river. It was one of the splendid works overseen by General Charles Vallancey, Engineer in ordinary in Ireland, and it was completed in 1780.

Shackleton's Mill at Lucan. Built in about 1800, it still uses water power with three turbines dating from respectively 1884, 1902 and 1906.

The first salmon of the year is always caught at Islandbridge.
Apart from salmon, the Liffey offers a rich harvest of trout, perch, eel and bream.

Perch

Eel

Bream

Dublin from Chapelizod by Wm. Ashford
c. 1800. Below is the weir at Islandbridge
and to the left the elegant single span of
the then new Sarah Bridge. The Royal
Hospital at Kilmainham is clearly shown.
(See also page 121).

Bridgefoot Street runs south from Liam Mellowes Bridge and in the nineteenth century was known as Dirty Lane. It is recalled in a song by Michael Moran, who was better known by his nickname Zozimus, about a bigoted Orangeman who had a particularly dirty appearance:

> At the dirty end of Dirty Lane
> Liv'd a dirty cobbler Dick McGrane;
> His wife was, in the old king's reign,
> A stout brave orange woman.
> On Essex Bridge she strained her throat,
> And six-a-penny was her note;
> But Dickey wore a brand new coat,
> He got among the yeomen.

In this century the street was the location of one of Dublin's 'hot walls' (it was hot because the furnace of a bakery was behind it) and against it the poor and unemployed could lean and talk in some comfort during the cold winter months. Thomas Dudley, known and loved as 'Bang-Bang' — from his mock gun-battles in the city streets — lived for some time in Bridgefoot Street flats.

The vista up the hill of Bridgefoot Street is closed by St Catherine's Church. This was built on the site of part of the Abbey of St Thomas which was founded in the twelfth century in honour of St Thomas à Becket. The present building was designed by John Smyth in the 1760s in a heavy Paladian style but the tower, which was meant to carry a steeple, was never completed. On 20th September 1803, Robert Emmet was executed in the street outside the church. In more recent years the church was used as an exhibition and community centre.

On the south side, down river from Liam Mellowes Bridge, is Usher's Quay. In 1737 a stage coach service started for Athlone from here at eight o'clock each morning. Soon there were coaches going as far afield as Belfast and Cork. Holmes' Hotel, one of the largest hotels in Europe when it was built, stood on the site of numbers 18, 19 and 20 Usher's Quay, behind which, up to the 1970s, the huge coachyard could be seen. Around 1843, the hotel was acquired by the White Quakers. This sect, which was always quite small, was established by Josua Jacob. He objected to the lavish life style of some members of the Society of Friends and in order that he might lead a simple life he publicly broke all of his mirrors, watches and clocks and disposed of all his property. Holmes' Hotel was demolished in 1977.

From the corner of St Augustine Street the Gothic spire of the Church of St Augustine and St John can be seen. The Augustinians have had a presence on this site for more than 300 years. In 1855, the architect Edward Welby Pugin was engaged to design a new church in Thomas Street but it was not until December 1895 that the exterior was completed. The most striking feature of the design, which is French Gothic of the thirteenth century, is the 223 foot oblong tower of granite and sandstone. The twelve large statues in niches on the tower were executed by the monumental sculptor James Pearse, father of Padraic and Willie Pearse. Since it is known that Padraic assisted his father in the workshop in the early 1890s, it is probable that he worked on some of these statues. Many of the labourers who built the church were members of the Irish Republican Brotherhood and they used to drill each evening in the home of their foreman in Pimlico. It is interesting to note that although the new church fronts on to Thomas Street it has continued to be known by the name of the lane where the original church stood — John's Lane.

drunk on it. Sir Walter Raleigh stopped off at Cork to receive a present of 'a 32-gallon cask of the Earl of Cork's home-distilled uisce beatha'. Peter the Great, Czar of all the Russias, said 'of all the wines, the Irish spirit is the best'.

To make it, the great distilling houses and the poitin-maker used the same principle. A mash of grain, some yeast, a container for the distilling and a still with a spout. Any grain will make whiskey, but Irish distillers have always preferred to use barley — a mixture of malted (partly germinated) and unmalted, to give the liquor its special flavour. Irish whiskey is uniquely refined in that it is distilled three times, and then only the middle part or heart of the run is considered fit for use. This new whiskey is filled into oak casks, where it lies for between 5 and 15 years, slowly maturing. For about two centuries, and until recently, at any one time about two million gallons of maturing whiskey were stored in enormous cloister-like vaults stretching far and deep under the streets of Dublin, while the busy city traffic rumbled above unknowingly.

John Jameson's distillery in Bow Street, on the north banks of the Liffey, was established in 1780. Members of the original Jameson family are still associated with the distillery today.

In 1966, to rationalize and strengthen their international trading position, the distillers of Ireland merged to form United Distillers of Ireland Ltd. A vast new modern distillery was built in Midleton, Co. Cork, and the great kilns and huge copper kettles of Jamesons, Powers and the others grew cold and still.

But the tradition of the original John Jameson, 'father' of the Irish distillers, has been maintained, insofar as the new head office of the united distilleries has arisen on the site of the old Jameson spirits store, next to Bow Street, close to the banks of the Liffey.

Visiting arrangements
At the 'Irish Whiskey Corner', which is located in one of the old warehouses at Bow Street, there is an exhibition and audio-visual theatre showing how it is all done. It is open to the public 7 days a week all the year through or, especially for groups, by arrangement. Tel. 725566 or write to Patricia Scally, Irish Distillers Ltd., Smithfield, Dublin 7.

Father Mathew Bridge was named in 1938 to commemorate the centenary of the signing by Father Mathew of his pledge of total abstinence which he did with the words 'Here goes in the name of God'. The bridge is a little to the east of the supposed site of the Ford of the Hurdles which gave the name Ath Cliath to the Gaelic settlement there. The bridge built here in 1215 by King John was swept away in 1385 and was replaced by the Friars Bridge which was built by the Dominicans in 1428 and on which tolls were collected. This was the only bridge on the Liffey until 1683. Friars Bridge was demolished by a great flood in 1802 and in 1816 the foundation stone of the present structure was laid. It was designed by George Knowles who was engineer to the Royal Canal Company. When the foundations for the bridge were being excavated it was discovered that the foundations of the old bridge were built on the ruins of an even older bridge, supposed to be that built by King John. These indicated that a still better bridge had been on the site in an earlier time. Like the Liam Mellowes Bridge, this bridge, which connects Bridge Street with Church Street, consists of three granite arches with a balustrade. It is known as Church Street Bridge.

Church Street, which runs north from Father Mathew Bridge, takes its name from St Michan's Church, said to have been founded in 1095 by Michan, a Danish bishop. In the

View from the roof of what used to be Powers Distillery and is now the National College of Art and Design. Two distilling vats are in the foreground, and the dome of The Four Courts in the distance.

spacious interior there is a tomb reputed to be that of St Michan. On the front of the organ case there is a fine carving of musical instruments in high relief. The vaults, which have a great attraction for the morbidly curious, are noted for their peculiar property of mummifying bodies. John and Henry Sheares, who as United Irishmen were executed for their part in the rebellion of 1798, are buried in these vaults. John Clayton, who was rector here in the early eighteenth century, was the first to discover coal gas and to appreciate its possible use as a source of light.

Bridge Street or Vicus Pontis, as it is styled in early documents, sweeps southwards up the hill towards Cornmarket. Here, set well back from the street, is the Brazen Head, the oldest inn in Britain or Ireland. There are records of an inn of this name here as far back as the early seventeenth century, although the original tavern is said to have been established in 1198. Down through the years it has been a favourite meeting place of revolutionaries. Robert Emmet used to frequent the inn and his writing desk is still to be seen there. Oliver Bond often came here since he lived just across the street in number 9 Bridge Street. He was a prosperous woollen merchant who became very active in the Society of the United Irishmen. In March 1798 he was arrested on the evidence of an informer, Thomas Reynolds, and condemned to death. The sentence was commuted but Bond died of apoplexy in Newgate Gaol in Dublin and is buried in the churchyard of St. Michan's.

Upper Bridge Street is close to the site of Keaser's Lane of which Richard Stanihurst, writing in Holinshed's Chronicle in 1577, said:

> This lane is steepe and slipperie, in which otherwhyles, they
> that make more haste than good speede clincke there bummes to
> the stones. And therefore the ruder sorte, whether it be through
> corruption of speache, or for that they gyve it a nickename,
> commonly terme it, not so homely, as truely, kisse arse lane.

Overlooking Merchants' Quay is the huge mass of St Audoen's Catholic Church in High Street. Patrick Byrne also designed this church and worked very well on the steeply rising ground. Although the church was built in the period 1841-1846, the Corinthian portico, which makes it one of the finest churches in the city, was not added until 1899.

The Norman (Protestant) church of St Audoen was founded in 1190. Prior to this time, the site had been occupied by a church dedicated to St Columcille. The only surviving relic of this church is an Early Christian gravestone which is known as the Lucky Stone. In 1309, the Lord Mayor, John le Decer, set the stone beside a water cistern which he had erected in Cornmarket so that it might bring luck to all those who drank the water. Many local merchants used come to touch the stone each day to ensure that their business would prosper. In 1826, the stone disappeared but eventually, in 1850, it was recovered and is now in the porch of the church. Within living memory local people used lay their hands or lottery tickets on it and wish. The church today consists of what was once the western end of the north aisle, while the remainder of the foundation is in ruins. There is a Norman doorway in the church and the original square bowl font may still be seen. The Norman tower, rebuilt in 1670, has a fine peal of six bells which is rung each Sunday. Three of these bells, cast in 1423, are among the oldest in the country.

At the foot of the steps by the church is the last surviving city gate, St Audoen's Arch. This was originally built in the twelfth century; unfortunately it was rebuilt and entirely altered by the Corporation in the nineteenth century. It was in a room in the original gate house that the first issue of the *Freeman's Journal* was printed in 1764. There

IN GOD IS ALL OUR TRUST

The Brewers & Maltsters Arms

is a long stretch of the city walls in Cook Street and this street was the centre of Dublin's coffin making trade in the early nineteenth century.

On the other side of the river is the Four Courts. In 1202 the Cistercians founded the Friary of Saint Saviour on this site but in 1224 it was taken over by the Dominicans. In 1506, Patrick Hay, the last prior, surrendered the monastery to the Crown. The foundation of the present building was laid in 1786 and it took fourteen years to complete at a cost of more than £200,000. The architect was Thomas Cooley, but on his death James Gandon revised the plans and finished the building. The central block is flanked by courtyards bounded on three sides by legal offices and separated from the street by arcades of rusticated masonry. Above the pediment of the main building is a statue of Moses holding the Tables of the Law and flanked by the figures of Justice and Mercy. The statues on either side are of Wisdom and Authority. Above this is a circular lantern surmounted by a massive dome. The quay wall is an iron balustrade some 800 feet long with corresponding balustrades on the bridges at each end. This is a fitting foreground for this splendid building when it is viewed from the other side of the river. The four courts were those of Chancery, King's Bench, Common Pleas and Exchequer.

The building was occupied by the 3rd Battalion of the Dublin Brigade of the IRA on 14th April 1922 in protest against the signing of the Treaty. The Provisional Government made no move until the 28th June when they mounted an artillery attack. The garrison surrendered on 30th June but before doing so they mined the building and so destroyed the country's greatest archive of legal and historical documents which dated back to the twelfth century.

The building was later restored but with some alterations to Gandon's design. One bay was removed from both the east and west ranges and, over the gates, the crowns on the trophies of arms were removed and replaced by incongruous balls.

The Four Courts to Capel Street

O'Donovan Rossa Bridge is a little upstream of the site of Ormond Bridge which was built in 1683 and was swept away one hundred and twenty years later. It was replaced by Richmond Bridge which was designed by J. Savage. This stone bridge, with three segmental arches, is decorated with six carved heads by Edward Smyth on the keystones. Those on the west side are of Peace, Hibernia and Commerce and those on the east are of Plenty, the Liffey and Industry. It is now officially named after Jeremiah O'Donovan Rossa, the Fenian, but is usually known as Winetavern Street Bridge.

Winetavern Street, south of the bridge, was, in medieval times, the centre of the wine trade although today it is one of the few streets in the city without a public house. Here, in 1597, one hundred and forty-four barrels of gunpowder, which had been unloaded from a ship, exploded killing one hundred and twenty people and levelling a great part of the surrounding area.

St Michael's Hill leads to Christ Church Cathedral which was founded in 1028 by Bishop Donatus and King Sitric of Dublin on the site of an earlier Gaelic church. Here, in 1487, Lambert Simnel was crowned Edward VI with the support of the Anglo-Irish lords. The Chapter House, which incorporates the tower of the old St Michael's church, and the bridge spanning St Michael's Hill, were erected when extensive rebuilding work was carried out in 1871 at the expense of the Dublin distiller, Henry Roe.

Immediately below Christ Church were the remains of one of Europe's finest Viking settlements. The officials of Dublin Corporation decided that it was more important that new civic offices be built here than that this site should be preserved.

St Augustine's and St John's, Thomas Street.

Mature and Stately, through Dublin City

Fishamble Street was where fish was sold in the fifteenth century. The lower part of the street is on reclaimed land. In a corner, half way up the street, is Kennan's Foundry on the site of the old Musick Hall where Handel's Messiah was first performed on 13th April 1742. Further up the street is Copper Alley, formerly Preston's Inns, a medieval street which is marked on Speed's map of 1610. Number 26 Fishamble Street, on the corner of West Essex Street, is believed to be the oldest house in Dublin, dating at least from the seventeenth century. At present it has to be buttressed following the demolition by the Corporation of the house next door.

Set back from Essex Quay in Lower Exchange Street is the church of SS Michael and John on the site of the Smock Alley Theatre. Smock Alley is now West Essex Street where the theatre was opened in 1662 by John Ogilby, Master of the Revels. David Garrick and

Christ Church Cathedral, from Brooking's Map of 1728. For a period it was called Holy Trinity.

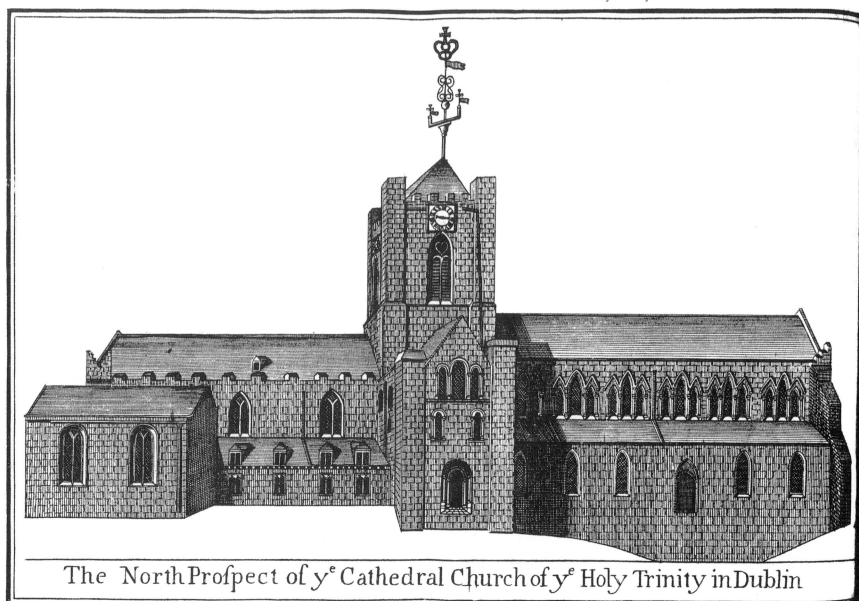

The North Profpect of yᵉ Cathedral Church of yᵉ Holy Trinity in Dublin

The Book of the Liffey

Peg Woffington appeared here in 1742. SS Michael and John's, which was designed by J. Taylor, was built principally by the voluntary work of Dublin tradesmen and was completed in 1815. The bell of the church was the first to ring the Angelus in Dublin since the Reformation. Alderman Carleton took exception to this and instituted legal proceedings to have the bell silenced but withdrew when the clergy of the parish engaged Daniel O'Connell to defend the case. A picture of this bell was used as a logo for the centenary celebrations of Catholic Emancipation in 1929.

The Bradogue River rises near Cabra and enters the Liffey at Ormond Quay. Chancery Street is on the site of the Pill or estuary of the Bradogue and is shown on Speed's map. The Pill was developed by the Cistercian monks and was known as the Little Harbour of St Mary's Abbey. In 1487, Lambert Simnel was vigorously supported in his claims to the English throne by Abbot Champfleur and was crowned with a diadem which is said to have been taken from the statue of Our Lady in St Mary's Abbey.

At the time of the Dissolution of the Monasteries in the 1530s, St Mary's Abbey was one of the wealthiest religious houses in Ireland but the religious fervour of the monks was at a very low ebb. The Chapter House was often the meeting place of Parliament and the Privy Council. In 1534, Garret Og, the Earl of Kildare, was summoned to London to answer a charge of high treason. While he was there it was falsely reported to his son, Silken Thomas, that the Earl had been executed. Thomas went to a meeting of the Privy Council, which was being held in St Mary's Abbey, and announced the commencement of his ill-fated rebellion.

All that remains of the monastery today is the Chapter House in Meetinghouse Lane and readers of *Ulysses* may remember how, in the 'Wandering Rocks' episode, J. J. O'Molloy comes here to have Ned Lambert guarantee a loan. Later in the novel, in

Smock Alley Theatre stood where the church of SS Michael and John is today. It was a popular focus of social life in the Dublin of the 17th century until, in 1701, the gallery collapsed causing several fatalities.

The Statue of KING GEORGE ye 1st on ESSEX BRIDGE

Essex Bridge. The flooding Liffey took care of both bridge and statue in 1751.

the 'Sirens' episode, the Reverend Hugh C. Love is seen at the corner of Capel Street having visited the Chapter House in the course of his historical research.

On 7th December 1922 gunmen killed Sean Hales, TD, and wounded Padraig O'Maille, the Deputy Speaker of the Dail outside the Ormond Hotel on Upper Ormond Quay. The Cabinet met that evening and decided that 'as a solemn warning to those . . . engaged in a conspiracy of assassination against representatives of the people' four of the Republican prisoners should be shot. Kevin O'Higgins signed the death warrants. The following morning Rory O'Connor, Liam Mellowes, Joseph McKelvey and Richard Barrett were executed. Rory O'Connor had been best man at the wedding of Kevin O'Higgins. The murderers of Sean Hales were never found.

Essex Bridge was built by Sir Humphrey Jervis in 1676 with materials from the ruins of St Mary's Abbey. In 1687 flood waters scoured the foundations of one of the piers and the ten-year-old bridge collapsed. The bridge was repaired and in 1722 an equestrian statue of George I was erected on it. In 1751 the bridge again collapsed and George Semple was engaged to carry out temporary repairs. Subsequently he was asked by the Corporation to submit a design for a new bridge. To ensure that the piers of this bridge would not be washed away he decided to use cofferdams to get down to the rock foundations. The bridge, which was modelled on Westminster Bridge, was completed in two years at a cost of £20,000. Based on this experience, Semple published in 1774 in Dublin one of the first important textbooks on Civil Engineering – *A Treatise on Building in Water*. The present bridge dates from 1875 and is named in honour of Henry Grattan. It is known as Capel Street Bridge.

Essex Bridge was a favourite pitch of Michael Moran - 'Zozimus' - whom W.B.Yeats called 'the last of the gleemen'. He was born in 1790 in Faddle Alley, off Blackpitts in the Liberties. Shortly after birth he became blind. Later he supported himself as a street

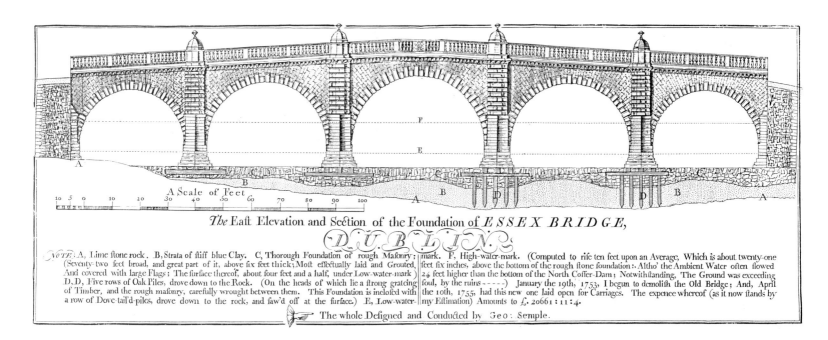

The East Elevation and Section of the Foundation of *ESSEX BRIDGE, DUBLIN.*

NOTE: A, Lime stone rock. B, Strata of stiff blue Clay. C, Thorough Foundation of rough Masonry; (Seventy-two feet broad, and great part of it, above six feet thick; Most effectually laid and Grouted, And covered with large Flags; The surface thereof, about four feet and a half, under Low-water-mark) D, D, Five rows of Oak Piles, drove down to the Rock. (On the heads of which lie a strong grating of Timber, and the rough masonry, carefully wrought between them. This Foundation is inclosed with a row of Dove-tail'd-piles, drove down to the rock, and saw'd off at the surface.) E, Low-water-mark. F, High-water-mark. (Computed to rise ten feet upon an Average, Which is about twenty-one feet six inches, above the bottom of the rough stone foundation: Altho' the Ambient Water often flowed 24 feet higher than the bottom of the North Coffer-Dam; Notwithstanding, The Ground was exceeding foul, by the ruins - - - - -) January the 19th, 1753, I begun to demolish the Old Bridge; And, April the 10th, 1755, had this new one laid open for Carriages. The expence whereof (as it now stands by my Estimation) Amounts to £. 20661 : 11 : 4.

The whole Designed and Conducted by Geo: Semple.

rhymer by reciting ballads and stories which he learned by rote. The name Zozimus comes from a poem by Dr Coyle, Bishop of Raphoe, on the 'Life, Conversion and Death of St Mary of Egypt, who was Discovered in the Wilderness by the pious Zozimus'. Some of Moran's own songs are still popular in Dublin, in particular 'The Finding of Moses':

> In Agypt's land contaygious to the Nile,
> Old Pharo's daughter went to bathe in style,
> She tuk her dip and came unto the land,
> And to dry her royal pelt she ran along the strand.
> A bull-rush tripped her, whereupon she saw
> A smilin' babby in a wad of straw .
> She tuk it up and said in accents mild
> 'Tare-an-ages, girls, which o' yez owns the child?'

Michael Moran died in 1846.

Capel Street to the Ha'penny Bridge

Jervis, having built Essex Bridge, went on to develop the part of the lands of St Mary's Abbey on which Capel Street, Mary Street and Jervis Street now stand. Capel Street rapidly became the most fashionable residential street in the city and, surprisingly, was considered to be both wide and commodious. Here the Mint, which issued the infamous brass money of James II, was built on what is now numbers 27 and 28 Capel Street. In the eighteenth century the street was the centre of the printing trade and in the nineteenth century O'Connell's Repeal Association was founded here. In the late eighteenth century the State Lottery Office was near the corner of Lower Ormond Quay. Fascination with the Lottery was so great that one enterprising imposter made some money by putting himself on show as one who had won £20,000.

Parliament Street, on the south side of the bridge, was the first street to be laid out by the Wide Streets Commissioners who were appointed by Parliament in 1757 to open a way from Essex Bridge to Dublin Castle. Sunlight Chambers are on the corner of Essex Quay. This extraordinary building, with its Florentine facade, was designed early this century as the Irish headquarters of Lever Brothers, the makers of Sunlight soap. Its two colourful friezes illustrate in terracotta the manufacture and the uses of soap. George Faulkner, the 'Prince of Dublin Printers' and the Dublin publisher of Jonathan Swift, lived on the corner of East Essex Street. Read's, the cutlers at number 4, is one of the oldest firms in the city, having been founded in 1670. It is said that this is the only shop in Dublin in which a left-handed potato-peeler can be bought.

The City Hall, which closes the view from Grattan Bridge, was designed by Thomas Cooley in 1769 as the Royal Exchange. Parliament provided the money for the site on Cork Hill and the building costs were raised through lotteries. In 1852 it became the City Hall. The Corporation meetings are held here and the mace and sword of the city and the records of the Corporation are kept in a safe in the Muniment Room.

The river at Wellington Quay, where the Custom House stood since 1620, was always congested with ships as many as eight deep at the quay. It was generally agreed

Mature and Stately, through Dublin City

A Prospect of the Custom House and Essex Bridge, DUBLIN. | Vuë de la Douane, et Dupont d'Essex, a DUBLIN.

The old Custom House which stood on Essex Quay, before the present one was built in 1791, further downriver to provide easier access for shipping. All buildings which stood directly over the river, as the one in centre picture here, were demolished in the mid-17th century to allow the clear passage along the quays which we enjoy today.

that the Custom House was too far up the river because of the danger of larger ships striking 'Standfast Dick', a rock in the channel opposite Liffey Street as already mentioned, when it was decided to build the present Custom House further down the river. It caused a storm of protests from all classes in the city and, in September 1781, Napper Tandy, then a member of the Corporation, led a mob to destroy the newly laid foundations of the building. Nevertheless, the building went ahead.

On Wellington Quay, near Eustace Street, the Poddle River passes unobtrusively through a grating into the Liffey. There is no trace now of the dark pool which, in ancient times, was formed by the confluence of the Poddle and the Liffey and which gave the city the name Dubhlinn. Over the centuries, as it flowed from Tallaght through Pimlico, the Coombe and Patrick Street, this little river provided water for the city and later served as its principal sewer.

The streets around Temple Bar still retain their seventeenth-century layout and their cobblestone paving. In 1259 an Augustinian monastery was founded between what is now Crow Street and Temple Bar. Later, in 1731, this site was occupied by the Crow Street Theatre. At the top of Fownes Street there are some eighteenth-century houses with their wide windows and panelled hall doors with cut stone surrounds. Brick built warehouses of the late eighteenth and early nineteenth centuries can still be seen in Temple Lane and Cecilia Street.

The fifteen-storey Central Bank seems to tower over the whole district. Designed by Stephenson Gibney and Associates, it was completed in 1978. As a building in Dublin it is unique insofar as all the floors are suspended from the roof. From the outset it was dogged by controversy and when the building was almost finished it was found to be almost thirty feet higher than the planning permission allowed. This has resulted in the steel roof girders being left uncovered which, from a distance, gives the building an unfinished appearance.

Lower Ormond Quay still has enough old houses to give people a romantic image of what the quays used to be like, but these houses, too, are soon to be demolished. Looking north from Swift's Row, the red brick mass of what was Jervis Street Hospital can be seen. Founded in 1718 by six Dublin surgeons, the Charitable Infirmary moved a number of times before it came to Jervis Street. In 1742, the proceeds of the first performance of Handel's Messiah were shared equally between the Society for Relieving Prisoners, Mercer's Hospital and the Charitable Infirmary. Jervis Street Hospital was closed in 1987.

Before Ormond Quay was built, Strand Street was one of the city's fashionable promenades. In 1933 the street was the scene of what later became known, rather grandly, as the Great Strand Street Siege. Some socialists had rented number 64 as their headquarters. In Lent, Cardinal MacRory, speaking of communists, said 'there is no room for them or their blasphemies among the children of St Patrick'. On 27th March the house was attacked by a crowd of about 200. The next evening the attack was renewed but by this time those inside were armed with three hand guns and an assortment of missiles which were hurled at the attackers before they succeeded in setting fire to the house. When the police arrived the socialists demanded, and eventually got, police protection and the mob dispersed quietly.

The Ha'penny (or Metal) Bridge was built in 1816 as a toll bridge to replace one of the Liffey ferries. It was one of the earliest cast-iron bridges in the world, and its elegant single span can be appreciated in this aerial view.

Mature and Stately, through Dublin City

Liffey Bridge, formerly Wellington Bridge or the Iron Bridge and now known as the Metal or the Ha'penny Bridge, was built in 1816 at the Bagnio's Slip ferry which is shown on Rocque's map (1756). Alderman Beresford and Mr William Walsh bought the tolls of the ferry and erected the bridge at a cost of £3,000. Originally it was intended as a short cut to the Crow Street Theatre and a toll of a ha'penny was charged. Various attempts to abolish the toll failed and the lease expired only in 1916. In 1913 a bizarre idea was mooted of building an art gallery over the river at this point, like the Ponte Vecchio in Florence, to house the collection of Sir Hugh Lane. W. B. Yeats, who said that he could see no merit in the Ha'penny Bridge, supported the idea and plans for the gallery were prepared by Sir Edwin Lutyens, but the proposal came to nothing. Lane, believing that a proper gallery for his collection would not be provided in Dublin, made a will leaving his pictures to the Tate Gallery in London.

The Ha'penny Bridge to O'Connell Street

On the open space outside the Dublin Woollen Company at the Ha'penny Bridge every weekend, fast talking salesmen sell an assortment of goods ranging from an all-purpose glass cutter to 'discontinued stock' from a continental chocolate factory. On Sunday mornings the star attraction used to be Hector Grey. Standing on a box, he demonstrated the quality of all his goods before offering them at bargain prices to his almost exclusively male audience. He was a Scotsman who went to sea when he was fourteen. He settled in Dublin in 1928 and set up business in Middle Abbey Street. He went on to become the millionaire doyen of the Irish toy trade and a household name in Dublin. He died in 1985.

A rare photograph of millionaire toy-merchant Hector Grey, at his regular Sunday morning post outside the Woollen Mills on Lr. Ormond Quay, offering bargains to Dubliners.

The fine granite building on the south side of the bridge is the Merchants' Hall which was designed by Frederick Darley and built in 1821. Merchants' Arch, which runs through the building, is the location of the bookshop where in *Ulysses* Leopold Bloom buys a book, 'The Sweets of Sin', for his wife, Molly.

In the nineteenth and early twentieth centuries, Aston Quay and Crampton Quay were the centre of the secondhand book trade. The Ballast Office was at the corner of Westmoreland Street and housed, before it was rebuilt, the headquarters of the Dublin Port and Docks Board. The clock, which is now on Aston Quay, was then on the Westmoreland Street front and was the most accurate public clock in the city. A time ball on the roof used fall at a signal from Dunsink Observatory at 1 pm Dublin time and later it fell at 1 pm Greenwich Mean Time. Two messengers were employed to bring a watch each day from Greenwich to check the accuracy of the clock.

Bachelors Walk was never a promenade for eligible young men but got its name from the property owner named Batchelor. In 1818, number 11 was the residence of Captain John d'Esterre, a member of Dublin Corporation. He was mortally wounded in a duel with Daniel O'Connell, because of a reference O'Connell made to 'the beggarly Corporation' of Dublin. There is no evidence to support the belief that after the duel O'Connell always wore white gloves when going to communion but it is recorded that O'Connell did settle an annuity on d'Esterre's daughter.

Carlisle Bridge was built in 1794 when the Custom House was moved to its present site. It was designed by James Gandon and was decorated with keystone heads, representing the Liffey and Neptune, by Edward Smyth. In 1880 it was rebuilt and widened to align with the width of Lower O'Connell Street, and Westmoreland Street and D'Olier Street which were laid out by the Wide Streets Commission in 1784. This redesigned bridge brought the axis of the city east to O'Connell Street.

The Anna Livia Water Feature, presented to the people of Dublin by Jefferson Smurfit Group plc. It was designed by Eamonn O'Doherty and erected in June 1988.

Down by the Liffey Side

Oh 'twas down by Anna Liffey
   my love and I did stray.
Where in the good old Liffey mud
   the seagulls sport and play.
We got the whiff of ray and chips
   and Mary softly sighed
'Yerra, John, come along for a one and one
   down by the Liffey side.'

And up to Rabiotti's together we did go.
And the rapture there that filled our hearts
   no poet e'er could know.
We started eating one and ones
   and Mary softly sighed
'Oh I'd live for ever eating chips
   down by the Liffey side.'

Then out along by George's Street
   the loving pairs to view
While Mary swanked it like a queen
   in a suit of royal blue.
Her coat was newly turned
   and her blouse was newly dyed
And you couldn't match her amber locks
   down by the Liffey side.

And it's on her oul' melodeon
   so sweetly she did play
'Goodbye and don't sigh'
   and 'Rule Britann-i-ay'.
But when she turned Sinn Féiner
   sure me heart near burst with pride
For to hear her sing the Soldier's Song
   down by the Liffey side.

And on Sunday morning early
   to Meath Street we will go
And it's up to Father Murphy
   we both will make our vow,
And he'll join our hands in wedlock bands
   and soon we'll be outside
For the whole afternoon on our honeymoon
   down by the Liffey side.

The O'Connell Monument by John Henry Foley was erected in 1854. The larger than life-size figure of O'Connell stands over a drum which depicts the Irish people in thirty figures. Around the base are four winged Victories which also represent the attributes of the Liberator Eloquence, Fidelity, Courage and Patriotism. As a result of the fighting in 1916 there are bullet holes in the figure of O'Connell and in three of the winged figures.

Carlisle Bridge to Dublin's Dockland

Eden Quay, which at one time formed part of Bachelors Walk, was first called Iron Quay and derives its name from William Eden who was Chief Secretary in 1782. The cinema, Screen at O'Connell Bridge, was formerly The Corinthian but was known to young cinema goers as The Ranch because it specialised in cowboy films starring Roy Rogers or William Boyd, who played Hopalong Cassidy. Around the corner in Marlborough Street is the Abbey Theatre. In 1904, W. B. Yeats and Lady Gregory, with the generous financial support of Mrs Annie Horniman, were two of the principal founders. The Abbey's first great period came after the riots of 1907 over J. M. Synge's comedy 'The Playboy of the Western World'. This play established the theatre's international reputation which was confirmed with the production of Sean O'Casey's three masterpieces 'The Shadow of a Gunman', 'The Plough and the Stars' and 'Juno and the Paycock'. The original building was burnt down in 1951 but was redesigned by Michael Scott and the new theatre was opened in 1966.

At the turn of the century the Northumberland Hotel stood at the corner of Eden Quay and Beresford Place. In March 1912 it became Liberty Hall, the headquarters of the Irish Transport and General Workers Union which had been established in January 1909. It was from here that the workers were organised during the 1913 Dublin Lock-out. On Easter Sunday 1916 the Proclamation of the Irish Republic was printed here. On Easter Monday the main column of the Irish Volunteers and Irish Citizen Army, under the command of Padraic Pearse and James Connolly, marched from here to take possession of the General Post Office in O'Connell Street. Although only a caretaker had been left in the building, it was shelled on Wednesday, 26th April, by the British gun-boat 'Helga'. The old building was demolished in 1964 and the present glass and concrete structure, designed by Rea O'Kelly, was erected in its place. At the time a humorous magazine commented that as a union headquarters it seemed to lean a little to the right.

On Burgh Quay at the junction of Hawkins Street an unattractive squat memorial commemorates the bravery of Constable Patrick Sheahan of the DMP. At this spot on 5th May 1905 he succeeded in rescuing two men who had been overcome by sewer gas down a manhole before he himself collapsed and died.

In 841 the Vikings marked their first landing place in the Liffey Estuary by setting up their Long Stone or Stein at what is now the southern end of Hawkins Street. This stood here well into the seventeenth century. In 1985 a new Stein by sculptress Cliodna Cussen was erected to mark this spot.

The facade of the Merchants' Warehousing Company on Burgh Quay is typical of the shop fronts that were specified by the Wide Streets Commission in the eighteenth century. These usually consisted of a large window with a door on either side, one of which was the entrance to the shop.

During the nineteenth century in a large hall in the Corn Exchange Building, which was erected in 1816, samples of corn were exhibited on market days. Only the facade of

The Wreck of the Vartry

It was the good ship *Vartry*
 That sailed the sweet Liffee,
And the Skipper had taken the casks aboard,
 A goodly companee.

Blue were the labels, an azure blue
 Proclaiming the Double X,
But nayther the Skipper nor the crew
 Had dreamt of storms or wrecks.

Now as she steam'd by the Ha'penny Bridge,
 The engine raised a row,
While a cloud no bigger than a midge
 Loomed up on the Starboard bow.

And as they steered by Aston's Quay,
 The look-out man grew pale,
'I feared we'd not escape,' says he,
 'MacBirney's Summer Sale!'

And ere they reached the Customs House,
 Down in a wild vortex,
The *Vartry* plunged, the cause was plain,
 She'd too much Double X.

All ye who drink of James's Gate,
 (No matter what your sex),
Take warning by the *Vartry*'s fate,
 Thro' too much Double X!

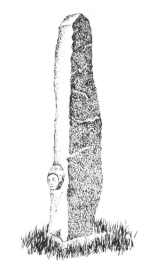

The new 'Stein' by Cliodna Cussen stands at College Green, on the spot where the Viking founders of Dublin erected their Long Stein or Stein soon after their arrival, and where it stood for over 700 years.

the building now remains. Next door was Conciliation Hall, now the Irish Press office. Daniel O'Connell, who built the Hall as the headquarters for his Repeal Association in 1843, addressed many meetings there. Later it was used as a corn store before it was converted into the Tivoli Music Hall in 1897. It was taken over by the Irish Press in 1931. The ground floor shows some remnants of the original facade.

Butt Bridge was built in 1878 but was then popularly known as the Swivel Bridge and was described as being useful rather than decorative. It was rebuilt as a conventional bridge in 1932 and was renamed Congress Bridge but continued to be known as Butt Bridge.

In 1891 the Loop Line Bridge was built to connect Pearse Station (Westland Row) with Connolly Station (Amiens Street). While it was being built some publicans in the area sold porter at a discount of a ha'penny a pint (1½d instead of 2d) to the labourers working on the line and those pints were known as 'loopliners'.

The Custom House is probably the most imposing building in Dublin. The architect, James Gandon, came to Ireland in 1781 on the invitation of the Rt. Hon. John Beresford, to oversee the completion of the building. The central portico is surmounted by a statue of Commerce, with her anchor, on an impressive dome. The tympanum, over four doric columns, shows Hibernia embracing Britannia while Neptune drives off Despair and Famine, which must have seemed ironic during the 1840s. This is by Edward Smyth as are the royal arms on the pavilions and the riverine heads on the keystones of the ground floor. The rivers depicted in these heads, starting at the main door and going left are: the Liffey, Erne, Foyle, Slaney, Nore, Suir, Lagan, Lee, Shannon, Bann, the Atlantic Ocean, the Blackwater, Barrow and the Boyne. The four figures on the north elevation represent Europe, Asia, Africa and America.

The Custom House was burnt on 25th May 1921 in an effort to bring the civil administration of the country to a halt. The IRA men arrived in lorries and ordered the staff out before setting the building ablaze. The time taken by the evacuation enabled the Black and Tans to come on the scene and a battle ensued in which five IRA men were killed and a further eighty were wounded. In the garden on the north side of the building there is a memorial to the men who died.

Behind the Custom House is the Busaras, the central bus station, which was designed by Michael Scott and built in 1953. At the time it caused as much controversy as the Custom House had in the 1780s but today, in spite of its awkward siting, it is recognised as one of the better post-war buildings in the city.

(Opposite) A lively view of Burgh Quay, the Corn Exchange, in 1820, with the 'new' Custom House in the background (by Brocas). The White House pub still juts out from the line of buildings, as shown here. The Tivoli Theatre stood where the Irish Press building is now. Notice the then 'new' style of door and window design as recommended by the Wide Streets Commission, and still to be seen on the Merchants' Warehouse building.

The Custom House bears sculptured heads by Edward Smyth representing the Irish Rivers. The impressions shown on these pages are by Jan de Fouw.

LIFFEY   ERNE   FOYLE   SLANEY

Mature and Stately, through Dublin City

NORE

SUIR

LAGAN

LEE

Contrast in styles: the Custom House and Liberty Hall.

SHANNON

BANN

BLACKWATER

BOYNE

(Top left) The Irish House stood on the corner of Wood Quay and Winetavern Street. It was demolished to make way for the Civic Offices.

Below:

(Left) The Ashling Hotel, Parkgate Street. The philosopher Ludwig Wittgenstein spent much of the years 1948 and 1949 living in Dublin, in this hotel which was then known as Ross's. His work during that time is regarded as having changed the whole nature of philosophical thought. A plaque was erected in his honour in May 1988.

(Right) The proposed Custom House Docks Development, begun in 1988.

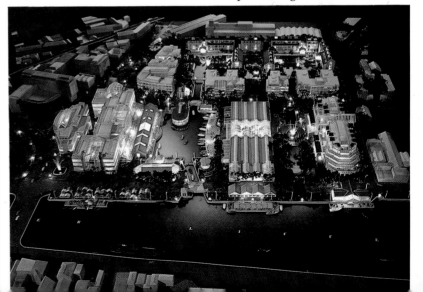

Sunlight Chambers, on the corner of Essex Street. Its wonderful terracotta friezes illustrate the manufacture and use of soap.

Read's the Cutlers, at No. 4 Parliament Street, pictured here with its proprietor, is one of the oldest shops in Dublin.

The Earliest Vikings?

When the Garden of Remembrance was being laid out at Islandbridge, a number of Viking graves were found. They seemed to belong to a cemetery associated with the very earliest Viking arrivals in Ireland, dating to the early part of the ninth century.

In the last century a large group of Viking graves were found not far away in Kilmainham, and near the railway-line foundations. These produced a rich hoard of weapons and jewellery, much of it now in the National Museum. The immensely rewarding excavations in the Christ Church area have so far not yielded material earlier than the 10th century. This would seem to indicate that the Islandbridge/Kilmainham settlement was the first base of these rovers, even before they set up the settlement on the shallow tidal banks down-river which were gradually embanked to form Wood Quay.

The Irish National War Memorial

Sir Edwin Lutyens designed the Garden of Remembrance at Islandbridge. It commemorates the almost 50,000 Irishmen who were killed in the 1914-18 War.

It occupies an area of about 20 acres, and is overlooked by Magazine Hill in the Phoenix Park. Lutyens' ground plan shows the avenues of trees leading to the gardens, but the scale is deceptive, insofar as the actual garden occupies only a small portion of the plan.

The great central cross, the pavilions, pools, terraces, fountains and pergolas are of noble proportion. The entire construction was undertaken by hand in order to give as much employment as possible, and the workforce was made up half and half of ex-soldiers from the British and Irish armies. The ground had to be levelled to a depth of 15 feet, and some of the stones, which had to be manoeuvred into places using only primitive hand-winches and a couple of telegraph poles, weighed up to eight tons. The Memorial was completed in 1937.

The Gardens fell into decay over the years and were greatly vandalized. The Office of Public Works has recently refurbished and replanted them and, with the banks of roses and avenues of flowering shrubs flourishing, it is a place of great calm, dignity and beauty. It deserves to be better known, and visited by more people.

The main gateway is on Con Colbert Road, but this is a difficult place to park a car. The best entry is by the hurling field off the South Circular Road, opposite Clancy Barracks, about 100 yards down from Islandbridge. A proper car park is planned for the riverside.

In 1978 the Talbot Memorial Bridge was opened. This functional concrete structure commemorates Matt Talbot, a Dubliner whose case for beatification is being examined in Rome.

Custom House Quay was, until 1978, the berth for the Guinness cross channel ships and the quayside was usually stacked high with barrels. Some of the old men who habitually played cards in the western arcade of the Custom House were known as 'Hoggers' in the 1940s. They used to drink the dregs from the empty hogsheads which they emptied into the rim of an upturned barrel. Unfortunately for them the rims were marked with a paint which left tell-tale marks on their clothes and faces. When a British photo-magazine ran a feature on them the police descended on the Hoggers and brought their drinking to an abrupt end.

The Custom House Docks are a complex of bonded warehouses grouped around St George's Dock and the Inner Dock. Ships with wine, spirits or tobacco and later some of those with coal used to dock here. There is now a huge development plan for the area under which the existing waterways are to be preserved while around them a financial centre, a museum of modern art, an hotel, and a residential and shopping area are to be built. The whole development will take five years to complete and should be a major factor in moving the axis of the city further east along the river.

Today the warehouses along the North and South Walls are empty and derelict but when the quays were in use the South Wall generally catered for ships carrying fruit, coal and general cargoes, while the North Wall dealt with passenger ships for Liverpool and the Isle of Man, and the ships carrying cattle to Britain and horses to the continent.

Near New Guild Street on the North Wall is the lifting bridge which gives on to Spencer Dock and the terminus of the Royal Canal. There is a major marshalling yard for container traffic near New Wapping Street and in front of the Transtrack depot there is a tree – admittedly it is a pitiful specimen, but it is the only one in the whole of the North Wall area. A little further east are the offices of Irish Rail in what used to be an hotel for cross channel passengers to and from this country. The rather comic statue of the Mariner by John Behan is at the corner of Castleforbes Road and what used to be the railway depot is at the point of the Wall.

The public houses in the docks area may open at 7.30 a.m. as the licence in Kennedy's of George's Quay reads: ' for the considerable number of persons following their lawful trades and callings in the vicinity of this premises'. For the most part, the early morning customers are night workers, such as hotel staff, going off duty.

The Gothic church of the Immaculate Heart of Mary on City Quay was built in 1863 to serve the needs of the dockers and those living nearby. Today the dockers work more than a mile down river and many of the local people have been moved to remote areas on the outer edges of the city. Some have been fortunate enough to be rehoused in one of the Corporation's more imaginative schemes further down the quay.

Windmill Lane, off Sir John Rogerson's Quay, recalls the windmill which stood here until quite late in the nineteenth century. It figured in an engraving of a view from Westland Row Station when the Kingstown Railway was opened in 1834.

Numbers 30-32 of Sir John Rogerson's Quay incorporate the massive keystone heads of Neptune and the Liffey from the old Carlisle Bridge.

The gasometer on the corner of Cardiff Lane, long since disused, is still a city landmark. All gasometers are obsolete since natural gas is now piped directly from the fields off the Cork coast. Rumour has it that a brewing company wished to paint the gasometer as a colossal pint of beer but planning permission was refused.

From here to the Point of the South Wall, most of the streets are cobbled and

The Liffey Ferries

The last of Dublin's ferries made its final crossing on Sunday the 21st of October 1984, from Sir John Rogerson's Quay to the North Wall. For the sad and merry occasion, the citizens of Dublin were invited to travel free. They turned up in style, young and old, rich and poor, and on that last morning several crowded crossings were made, presided over by Lord Mayor Michael O'Halloran.

The ferry had served Dublin well for over four hundred years, from 1668 when there was only one bridge across the river, the one built around 1215 where Fr. Mathew Bridge now stands, linking Church Street and Bride Street. Under a Charter issued by King Charles II (it is now preserved in the Archives at the City Hall) the ferry was to start one hour before sunrise and stop one hour after sunset. The passenger fare was to be one halfpenny, and for a horse, one penny.

Through most of those centuries there were three different ferry-points and, as new bridges were added, the ferries moved downriver towards the sea.

When Carlisle Bridge (now O'Connell Bridge) was built in 1794 it took a lot of traffic away from the ferries so that it was proposed to scrap the upper routes altogether and build a new toll-bridge for the use of pedestrians. This was how the desolate. One of the streets is aptly named Misery Hill. Forbes Street still has a length of track for a miniature railway which hauled the coal to the yards behind the quays as it was unloaded by hand from the ships. Today six four-ton cranes stand marooned on the quayside. The whole area shows the dereliction typical of a transition period when a locality is undergoing a change of use.

The Harbour Master's house is boarded up at the entrance to the Grand Canal Docks. The docks were built in 1796 but were never a commercial success due to the silting of the entrance by the Dodder River. The names of the three locks are incised on the stone — Westmoreland Lock, Buckingham Lock, Camden Lock — and each is dated 1796.

Looking south, the tidal reaches of the Dodder are elegantly framed by Ringsend bridge, built in 1802.

Ringsend still retains a community atmosphere. The natives of Ringsend, or Raytown as it is sometimes known, always regarded themselves as a race apart and did not approve of one of their own marrying an outsider from 'over the bridge'. Between the seventeenth and the eighteenth centuries the packet boat from Britain arrived here before it was moved, first, to Howth and then to Kingstown (Dun Laoghaire). One of the more unwelcome visitors to arrive here in 1649 was Oliver Cromwell with 12,000 men and artillery.

In 1984 the East Link Toll Bridge, which connects East Wall with Ringsend, was opened to give easy access from the north-eastern suburbs to those in the south-east of the city and it opened up a real possibility of the development of the areas on the Liffey below the Talbot Memorial Bridge. ●

Metal Bridge came into being. It was opened in 1816 and, as users were to be charged the same amount as for the ferry crossing, it became known ever after as the Ha'penny Bridge.

During the 19th century ferries plied between City Quay and the Custom House and between Sir John Rogerson's Quay and the North Wall. The opening of Butt Bridge in 1879 almost sounded the death knell of the Liffey ferries, but to maintain the service Dublin Corporation took over the operation. In 1952 the number using the ferry was 434,000, in 1984 it was only 15,000. The fare had risen in four centuries from ½p to 10p!

The opening of Matt Talbot Bridge in 1980 and, finally the Toll Bridge on 21st October 1984, brought about the inevitable.

The last ferry sailed at 2.30 pm on Sunday 21st October, to the cheers and songs of Dubliners. ●

The East Link Toll Bridge.

. . . and to the Sea

It is at the place where the Liffey meets the sea that it had been transformed most radically. Three hundred years ago the mouth of the river looked much as God made it. Few signs of man were visible other than the occasional small ship traversing the winding, shallow channels or anchored in one of the pools near where the Liffey's last tributaries, the Tolka and the Dodder, join it from the north and from the south. The full story of the creation of Dublin Port is told in detail elsewhere. I hope to show, in a short space, how the Liffey and Dublin as a port were in conflict and in harmony down the centuries.

There was sea trade at Dublin before the Norsemen came. It was a natural place for it with its easy access to the hinterland. The Norse Kingdom of Dublin had its tiny port with wharves and jetties at Wood Quay and from this nucleus there grew, very slowly at first, the great Port of Dublin.

By the 12th century Dublin had about 200 ships trading with Britain and the Continent. Wine, wool, spices and other luxuries moved up river and hides, livestock and surplus food moved down. Through the Middle Ages the frontage on the river hardly grew. The first quays were built in the early 17th century after an explosion of gunpowder had devastated the old port area in 1597. The north side was still fretted with little inlets which are shown in Speed's map of 1610, but later in the century the walling of each side of the Liffey here began to give it something of its present aspect.

Trade was good in those days. In 1652 Gerard Boate was writing that Dublin was 'frequented with more ships and hath greater importation of more things than any other harbour in the Kingdom'. This was in spite of political upheavals. There was, in fact, no longer a Kingdom and Cromwell had landed only three years before at Ringsend with his 12,000 troops.

The Liffey was now embanked down to the present Townsend Street and Burgh Quay area, near where lepers sailed for Compostella in the Middle Ages, Lazar Hill. From there a great stride towards the sea was made when Sir John Rogerson walled in the strand as far as the Dodder, where the quay that bears his name now stands.

But the Harbour of Dublin was in a wretched state. There was no safe anchorage and it was so shallow that ships preferred to discharge part of their cargoes at Dalkey or into lighters in the lower part of the river. In 1674 the engineer Andrew Yarranton reported that 'the badness of the Harbour did occasion the decay of trade'. It was 'wild, open and exposed to every wind'. The sandbanks were constantly shifting and the largest of these sandbanks, known as the North and South Bulls, 'had been the graves of thousands'. At low tide one could walk dry footed around ships at anchor.

The river, furthermore, had been much damaged by the removal or dumping of gravel which was used for ballast in those days.

The work of rectifying all this, a formidable task, was given to a committee of the City Corporation in 1707. The Ballast Committee built gabbards, or barges, to supply ballast to ships at a fee. There was also some primitive dredging and the channel was deepened a little to prevent the river spreading out into many branches across the sands.

The strand between the Liffey and the Tolka began to be reclaimed and the beginnings of the North Wall were laid down in the form of a line of wicker baskets filled with stones. Between the north and south walls the Liffey was now straight where previously it was divided into two curving streams.

Then the Ballast committee turned its attention to the river beyond Ringsend. It was hoped that a line of piles driven into the bed might restrain the movements of sand from the South Bull into the river and straighten the channel. The piles proved expensive to maintain and not very satisfactory in keeping out the creeping sands. Something better was called for.

The Great South Wall was a mighty undertaking and when completed towards the end of the 18th century it was one of the longest sea walls in the world. On the one hand its blocks of Dalkey granite had stopped the drifting sand and given some small shelter to ships as well as making the river a little deeper by concentrating the current. On the other hand it cost about £200,000 to build and took a very long time to complete.

Waxie's Dargle

Says my aul' one to your aul' one
Will yeh come to the Waxie's Dargle
Says your aul' one to my aul' one
Shure I haven't got a farthin'
I've just been down to Monto Town
To see young Kill McArdle
But he wouldn't lend me half a crown
To go to the Waxie's Dargle

Chorus
What are yeh havin'
Will yeh have a pint
Yes I'll have a pint
With you sir
And if one of yeh doesn't order soon
We'll be thrown out of the boozer

Says my aul' one to your aul' one
Will yeh come to the Galway Races
Says your aul' one to my aul' one
With the price of me aul' lad's braces
I went down to Capel Street
To the Jew man money lenders
But they wouldn't give me a couple a bob
On my aul' lad's red suspenders

Chorus
Says my aul' one to your aul' one
We have no beef or mutton
But if we go down to Monto Town
We might get a drink for nuttin'
Here's a piece of advice
I got from an aul' fishmonger
When food is scarce and you see the hare
You'll know you have died of hunger

The Waxie's Dargle was the strand or foreshore at the Irishtown end of Sandymount. The Waxies were the shoemakers. The 'quality' had their picnics at the Dargle Valley in Wicklow. The waxies couldn't afford to travel so far, and happily made do with Sandymount. An inscribed granite boulder erected by Dublin Corporation honours the spot, now part of a large area of reclaimed land.

In fact it was completed by a body other than the Ballast Committee. An independent authority had been created to undertake the running of the Port of Dublin.

John Beresford was a power in the land in the late 18th century. He was much involved in Port matters, from laying the foundation stone of Carlisle Bridge, which was to cut off the old port area from shipping, to inviting Gandon to build the splendid new Custom House downriver. The merchants had opposed him to the extent of rowdy demonstrations against moving the centre of gravity of maritime Dublin away from their old haunts. In his next enterprise they supported him. He promoted a Bill in Grattan's Parliament to create the Corporation for Preserving and Improving the Port of Dublin. This replaced the rather discredited Ballast Committee. Beresford went on to help abolish the Irish Parliament, but he had put the Port on a new course.

It was in 1786 when the new authority, usually called the Ballast Board for obvious reasons, was set up. It faced massive problems. Trade was expanding, ships were larger than ever before, the Custom House had given a magnificence to the river, but commercial expansion was being frustrated by the still shallow Harbour, the sandbanks and that wide expanse of sand across the entrance to the Liffey, the bar.

Sand bars are produced by the action of a river current and tidal currents where it joins the sea. The depth on the Dublin bar at low water was a paltry six feet. Even relatively small ships had to wait in the hazardous Bay for high tide; large ships could not come up to Dublin at all. In the last year of the 18th century ships to the value of £113,000 had been lost in Dublin Bay. As late as 1807 hundreds of bodies were strewn along the sands of Merrion from the wreck of two troop-ships.

As is the custom today, consultants were called in. The most famous of these was Captain William Bligh R.N., late of H.M.S. 'Bounty'. Bligh produced the first modern-style chart of Dublin Bay and prepared a long report. Most of the experts, including Bligh, suggested some form of wall on the north side of the river to increase its flow and remove sand from the bar by tidal scour. There was no agreement on where the wall should be placed. The great engineer John Rennie declared the whole question to be one of the most difficult to face a civil engineer.

Some of the consultants wanted to circumvent the whole problem by having a canal built from Dun Laoghaire or some other outport to Dublin on which goods could be transported by barge from ships offloaded there. Bligh rightly attacked this once seductive idea as being ultimately destructive to Dublin Port.

In the end the problem was solved by the Ballast Board's own engineer, George Halpin, who built the Bull Wall in the early 1820s on a plan previously suggested by others but brilliantly modified and executed by him. By enclosing a great body of water within the Harbour which, on the turn of the tide would produce a long, steady and powerful outward current, the Bull Wall brought about a dramatic lowering of the level of the bar in the years that followed its completion. It also prevented the encroachment of the North Bull sands into the river and, in time, caused the creation of Bull Island, to the great benefit of the citizens of Dublin.

Meanwhile expansion had taken place in the Port. The Grand Canal Docks had been opened with great pomp in 1796 but they never prospered. The Custom House Docks, opened in the 1820s, had more success and in its early years was an important part of the Port. Later the importance of the Docks dwindled as ships grew too big to enter them but the surrounding warehouses became ultimately the largest warehouse complex in Ireland.

The effects of the Bull Wall and the subsequent extensive dredging operations so increased the depth at the entrance to the Port that by 1886 the largest ship in the world,

The Grand Canal Docks is an intriguing backwater little visited by Dubliners. The beautifully constructed triple lock system is worth inspecting.

Captain Bligh sailed in Dublin Bay

Cruel, rigid, tyrannical: that is the popular image of Captain William Bligh (1754-1817), a man whose mastery of the H.M.S. Bounty was so brutal that his crew were driven to mutiny, a step punishable by death.

The bones of the story of which a famous film was made were true, but the character of Bligh was somewhat maligned as portrayed by Charles Laughton. A rigid disciplinarian, he was also a distinguished and courageous commander and a brilliant navigator. His rough ways did earn him the name of Bully Bligh. He was also called Bread-fruit Bligh, a name he earned as a naval rating when he travelled with James Cook on his second voyage around the world, the trip on which bread-fruit was discovered.

His involvement with Dublin Bay arose through the seemingly endless efforts over the centuries to make Dublin Bay, with its shoals and shifting sandbanks, safe for shipping, as ships got bigger.

Bligh, because of his reputation as a skilled navigator and surveyor, was commissioned in 1800 to survey the mouth of the river and, in his own words, 'to state whatever may occur to me as likely to be of advantage in improving the harbour, assisting the navigation or affording shelter and safety to vessels under circumstances of distress or hazard'.

His map and report of the harbour and bay is today in the archives of Dublin Port and Docks Board. It is regarded as a model of its kind.

The subsequent building of the Bull Wall and the South Wall, so making Dublin port at last safe and accessible to shipping, owes much to his charting and his recommendations.

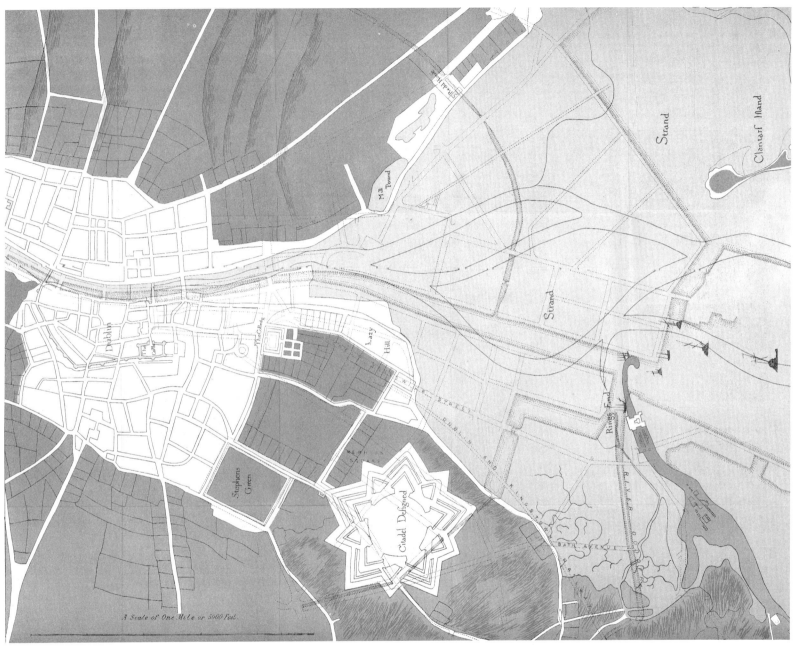

In this Map by de Gomme dated 1673, the isolated position of Ringsend can be clearly seen, and the mudflats which separated it from Dublin.

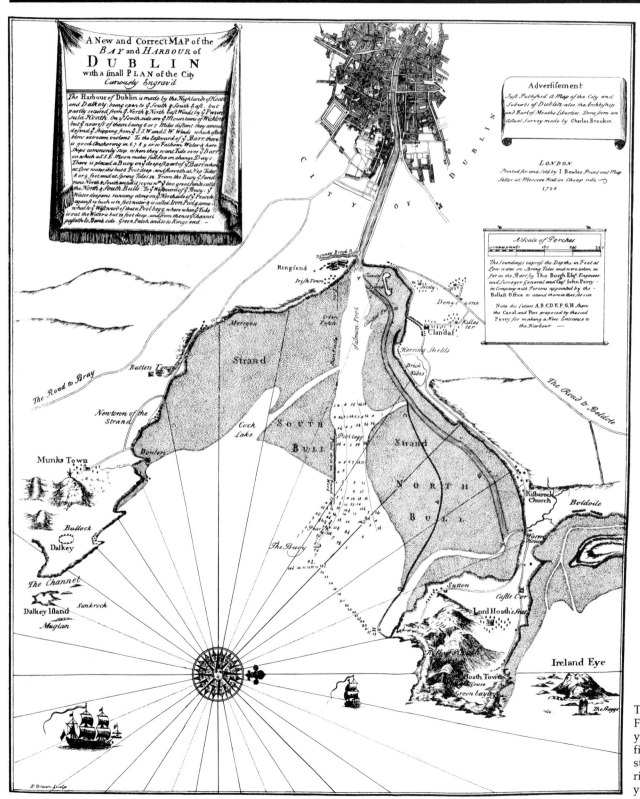

Map of Dublin City and Bay
'from an Actual Survey made
by Chas. Brookin in 1728.'

Bay and Harbour of Dublin.
A.D. 1728.

The city is now rapidly expanding
From a population of 40,000 in the
year 1700, it jumps to 150,000 just
fifty years later. Open countryside
still extends to the mouth of the
river shown as the 'Salmon pool' if
you please!

. . . and to the Sea

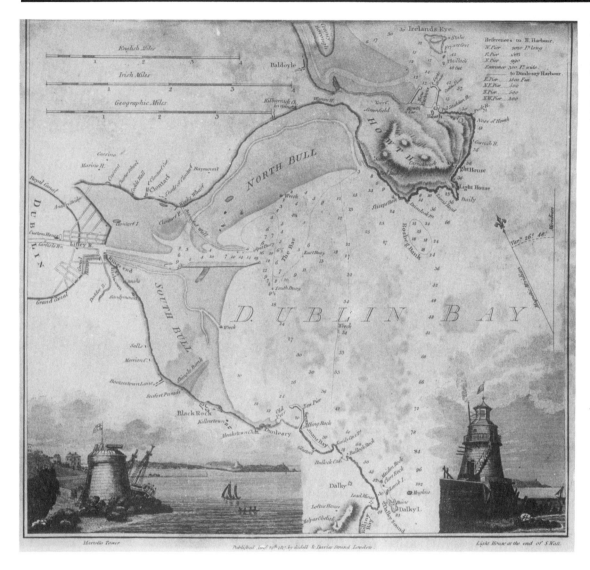

By the time of this map, 1817, the South Wall was completed. The 'Intended Wall' shown on the north side had been proposed by several people, including Bligh, with variations. The Wall as finally built in the early 1820s was designed by the Ballast Board's engineer, George Halpin.

the 'Great Eastern', could come safely up to the North Wall Extension where, it might be added, it wasn't wanted by the Port Authorities!

The great expansion of the Port of Dublin, begun by the Ballast Board, was accelerated by its successor from 1867, the Dublin Port and Docks Board. The originality of engineers and the labour of armies of men made a new Port, mostly out of the mud of the Liffey itself. The Alexandra Basin was formed, surrounded by quays and to its north and east land reclamation on a huge scale was undertaken. In the 1870s the North Wall Extension was built by machines designed by the Port Engineer, Bindon Stoney, and on advanced principles. From 1922 a revolutionary method of constructing quays was employed involving the building of huge concrete caissons, launched like ships, towed into position and sunk in rows. It was the same idea as was used in 1944 during the Normandy invasion, but well ahead of its time. This system of quay construction was used in Dublin with great success until long after the Second World War.

Reclamation was carried out on the Dutch system, and indeed was assisted at times by Dutch dredgers. This involved the building of walls enclosing large areas of shallow water which were then covered by Liffey mud pumped in. The new land thus created became the foundation of a great Port complex. On it rose sheds, warehouses, storage areas and quay areas served by roads and railways.

After the War a second Graving Dock was built. The first, opened in 1860, is still operating. Oil berths and a huge oil zone were completed. In more recent times the B & I and Sealink berths were built where there had been sea in the 1950s. Later again a whole new section of the Port was created on the south side for containers.

All change causes disruption. The river in Victorian times was packed with shipping. From O'Connell Bridge a forest of masts stretched towards the sea. Amongst the ships moved tugs, little boats, shuttling ferries. When sail gave way to steam, lines of steamers crowded the berths on the river and in the Basin. The older Dubliner will recall the Guinness barges carrying the barrels from the brewery to the Port. 'Bring us back a parrot', the children would shout as they puffed by and they would watch keenly to see if the crew would forget to pull down the hinged funnel in time before it struck one of the bridges. All this has gone and the relatively empty quays near the City cause people to think that the Port is dead. The opposite is true.

In the old days ships were many but they were small. Hundreds passed in and out of Dublin in a week but they carried far less than the fewer but much greater vessels of today. Being big, the modern ships must berth at deepwater berths down river, almost out of sight of the Dublin man-in-the-street. In spite of recent setbacks more tonnage than ever before now passes through Dublin Port.

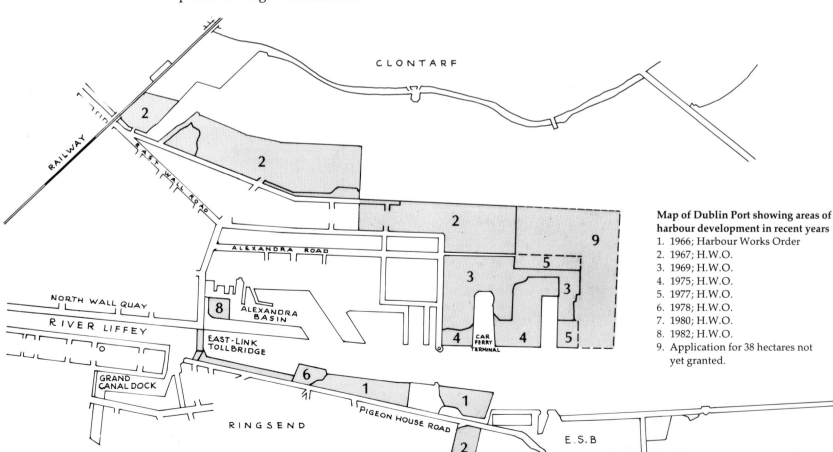

Map of Dublin Port showing areas of harbour development in recent years
1. 1966; Harbour Works Order
2. 1967; H.W.O.
3. 1969; H.W.O.
4. 1975; H.W.O.
5. 1977; H.W.O.
6. 1978; H.W.O.
7. 1980; H.W.O.
8. 1982; H.W.O.
9. Application for 38 hectares not yet granted.

. . . and to the Sea

Once the Liffey quays were bustling, crowded, noisy, dirty, full of men, carts, confusion. All this has gone. Modern cargo handling and the container revolution has transformed the scene in Dublin as in all other major ports. Jobs have gone too, but so also has back-breaking labour, dirt, dire poverty, much danger and often early death. The old days were not all that good for those who lived and worked down by the Liffeyside, however colourful they may seem in retrospect.

Not all activities on the Liffey are commercial. For centuries people have boated, sailed, fished and swum here. The Ringsend Regatta and the Liffey Swim were part of the annual calendar of Liffey life. Clusters of yachts are moored near East Link Bridge. Pleasure steamers have carried crowds from the Liffey quays for trips in the Bay or along the coast. Even in the distant past the pleasures of the Liffey were known to Dubliners. In the 1760s boatloads of sightseers were carried down to view the Poolbeg Lighthouse under construction. Perhaps the Norsemen too enjoyed the occasional pleasure trip.

The deadly Dublin Bay has lost its terrors. Modern vessels, power-driven, with all the navigational aids of modern technology, in constant communication with the Port, piloted by Port Board pilots and supplied with tugs as required, find Dublin amongst the easiest ports in which to navigate. This is true even of those car-carriers of awe-inspiring bulk that river-side wits have called 'Liberty Hall on its side'.

Those picturesque maps of the 17th and 18th centuries which show such places in Dublin Bay as Cock Lake, Clontarf Island, the Green Patch and the Poolbeg, the oyster beds and the great sand banks, bear no resemblance to modern charts of the Bay. It seems to be a different place, and perhaps it is.

And so Anna Liffey's marriage to Neptune, once a stormy and troubled one, has been transformed by men, many men, into a union which is fruitful and prosperous.

Like all rivers always present yet always passing, the Liffey, our quiet benefactress, moves silently through the great Port and out between the lighthouses and the nodding buoys to melt and vanish into the great waters. •

Custom House Conversation Piece. Britain and Ireland united, seated on a marine chariot drawn by seahorses, while Neptune banishes famine and despair!

South Wall - the ultimate wilderness

The great South Wall separates the sands of Dublin Bay from the main stream of Anna Liffey. In the days of her freedom, she wandered across the sand flats, until the harbour engineers of the 18th century constrained her. They created a final stretch of wilderness, a wonderful mile and a half of footpath, free from cars and so uneven and unsheltered that none but the most enlightened of wayfarers use it. The breakwater is made mainly from granite boulders, with a paving of roughly dressed stone. On the outer side of the wall, enormous hewn blocks of granite, limestone and andesite are piled to absorb the force of the waves. It is not an ideal spot for finding wild flowers, though a few grasses and the white-flowered scurvy grass somehow find a living space in the crevices of the paving.

From early autumn until springtime, the South Wall is an excellent spot for looking at a variety of seabirds. At low tide, the sand flats are busy with many gulls, with large flocks of oyster-catchers and smaller numbers of sanderling. The oyster-catchers are black-and-white, with strong red bill. They find few oysters, but thrive on the enormous population of cockles which bury themselves a little below the surface of the sand. The sanderling are small, silver birds which dash about at the edge of the tide, catching tiny shrimps. The scientific name of the sanderling is *canutus* because, like the good king, they defy the tides.

Seaweeds grow on the stones at the edge of the breakwater. They are the haunt of the turnstone and the purple sandpiper. The turnstone has bright, tortoise-shell colouring, while the purple sandpiper is a greyish purple. Other birds swim in the Liffey or in the deeper water outside the wall. The cormorant is the most regular visitor, but in winter there is nearly always a merganser, a scruffy duck with a red bill which eats fish. As well as the regulars, most of the birds which visit the North Bull nature reserve stop by the South Wall now and again.

In the warmer months the birds of the sand flats go away to breed in distant lands to the north. They are replaced by the terns, graceful white, swallow-tailed birds which swoop down to snatch small fish from near the surface. Some of the terns nest on an island within the river mouth. And there are fish in the river, too, most of them invisible except for the mullet which swim close by the wall.

And from the Poolbeg lighthouse, you can lift up your eyes unto the hills from whence cometh Anna Liffey. You can't quite see the slopes where the Source is. But you know that, somewhere up there, lies that deep, dark pool and the mountain stream without whose aid Dublin's fair city would never have begun. ●

Christopher Moriarty

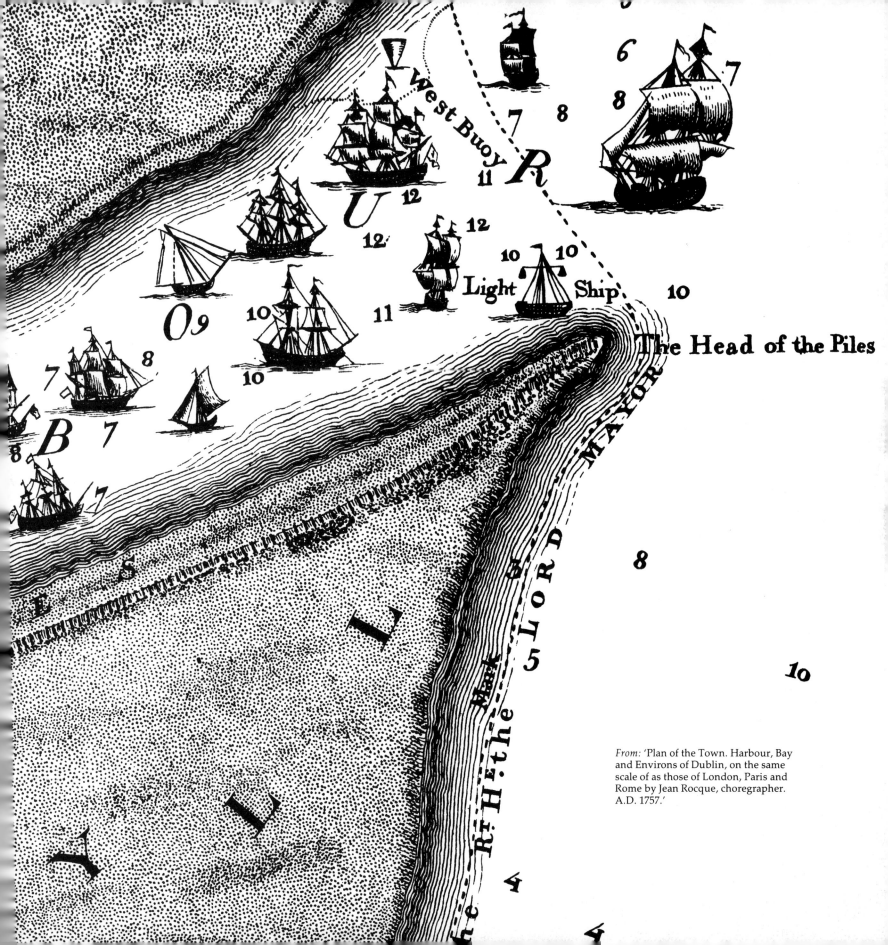

West Buoy

R

U   12

O 9

B 7

The Head of the Piles

Light Ship

LORD MAYOR

From: 'Plan of the Town. Harbour, Bay and Environs of Dublin, on the same scale of as those of London, Paris and Rome by Jean Rocque, choregrapher. A.D. 1757.'

Fountain head of 'Anna Livia',
Water Feature in O'Connell Street.

The Pigeon House: a painting by William Sadler (1782-1839). Soldiers escort a wagon towards the Military Barracks. A very handsome ship has docked. Its passengers may take themselves to Mr. Pidgeon's House for rest and refreshment.

'Plucking the Pigeons'

In 1833, the Dublin Penny Journal was able to say:

The improvements made in the harbour of Dublin within the last sixty years (or thereabouts), cannot fail to fill the beholder with admiration. Every way the eye turns the taste and spirit of our fellow-citizens are displayed – beauty is combined with utility. The feeble citizen of four-score, as he saunters along the quay of the north or south wall, recalls to his memory, that in his boyhood those beautiful walks which he now enjoys were swampy impassable strands – that from Ballybough to Ball's Bridge and from Mark's Church to Ringsend, were under the domination of the waves of the Atlantic. Ringsend might then be deemed an island, for, before the Dodder River was enclosed by banks, the sea rolled over where rich pastures now relieve the eye in the vicinity of Irishtown . . .

Access from Dublin to Ringsend across the tidal headwaters was safeguarded only in 1711, when the Liffey was embanked and the South Lotts reclaimed – well, partly safeguarded, as two successive bridges were swept away before the present one was built.

The building of the South Wall, from Ringsend into Dublin Bay, was undertaken in two stages, the first stage over 3 miles as far as the Pigeonhouse where there was a floating lightship in 1735, and later, to give better protection to the harbour, it was extended two miles farther into the Bay, originally as a wooden structure and later, with the building of the Poolbeg Lighthouse, by the massive stone structure we know today.

The Pigeonhouse was originally a watch house and storehouse, and was used also as a refuge by passengers forced

by bad weather to land there. While the Wall was being built, crowds of sightseers used to come by boat to view the work in progress. The Caretaker, whose name was Pidgeon, decided to take advantage of the situation and, with his family, started to provide meals, refreshments and accommodation. Obviously a believer in free enterprise, he gradually expanded his services and acquired a pleasure boat of his own for hire. A trip to Pidgeon's House became one of the most popular outings in the Dublin of the day.

Cross-channel passengers frequently disembarked at the Pigeonhouse. Here they had to pay landing dues, customs fees and further transport costs, and in addition ran the risk of being held up by bandits as well on the way to Dublin. All of this merry extortion was known as 'plucking the pigeons'.

And it's old and old it's sad and old it's sad and
weary I go back to you,
my cold father, my cold mad father, my cold mad feary father,

I am passing out. O bitter ending!
I'll slip away before they're up.
They'll never see. Nor know. Nor miss me.

. . . and I rush, my only, into your arms.
I see them rising!

Save me from those therrble prongs!

Whish! A gull. Gulls. Far calls. Coming, far! *End here. Us then. Finn, again!*

A way a lone a last a loved a long the

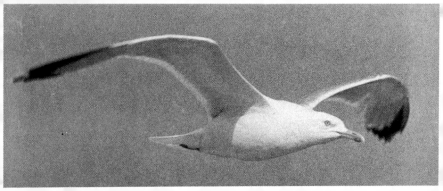

The Liffey as Playground

The Liffey flows out to sea but, as in Joyce's 'commodius vicus of recirculation' the next tide or the next shower replenishes it and brings it back again: a new river, newly bountiful, a sporting river.

Sixty miles of it and all of its broad lakelands beckon to lovers of the great outdoors, and they come and spread themselves over its bountiful acres, to play and sail and ski and wander and make picnics and sandcastles. The Liffey embraces them all, divides her territory judiciously among them. Her moods offer a changing delight to all of them: capricious and calm, wide and narrow, shallow and fierce. And she has space and freedom for many more visitors and friends.

WATER SPORTS

CANOEING

The great way to see the Liffey is, of course, by travelling the river itself. As a canoeing river, the Liffey is unique among Irish waterways. It packs all the interesting aspects of other rivers into less than 60 miles of its 82 miles of overall length. Lakes, rapids, weirs and slow meanderings are all met with along its course. In addition, because of the weirs and the ESB dams, the water flow is relatively stable. During summer months when other rivers run dry, the Liffey can be paddled from Oldcourt Bridge above Blessington all the way to the sea. And when high water is needed for competitive events, this can usually be arranged between the Irish Canoe Union and the ESB.

There are canoeing clubs at Kilcullen, Newbridge, Clane, Celbridge, Leixlip, Lucan, Palmerstown and Chapelizod. All in all there are perhaps 500 members of canoe clubs on the Liffey, not to mention visiting groups and training courses, and there is hardly a day or week-end throughout the entire year when canoes cannot be seen skimming along Liffey waters.

The 17 miles between Straffan Weir and Islandbridge, the course over which the famous International Liffey Descent takes place, is regarded as one of the finest canoe courses anywhere. Within that distance there are 10 weirs to contend with, two stretches of rapids, a punishing portage and a daunting stretch known to regulars as the 'Jungle'. This important event is held in September every year, to large and vociferous groups of spectators at every viewpoint. To add extra drama to the occasion the ESB releases 30 million tons of water through their hydro stations, to create a massive and powerful flood.

To go over that course in some detail is like going through a demonstration course in all types of canoe hazards, problems and delights. Straffan Weir itself, especially with a couple of hundred canoes charging towards it immediately after the start of the race, sorts out a lot of the contenders: it is a wide weir with fish tanks, standing waves, deep holes and rocks. From there you arrive in the 'Jungle', two or three miles of swirling currents and encroaching trees. Two more weirs and an area of exciting rapids in front of Castletown House, with standing waves at the bottom as the water rushes into the calm of Leixlip Lake. The dam at the end of the lake demands a gruelling 500-yard portage. Seven more weirs, each demanding a completely different approach and technique – the most notable being the Wren's Nest and Palmerstown which are turbulent 'V' weirs – sorts out such paddlers as are still in the race.

All this sounds daunting, but it shouldn't put off the beginners, who should perhaps regard it as something to aspire to, while being reassured that there are delightful calm and serene stretches, particularly on the lower part of the river between weirs along the Strawberry Beds road, to learn the trade on, gain experience and learn to enjoy the sport without anxiety or any sense of challenge.

Leixlip Reservoir provides another nice wide stretch for easy paddling, and it has its own canoe club at the Newbridge end. Further downstream, the Irish Canoe Union Training Unit runs courses during the summer. The Blessington Lakes are, of course, immediately accessible – but take care, these are large stretches of water, with the attendant hazards.

The Liffey Descent is taken as a hard-run race, but the same course, taken more gently, is a nice experience in long-distance touring, and is often undertaken non-competitively by groups such as scouts, youth clubs and business clubs. White-water racing is carried out mainly between Temple Mills (just above Celbridge) and Palmerstown, and there are several different locations for slalom events.

Joining in. In order to join in this or any of the other water-sports on the Liffey, the best advice is JOIN A CLUB .

The Irish Canoe Union, 4/5 Eustace Street, Dublin 2. Tel. 01-719690, controls the sport in Ireland, and offers guidance, encouragement and advice. Many schools have canoeing as part of their sports programme, but if yours (or your children's) doesn't, contact the Union, as above.

AFAS (The Association for Adventure Sports) runs courses throughout the year in canoeing and other water sports. Taking a course with them, of a week or weekend, gives you a chance to try it out and see whether it really is the sport for you, before you spend money on equipping yourself. You can contact AFAS at Tiglin Adventure Centre, Ashford, Co. Wicklow. Tel 0404-40169.

Beginners **should not** just buy or borrow a canoe and take it out alone, no matter how sunny the day or how tempting the idea.

ROWING

'Resolved that any member marrying shall forfeit a dozen of champagne to the club which shall be drunk by the members of the club at such time and place as shall be agreed upon by them.'

150 years may have passed since the Pembroke Club, perhaps the earliest rowing club on the river Liffey at Dublin, voted in this resolution penalising matrimony; but it's a sentiment that would be appreciated by some of the Dublin rowing clubs even now! The sport of rowing is *that* demanding, and definitely not for those – like Ratty in *The Wind in the Willows* – who love the idea of 'simply messing about in boats.'

No, the equipment is far too expensive for that. The cost of latest designs in fours, eights, sculls and pairs, with sliding seats, riggers (for oars) and foot stretchers, run into four and five-figure sums. Thus, demand on equipment among the eleven rowing clubs based on the Liffey at Islandbridge, opposite the Phoenix Park, is always at a premium. Training sessions on the river at 6.30 a.m., in the middle of winter, are quite normal if a boat has to be shared among crews!

The training for the sport also favours the celibate life. Rowing has been a competitive sport in Ireland for more than a hundred years and international standards have pushed training levels up. It is now ranked with cycling as one of the toughest forms of exercise, and with a six-day-week land and water training programme to suit accordingly.

The eleven Liffey clubs, based in six boathouses along the flat Islandbridge stretch at just under 2,000 metres to Chapelizod, comprise a fraction of the 3,000 active oarsmen and women throughout the 32 counties, affiliated to the Irish Amateur Rowing Union. Winter training begins about September for the regatta season which lasts from April to August of the following summer. Regatta races take place at various venues throughout the country over courses of 1,500 to 2,000 metres. Prior to that there are pre-season Heads of the River, over longer distances of one to twelve miles.

The big events on the Liffey reaches include the Dublin Head which (usually) takes place every year around about the end of March. Tides determine the precise date, for it is held over the tidal stretch of the river from a start below Islandbridge weir to a finish just past O'Connell Bridge. This Head is for eights only, and competitors, being both male and female crews, are set off at timed intervals.

The first regatta of the season in recent years has been on the Liffey at Islandbridge, hosted by Neptune Rowing Club, with another event run by neighbouring Commercial Rowing Club the following day. Trinity Regatta, hosted by the oldest club on the river, Dublin University Boat Club, has become a Maytime institution. Emphasis here is not only on the sporting but the very social. Trinity Regatta tries its best to be an Irish Henley. It is held at the beginning of Trinity Week and, weather permitting, is an occasion for blazers, boaters, champagne and strawberries.

Then there's the Dublin Metropolitan Regatta on the Blessington reservoir in June, which allows for a more equitable six-lane course, compared to the two-boat racing on the Liffey. This is often followed, fixtures calendar permitting, by the National Championship regatta near the end of the season in July.

But it is the Islandbridge stretch on the Liffey that has seen so many events, as documented in the one and only history of the sport to date, T. F. Hall's *The History of Boat-Racing in Ireland*, written in 1937. Mr. Michael Johnston, the sport's archivist, may be persuaded to publish an update soon!

For information on rowing at Islandbridge and advice on clubs to join, the Irish Amateur Rowing Union can be contacted at Hogan House, Grand Canal Street, Dublin 2. or Ardee Road, Rathmines, Dublin 6. (Tel. 01-613022/631294).

Take a walk along the southside (Trinity) towpath on a Saturday or Sunday morning if you want to see what it's all about. But beware of zealous coaches tearing up and down on bicycles, yelling at crews in what sounds like a foreign language: 'sit it level!' (steady the boat up), 'head sculler!' (warning to cox and to sculler ahead) and 'get the lead out!' (which means what it says) being among the most common exhortations.

Ringsend Rowing

Outrigger rowing should not be confused with coastal rowing, a sea sport which also features on the Liffey near its mouth at Ringsend. Coastal rowing is organised on a local basis and takes place in fibreglass and wooden fixed-seat skiffs, 4-man crews with cox'n, on courses varying from 800 to 1200 yards – and some include a turn at the host club's discretion. It provides for both mixed and single sex crews and the racing season usually spans from late June until late August. Great emphasis is placed on the training of young people.

There are two clubs based at Ringsend, the Stella Maris, based at the South Bank, and St. Patrick's, based on the Dodder. Both have recently celebrated their 50th Anniversary. It is claimed that the rowing here originated with the 'hobblers' or dockers well over a century ago. They used to row out to sea to intercept incoming schooners. The first boat to get their grappling iron and line aboard got the right to discharge its cargo in Dublin Port. (See also 'Blessing of the Boats', page 187).

The best way to find out more is to call to the Clubhouse of the Poolbeg Yacht and Boat Club on the South Bank. It is open every evening.

SAILING AND SKIING

Blessington Lakes

Experienced sailors who want to bring a boat to Blessington must apply for a licence to ESB, Fitzwilliam Street, Dublin 2, or alternatively join the Blessington Sailing Club. Being a club member offers the advantage of rescue services and other facilities being laid on, and the use of the Clubhouse.

Blessington Lake is in many ways an ideal training ground, because of its size and openness. It isn't crowded with other craft, there are no tides and there are no shipping lines to avoid – or get into! But quite a sea can be whipped up, often suddenly, with sharp choppy waves rather than the long rolling waves off the coast. Unlike the sea the wind can be very erratic here among the mountains. So aspirant sailors get good training in comparatively safe conditions – and in a Club, under proper supervision.

Blessington Sailing Club is the main club on the lake. It is located on the western side of the main lake, near Baltyboys. Contact must be made in advance (see below) as access to the area isn't possible without a member's key.

Membership is confined to boat-owners and their families. The designated dinghy classes are Optimists, Mirrors, Lasers and GP14s, but a certain number of other craft are allowed, including a small number of day-boats and cruisers. The racing programme extends from mid-April to the end of September, with fixtures on Sunday afternoons and Wednesday evenings. A lively Regatta Day happens on a July Sunday, and the Club holds one of the National Events as designated by the IYA.

Emphasis is placed on training, and there is a strong Junior Training Course, mainly in July, and training also for adults. There is always a powerful Rescue Launch on duty on sailing days. Membership fees are very reasonable.

This quiet part of the lake is a lovely

place to be on summer days, with the sandy shores extending in both directions and the mountains rising all around. It is very much a family club. Toddlers can paddle and make sandcastles while their elders sail or mess about in boats, and everybody gathers around the barbecue when sailing is over for the day.

Contact Mrs. Ann Smyth, 4 Dangan Drive, Dublin 12. Tel. 01-561090.

Board-sailing

Wind-surfing and board-sailing seem to have taken over the world, so it is no surprise to see these bright sails darting across the lake. The 'designated area' is close to Blessington, but they can often be seen in the Lackan area, especially in winter. Saturdays and Sundays are the popular days, and Wednesday evenings in summer. A marathon Circumnaviga-tion of the Lake is held in October – a tough outing which with average winds takes about 2½ hours.

The Blessington Board Sailing Club is a very socially-minded group. They travel a lot and organise frequent 'away' weekends. To make contact, look for the Noticeboard in West Wicklow House, the pub in Blessington. Some stalwarts of the club may be found there as well.

Dublin VEC Adventure Centre

Further along the lakeside towards the south are the premises of the Adventure Centre which is a joint venture between the City of Dublin VEC and the Curriculum Development Unit of TCD. The activities cover such sports as climbing and mountaineering as well as sailing and canoeing. The activities are built into the curriculum of 2nd level students, and is arranged for 3rd level students on request. All gear is supplied. Here again the emphasis is on training, and there are teacher training courses and some Youth Leader training. For information, contact: The Curriculum Development Unit, Trinity College, Dublin at 28 Westland Row. Tel. 01-772941.

Wicklow VEC operates sailing courses through the Blessington Sailing Club. contact: the VEC Principal, at 045-65170.

WATER-SKIING

Between Pollaphuca and Ballymore Eustace lies the little Golden Falls lake, which has a dam and power station. This is one of the prime water-skiing lakes in Europe, according to its members.

Water-skiing on the sea is great fun and great practice. But for training and for competition, what is needed is secluded and calm water, with no other boats about. Golden Falls has these advantages, plus a further possibly unique one – that is, because of the dams, and the generally benign co-operation of the ESB, the water level is controllable.

Facilities at Golden Falls represent a substantial investment. They include a 6-ton steel and fibreglass jump ramp and a 260hp V8 Competition Ski-boat which can pull up to 14 skiers at one time.

With all of this, a homolgated slalom course and a trick course, Golden Falls Ski Club is a remarkable facility within 50 miles of the Capital.

The season extends from Easter to November. There is skiing from midday till dark on Saturdays and Sundays, and on most evenings after 6 p.m. Life-jackets and all equipment is provided for trainees and others. Training for beginners is by arrangement – and children can be started as early as four years old.

The Big Event of the year is the Golden Falls Ski Jump Classic, held in September. Other events are as dictated by the Irish Water Ski Federation.

To make what would otherwise be an expensive sport more accessible, the Golden Falls Club offers an arrangement by which groups or individuals can 'pay as you ski' – a very favourable system which includes use of all equipment, and of the Clubhouse and Barbecue.

To make contact. The lake and club are signposted from Ballymore-Eustace. Before arriving, however, it would be useful to get further information. The best contact is the Chairman of the Irish Water Ski Association: Mr. Desmond Burke-Kennedy, Mount Salus, Knocknac-ree Road, Dalkey. Tel. 01-855205 (home) or 01-506533 (office).

RINGSEND

Down at Ringsend there is a very active and enthusiastic group of sports and social clubs whose members seem to work together with a great community spirit. The Poolbeg Yacht and Boat Club caters for all types of craft, from small dinghies to quite large cruisers, and they even include a couple of Galway Hookers. Even though their sailing ground is mostly Dublin Bay, they belong to the Liffey insofar as their fine new Clubhouse is located at South Bank on the Pigeon House Road. It has a good bar, open to members every evening. They like to think of themselves as a working man's club. Fees are kept as low as possible,'and mooring is free. A clause in their Constitution stipulates: 'the interest of the members with modest means to have priority when the occasion demands.'

Training sessions for young people are held on weekdays between April and September, and there is racing every Wednesday and Sunday. To make sure that youngsters are properly trained for the sport, swimming lessons are held at Markievicz Swimming Pool at Townsend Street.

Membership is not restricted to residents of Ringsend area: they come from all parts of the city and environs.

To find out more, drop along to the Clubhouse on the South Bank any evening, or telephone Robert Donaldson (of 2 Glendalough Road, Drumcondra, Dublin 9, Tel. 01-375207) who has been associated with the club since its foundation.

The annual Blessing of the Boats is a big event down here at the Liffey's mouth, giving a good start to the boating season. Boats from all parts of the bay and adjacent coast assemble to take part in an ecumenical service, after which the bedecked flotilla parades up river, and back to the clubhouse for 'refreshments'.

Angling

The rights to nearly all the best trout and salmon fishing on the Liffey are owned by angling clubs. Many of these are willing to issue fishing licences for a reasonable fee. There are notices at most of the points of access proclaiming ownership and, more helpfully, giving the name and address of a local person who can issue a fishing permit. The not-so-good fishing, especially in the upper reaches, technically belongs to the 'riparian owner', he who owns the land on the bank. As a rule the rights are not enforced and few people object to the efforts of the honest angler.

Angling permits for the lakes may be bought at many of the pubs, shops and hotels in Blessington, from various Dublin fishing tackle dealers or from the ESB, Ardnacrusha, Limerick. The simplest way of finding out where to apply for permission to fish on other stretches is to contact the Eastern Regional Fisheries Board, Balnagowan, Mobhi Boreen, Dublin 11. ●

The Book of the Liffey

Starting places for ramblers

1. Liffey Head Take the Military Road through Glencree towards Sally Gap. Liffey Head Bridge is 500 m downhill from the gate to Kipppure TV mast. Walk upstream to the Source and beyond to the summits of Tonduff. Downstream of the bridge follow the Liffey for 2 km in a hidden valley on the slopes of Kippure.

2. Coronation Plantation Begin where the road crosses the Liffey 2.5 km downhill from Sally Gap. A vigorous walk by the side of the river, often boggy and most easily managed by crossing and recrossing the stream.

3. Ballysmuttan Ballysmuttan Bridge is 9 km downhill from Sally Gap or 5 km uphill from Kilbride and has a lovely picnic place. Best walk is upstream on the right bank.

4. Three Castles Car park at the Castle, walk along old road to riverside and back along lake shore, the best place to see wild geese in winter and best spot for birds at any time.

5. St Boden's Well Signposted at Lackan on lake drive, car park and access to longest uninterrupted walks by sandy lake shore.

6. Ballyknockan No special parking places. Mountain track leads up from the Madonna, high on the side of Moanbane and a good starting point for higher mountains like Mullaghcleevaun.

7. Ballymore Eustace Iron gate by bridge on right bank gives access to path to Woollen Mills and millstream. Downstream of the village, you may follow the meanders in the flood plain.

8. Kilcullen Riverside park on left bank, upstream of bridge. Walk through park and along old path through fields to the cemetery.

9. Celbridge Abbey Access to river by gate of old National School, upstream of bridge on right bank.

10. Castletown Two possibilities: park at the gate or in front of the house. Walk along the left bank as far as Leixlip Reservoir.

11. Palmerston Take steep hill to riverside at Stewart's Hospital. Wicket gate at end of row of mill workers' houses gives access to disused millstream and right bank of river.

12. South Wall Drive through Ringsend past Poolbeg power station to car park at the beginning of the breakwater. •

Further Reading

As the story of Dublin and the story of the Liffey are closely interlinked, in any book relating to the city's history, the Liffey features prominently. Apart from the great epic of James Joyce's *Finnegans Wake*, however, which doesn't go very far in helping the general reader to discover the charms of the river, as far as literature is concerned the Liffey might not exist above Islandbridge.

Here is a short suggested reading list:

Conlon, Stephen and deCourcy, John. *Anna Liffey, the River of Dublin*. Dublin: O'Brien Press, 1988. Craig, Maurice. *Dublin 1660-1860*. London: The Cresset Press, 1952, reprinted Dublin: Allen Figgis, 1980. D'Alton, John. *The History of the County Dublin*. Dublin: Hodges and Smith, 1838, reprinted Cork: Tower Books 1976. Doohan, Tony. *A History of Celbridge*. Celbridge, 1984. Fagan, Patrick. *The Second City: Portrait of Dublin 1700-1760*. Dublin: Branar, 1986. Gilbert, J. T. *A History of the City of Dublin* (3 vols). Dublin: James Duffy, 1861, reprinted Shannon: Irish University Press, 1969, Dublin: Gill and Macmillan 1978. Haliday, Charles. *The Scandinavian Kingdom of Dublin*. Dublin: Alex Thom and Co., 1881, reprinted Shannon: Irish University Press, 1969. Joyce, Weston St. John. *The Neighbourhood of Dublin*. Dublin, Gill and Son 1939. Little, George. *Dublin before the Vikings*. Dublin: M. H. Gill and Son, 1957.

Acknowledgements

A great many people helped in the creation of this book. We are grateful to all of them. We would particularly like to express our appreciation, for their help and advice, to Liz O'Sullivan, Paddy Flynn and John Godden of the ESB; Willie Corby, James Fenwick and Clair Sweeney of Dublin Corporation; Eileen Twomey of the Dept. of the Marine; Charles Nelson of the Botanic Gardens; Pat Wallace of the National Museum and Paula Howard of the Gilbert Library. Also to Adrian Phillips, Edward Nolan, Oscar Merne, Eamon Cusack, Jean Archer, Rev. Richard Stokes, Anna Brindley, Jim O'Reilly, Richard Shackleton, Hugh O'Connor and Archdeacon W. B. Heney for their expert advice on a range of topics, and to Desmond Burke-Kennedy, Lorna Siggins, Anna White, Brian Pollock, Peter Reynolds and Robert Donaldson for their help on some sporting aspects. A special word of thanks to Robin Love for, among other things, a very happy day on the river – portage and all!

For permission to quote from his father's works, our grateful thanks to Oliver D. Gogarty SC. Extracts from James Joyce's works are by permission of the Society of Authors. The song Down by the Liffeyside is by permission of Walton's Musical Instrument Galleries Ltd.

For illustrations, we are indebted to the following:

Bord Failte: pages 2, 30, 42, 85, 103, 107, 118 (top), 134, 146, 150, 156, 157 (bottom), 160 (top), 171.
Mike Bunn: pages 8, 32, 84, 178, 179 (right), 180 and back cover.
Seamus Cashman: page 114.
Con Costello: pages 94, 95, 96, 97.
Jan de Fouw: Front cover, pages 1, 3, 4, 5, 12-13, 14, 17, 26 (bottom), 27, 28 (bottom), 31, 32 (bottom), 33, 38, 48, 51, 52, 62-3, 72, 87, 90, 115, 121, 154, 155 (bottom), 156 (bottom), 179 (left).
Remco de Fouw: pages 23, 59, 123 (bottom), 124, 142, 152, 158, 159, 162, 176.
Jenny Dempsey: marginal line drawings.
William Dick: pages 65 and 66.
Dublin Port and Docks Board: page 181.
Electricity Supply Board: pages 56, 82, 83, 84.
Frank Fennell Photography: page 118 (centre).
Geological Survey of Ireland: page 25.
Guinness Ireland Ltd: pages 131, 157 (top).
Hardwicke Ltd: page 157 (right).
Anthony Heade: page 138.

Elizabeth Healy: pages 164, 166.
© 1988 CNES and Maptec International Ltd: pages 182-3.
Christopher Moriarty: pages 19, 26 (top), 28 (top), 40, 45, 46, 47, 81, 101, 102, 104, 137 (bottom), 138, 139.
National Gallery of Ireland: pages 3 (right), 99, 122, 137 (top), 140, 177.
National Library of Ireland: pages 78, 79, 99 (right), 108, 123, 126, 127 (top), 133, 149, 155.
National Museum of Ireland: 116, 118 (bottom right).
Ordnance Survey Government Report No. 4998 (by permission of the Minister for Finance): pages 6-7.
Radio Telefis Eireann: page 127 (bottom).
Royal Irish Academy: page 92.
Royal Society of Antiquaries of Ireland: page 21.
Gerrit van Gelderen: pages 35 (bottom), 36 (left), 37 (bottom), 43, 172-3, 184.
Wendy Walsh: page 77.

Index

The Book of the Liffey